ILLUSTRATORS

of Books for Young People

Second Edition

by

MARTHA E. WARD

and

DOROTHY A. MARQUARDT

The Scarecrow Press, Inc.

Metuchen, N. J.   1975

Library of Congress Cataloging in Publication Data

Ward, Martha Eads.
    Illustrators of books for young people.

    1. Illustrators--Biography--Dictionaries.
2. Illustrated books, Children's--Dictionaries.
I. Marquardt, Dorothy A., joint author. II. Title.
NC45.W3 1975   741'.092'2 [B]   75-9880
ISBN 0-8108-0819-6

Manufactured in the United States of America

PREFACE

This is a revised and considerably enlarged edition of Illustrators of Books for Young People, originally published in 1970. A total of 750 biographies are included in the present work.

Biographical information for this volume was compiled in the Children's Department of the Quincy Public Library, Quincy, Illinois. Since publication of the first edition, a great deal of information has been received from various sources, including many of the publishers of illustrated books for children.

As before, all recipients of the Caldecott Medal (through 1974) have been listed. The Caldecott Medal is awarded annually "to the artist of the most distinguished American picture book for children."

Many of the biographical entries herein are followed by one or more of four symbols, shown below. These symbols refer to works in which additional information about an illustrator can be found.

ICB-1   Illustrators of Children's Books, 1744-1945, compiled by Bertha E. Mahony, Louise Payson Latimer, and Beulah Folmsbee (Boston: The Horn Book, 1947).

ICB-2   Illustrators of Children's Books, 1946-1956, compiled by Ruth Hill Viguers, Marcia Dalphin, and Bertha Mahony Miller (Boston: The Horn Book, 1958).

ICB-3   Illustrators of Children's Books, 1957-1966, compiled by Lee Kingman, Joanna Foster, and Ruth Giles Lontoft (Boston: The Horn Book, 1968).

ABYP-2   <u>Authors of Books for Young People</u>, 2d ed.,
          by Ward and Marquardt (Metuchen, N.J.:
          Scarecrow Press, 1971).

     An index to all titles of books mentioned in any of the
entries appears at the back of the book.

                              Martha E. Ward
                              Dorothy A. Marquardt

CALDECOTT MEDAL WINNERS

THE ILLUSTRATORS

ABRAHAMS, Hilary Ruth, 1938- . She was born in London, England, and later studied design at St. Martin's School. She has been a free-lance artist and has worked in black-and-white. She always considered herself fortunate to have worked under artist Edward Ardizzone, who taught art at the Royal College of Art. Her husband, Jan van de Watering, a Dutch typographer, has been a designer with the Cambridge University Press. They have lived in Cambridge, England. She illustrated A. Abrahams' Polonius Penguin Learns to Swim (Watts, 1964). ICB-3

ABRAMS, Lester. His home has been in Wellfleet on Cape Cod. Mr. Abrams studied at the Rhode Island School of Design. For young people he illustrated L. Alexander's The Four Donkeys (Holt, 1972).

ADAMS, Adrienne. Illustrator and teacher, born in Fort Smith, Arkansas, she grew up in Oklahoma. She attended Stephens College at Columbia, Missouri, graduated from the University of Missouri, and studied at New York's American School of Design. She married writer John Lonzo Anderson, and they have lived in Hunterdon County, New Jersey. Miss Adams' illustrations of several fairy tales were selected as "Notable Books" by the American Library Association. Juvenile books which she illustrated include J. Wahl's Cabbage Moon (Holt, 1965) and R. Godden's Candy Floss (a Junior Literary Guild selection; Viking, 1960). She wrote and illustrated A Woggle of Witches (Scribner's, 1971). ICB-2, ICB-3

ADAMS, Pauline Batchelder. An illustrator for several publishing firms, the artist received her training at the Chicago Art Institute. She lived near Chicago prior to making her home in Southern California. For young readers she illustrated M. Ericsson's About Glasses for

Gladys (Melmont, 1962); and C. Krum's Read with Me
(Children's Press, 1946). With Phoebe Erickson she
also illustrated M. Friskey's Farm Friends (Children's
Press, 1951).

ADAMSON, George Worsley, 1913- . Artist, cartoonist,
teacher. He was born in New York City and grew up
there and in Wigan, Lancashire, England. He attended
the Wigan School of Art, Liverpool University, and also studied at the City School of Art in Liverpool. He
later made his home in Exeter, Devon, England. George
Adamson served as a navigator and official war artist
with the R. A. F. during World War II. He has belonged
to the Society of Industrial Artists and he has worked
with both color and pen. The artist has worked in advertising in addition to illustrating books and magazines.
He illustrated W. Hall's The Royal Astrologer (Coward,
1962). ICB-2, ICB-3

AHRENHOLD, Novie Moffat. Illustrator, artist. Her husband has also been active in the field of art, and they
have lived in Gatlinburg, Tennessee. She formerly
made her home in Chicago. For young people she illustrated R. Carleton's Indoor Gardening Fun (Reilly,
1970).

AICHINGER, Helga. This painter and illustrator was born
in Linz, Austria, where she has continued to make her
home. Her paintings have been included in the permanent collections of the Harvard University Library and
the Museum of Modern Art in New York City. The
Stedelijk Museum in Amsterdam also has her work.
In addition to illustrating children's books, Miss Aichinger has written books for boys and girls. She illustrated L. Chaffin's Bear Weather (Macmillan, 1969).

AKINO, Fuku, 1908- . Artist and teacher, born in Futa-
mata, Tenryu City, Japan. She studied at the Sizuoka
Normal School and later attended private art classes
in Tokyo and Kyoto. In addition to drawing and painting, Miss Akino has been an elementary school teacher.
She later became Assistant Professor at the Municipal
Art Academy in Kyoto. The artist helped to organize
the Sinseisaku Association in 1948. She has been
the recipient of many honors including the highest award
presented to a woman artist, the Uemura Shoen Prize.
Juvenile books (all by B. Lifton) she has illustrated

include The Cock and The Ghost Cat (Atheneum, 1965);
The Dwarf Pine Tree (Atheneum, 1963); and The One-
Legged Ghost (Atheneum, 1968).   ICB-3

ALAIN see BRUSTLEIN, Daniel

ALAJÁLOV, Constantin, 1900- .   Artist, muralist, portrait
painter, world traveler.   He was born in Rostov on the
Don in Russia, received his education in Rostov, and
made his home in New York City after coming to America in 1923.   In addition to book illustration, Constantin
Alajálov has painted portraits and murals.   He became
well-known for his covers on the New Yorker magazine.
The artist has also taught in New York at the Alexander Archipenko's School and Phoenix Art Institute.   His
work can be found in private collections and Art Museums.   For children he illustrated A. Miller's Cinderella (Coward-McCann, 1943).   ICB-1, ICB-2

ALBION, Lee Smith.   She was born in Rochester, New York,
and later attended Radcliffe College and Columbia University.   She also attended New York City's Art Students League and the Art Center in Los Angeles.   Her
work has appeared in the Saturday Review, Jack and
Jill, and Scholastic magazines.   Wife of a Miami attorney, Lee Albion has illustrated many books including
M. Prieto's The Wise Rooster: El Gallo Sabio (Day,
1962).   ICB-3

ALCORN, John, 1935- .   He was born in Corona, Long Is-
land, New York.   Mr. Alcorn studied at Cooper Union.
His work has won awards from the Type Directors
Club, the New York Art Directors Club, the Society of
Illustrators, and the American Institute of Graphic Arts.
He has lived with his wife and four sons in Ossining,
New York.   His books include two of S. Joslin's, La
Fiesta (Harcourt, 1967) and La Petite Famille (Har-
court, 1964), and A. Hine's A Letter to Anywhere
(Harcourt, 1965).   ICB-3

ALEXANDER, Martha.   She was born in Georgia.   She has
illustrated the picture books of many leading authors.
At one time she lived in Hawaii, but in 1960 she came
to New York to make her home.   Later she lived in
Sag Harbor, New York.   Her work includes: J. Udry's
Mary Ann's Mud Day (Harper, 1967) and L. Hobart's
What Is a Whispery Secret? (Parents', 1968).   She

wrote and illustrated: <u>Bobo's Dream</u> (Dial, 1970), <u>I'll Protect You from the Jungle Beasts</u> (Dial, 1973), and <u>Sabrina</u> (Dial, 1971).

ALMQUIST, Don.   After graduating from the Rhode Island School of Design in 1951, he studied with Jose Guerrero.   His career as an artist has included magazine work, book illustration for children, and advertising. Mr. Almquist has lived in Bridgeport, Connecticut, but spent two years in Sweden as Creative Director for a publishing firm.   He has been the recipient of many awards and honors.   In 1956 he won the silver medal from the Philadelphia Art Directors Club.   For boys and girls he illustrated: W. Fink's <u>Getting to Know New York State</u> (Coward, 1971) and M. Craig's <u>Spring Is Like the Morning</u> (Putnam, 1965).

ALOISE, Frank.   Prior to his career in book illustration, he worked as an artist in television.   Mr. Aloise studied in New York at the Art Students League and the Workshop School of Art.   He has made his home in New York and has worked with blind children at New York City's "Light House."   He has illustrated many books for boys and girls and once said: "(children) are the truest, purest judges of what an artist must do in order to successfully illustrate a book for children." His work includes: A. Vorwald's <u>Computers</u> (Whittlesey House, 1964), V. Voight's <u>Nathan Hale</u> (Putnam, 1965), and M. Merryman's <u>Road to Raffydiddle</u> (Abingdon, 1966).

AMBLER, Christopher Gifford, 1886- .   He was born in Bradford, Yorkshire, England and later made his home in Oxford.   He received his art training at the Leeds School of Art.   His career began in the field of pottery design and modeling.   The artist was awarded several medals (Gold, Silver, and Bronze) for Decorative Design and Modeling in National Competition.   The Royal Academy and other galleries have exhibited his work. Prior to World War I, Mr. Ambler traveled to America and Canada.   After serving in both World Wars, he returned to book illustration and concentrated on dog and horse portraits.   In 1950 he was made an honorary life member of the Schipperke Club of America for which he designed a memorial medallion.   For young people he illustrated D. Clark's <u>Black Lightning</u> (Viking, 1954).   ICB-2

AMBRUS, Victor G.   He was born in Budapest, Hungary,
    where he later studied at the Academy of Fine Arts.
    He won the 1964 Carnegie Medal and several times was
    runner-up for the Kate Greenaway Medal.   He has been
    a lecturer at Guildford School of Art in Surrey.   His
    wife Glenys, who was born in the British Isles.
    an artist; and they have lived in Fleet, Hants, England.
    His books include: H. Kay's (pseud.) Henri's Hands
    for Pablo Picasso (Abelard-Schuman, 1966), R. Park-
    er's Private Beach (a Junior Literary Guild selection;
    Duell, 1965), and his own The Three Poor Tailors
    (Harcourt, 1966).   ICB-3

AMUNDSEN, Richard E.   Both a book and magazine illustra-
    tor, Richard Amundsen was born and educated in Cali-
    fornia.   He later made his home in Seattle, Washing-
    ton.   For several years, his wildlife illustrations have
    appeared in Field and Stream magazine.   His paintings
    can be found in private collections and have been ex-
    hibited throughout this country.   His illustrations in
    color appeared in E. Austin's The Random House Book
    of Birds (1970).

ANDERSON, Gunnar.   He was born in Berkeley, California.
    Following service in the Coast Guard, Gunnar Ander-
    son studied at the California School of Fine Arts and
    the Los Angeles Art Center School.   He has received
    recognition as a painter of children, and his work has
    been shown in galleries in Boston, New York, Phila-
    delphia, Chicago, Los Angeles, and San Francisco.
    Gunnar Anderson and his family have lived in Sonoma,
    California, where he has worked in a mountaintop stu-
    dio.   He illustrated F. Sayers' Oscar Lincoln Busby
    Stokes, (Harcourt, 1970).

ANDREWS, Benny.   He has been a teacher of painting and
    drawing at New York's New School for Social Research.
    His work has been exhibited at the Museum of African
    Art, the Brooklyn Museum, and the Museum of Modern
    Art.   His paintings have been included in the perma-
    nent collections of the Norfolk and Chrysler Museums
    and the Joseph H. Hirshhorn Collection.   His home has
    been in New York.   He illustrated I Am the Darker
    Brother, ed. by A. Adoff (Macmillan, 1968).

ANGEL, Marie.   Born in London, she received her educa-
    tion at the Royal College of Art in the School of Design.

Her special interest was in calligraphy. Her work has
been exhibited in England and in the Hunt Botanical Library in Pittsburgh. Her meticulous and sensitive illustrations and miniature paintings have received much
praise. For young people she illustrated The Twenty-
Third Psalm (Crowell, 1970).

ANNO, Mitsumasa. Artist and painter. He has belonged to
many Japanese artists' organizations. Mr. Anno has
devoted most of his time to book illustration and design. His drawings can be found in Topsy-Turvies
(Walker/Weatherhill, 1970).

APILADO, Tony. Born in Hawaii, the artist grew up in
California, and later made his home in New York City.
He graduated from Compton College and the Los Angeles Art Center School. Tony Apilado has been an art
director in an advertising agency in addition to being
a designer and illustrator. His drawings can be found
in B. Kohn's Easy Gourmet Cooking (Bobbs-Merrill,
1973).

APPLEYARD, Dev. He was born in Nebraska and later
made his home in Kenilworth, Illinois. Following
World War II, Mr. Appleyard studied at the Chicago
Art Institute. His illustrations have appeared in learning games and textbooks. He and his wife have enjoyed ballet, opera, the Beatles, and Bach. For boys
and girls he illustrated T. McGowen's The Last Voyage of the Unlucky Katie Marie (Whitman, 1972).

ARMSTRONG, Tom. Biblical art has been the specialty of
this artist, and he has illustrated several books on re-
ligion for young people. His drawings reflect the authenticity derived from careful research. For young
people he illustrated M. Jones' Bible Stories: God at
Work with Man (Abingdon, 1973), and Young
Readers Dictionary of the Bible, ed. by C. Wolcott
et al. (Abingdon, 1969).

ARNDT, Ursula. She was born in Germany and spent her
childhood in Düsseldorf. A student of etching, she
later came to America and made her home in Brooklyn, New York. Her illustrations have not only appeared in books for boys and girls but also in many
magazines. Her work includes: All the Silver Pen-
nies, ed. by B. Thompson (Macmillan, 1967) and E.
Coatsworth's Troll Weather (Macmillan, 1967).

ARNO, Enrico, 1913- . Artist and teacher, born in Mann-
   heim, Germany. He studied in Berlin at the State
   Academy. Enrico Arno came to the United States in
   1947 and has lived in New York on Long Island. His
   hobby has been puppetry. He has taught lettering and
   design and has been on the staffs of Pratt Institute in
   Brooklyn and Columbia University. In addition to
   books, he has illustrated book jackets, magazines, and
   record covers. For children he illustrated J. Curry's
   Down from the Lonely Mountain (Harcourt, 1965) and
   J. Craig's Pomando (Norton, 1969). ICB-2, ICB-3

ARUEGO, Jose. Illustrator, cartoonist, and designer. He
   was born in Manila, Philippines, and studied at the University of the Philippines where he received a degree
   in law. After practicing law for a short time, he came
   to New York and studied at the Parsons School of Design. In addition to illustrating books, his work has
   appeared in Saturday Review and Look magazines. For
   boys and girls he illustrated R. Kraus' Whose Mouse
   Are You? (Macmillan, 1970). He also wrote and illustrated: Look What I Can Do (Scribner's, 1971) and
   Pilyo the Piranha (Macmillan, 1971).

ASMUSSEN, Des. He has made his home in Fredensborg,
   Denmark. Mr. Asmussen's pen-and-ink drawings have
   appeared in the Saturday Evening Post. Known throughout Europe for his book illustrations, his work first appeared in an American book for boys and girls in Leo
   Tolstoy's collection Ivan the Fool, and Other Tales, selected and tr. by G. Daniels (Macmillan, 1966). He also illustrated L. Kingman's The Meeting Post (Crowell,
   1972).

AUSTIN, Phil. Watercolor artist, he studied at the University of Michigan and at the Academy of Art in Chicago.
   Vincent Price bought some of his paintings for the Sears
   Collection. His work has been exhibited at the Watercolor Society of New York and at the Chicago Art Institute. Maintaining a studio in Chicago, Mr. Austin and
   his family have lived in Waukegan, Illinois. For young
   people he illustrated two works by A. Carpenter, California (Children's Press, 1964) and Colorado (Children's
   Press, 1967).

AVISON, George, 1885- . He was born in Norwalk, Connecticut, and later studied at the Chase School of Art in
   New York. His drawings were used to create the

"Street of the Nineties" in the 1939 New York World's
Fair. In addition to illustrating books, he has painted
murals and designed houses. The artist has lived in
Rowayton and New Canaan, Connecticut. He illustrated:
L. Silliman's The Scrapper (Winston, 1946), A. Graham's
Thirty-Three Roads to the White House (Nelson, 1953),
and M. Miller's White Captive of the Sioux (Winston,
1953). He also wrote and illustrated Uncle Sam's Ma-
rines, How They Fight (Macmillan, 1944). ICB-1,
ICB-2

AXEMAN, Lois. Born in Chicago, she later married a designer. Lois Axeman was the recipient of an award in
the "1967-1968 New York Illustrators' Show." A free-
lance artist, she has been especially interested in artwork for children. She illustrated J. Blume's The One
in the Middle Is the Green Kangaroo (Reilly, 1969).

AYER, Jacqueline Brandford, 1930- . She was born in New
York City, and she later studied at Syracuse University,
Art Students League, Beaux Arts and École Paul Calin
in Paris. Both of her parents were Jamaicans, and
she has lived in both Hong Kong and Bangkok. Later
she lived in London and spent her summers in Bangkok. The Society of Illustrators has awarded her a
Gold Medal. In addition to illustrating children's books,
she has designed materials for Design-Thai. For boys
and girls she illustrated J. Grimm's Rumpelstiltskin
(Harcourt, 1967). ICB-3

AYER, Margaret. She was born in New York City, and
grew up in Mexico and the Philippine Islands, and later
made her home in New York and Connecticut. In addition to attending schools in Paris and Rome, she studied in Philadelphia at the Museum School of Industrial
Art. Many of her paintings were exhibited and sold in
the Orient when she lived there with her father who
was a doctor. Several of her pictures were purchased
by the King of Siam. Besides book illustration, Margaret Ayer has been the author of books and stories.
She illustrated three works by J. Bothwell, Little Boat
Boy (Harcourt, 1945), Peter Holt, P. K., (Harcourt,
1950), and River Boy of Kashmir (Morrow, 1946).
ICB-2

-B-

BACON, Peggy (Margaret Frances), 1895- . Artist, author,
teacher. She was born in Ridgefield, Connecticut, and
later made her home in New York City. She studied
in New Jersey at the Kent Place School and in New
York at both the School of Fine and Applied Art and the
Art Students League. She received a Guggenheim Fellowship and a National Academy of Arts and Letters
award. Her parents were the noted artists Charles
Roswell and Elizabeth Chase Bacon. In addition to illustrating books, Peggy Bacon has been an art instructor, contributed drawings to such magazines as the New
Yorker, and written books. Her work has been exhibited here and abroad, and many museums and private
collectors own her paintings. For young people she illustrated T. Robinson's Buttons (Viking, 1938) and C.
Govan's Number 5 Hackberry Street (World, 1964). She
also wrote and illustrated The Ghost of Opalina (Little,
1967). ICB-1, ICB-2, ICB-3

BAHTI, Tom. He has written several books pertaining to Indian crafts and tribes belonging to the Southwestern region of the United States. In addition, he has created
many drawings and outstanding prints. Mr. Bahti graduated from the University of New Mexico's Anthropology
Department. He used "amatl" paper, a handmade bark
paper made by the Otomi Indians of Puebla, Mexico for
his illustrations in B. Baylor's Before You Came This
Way (Dutton, 1969).

BAILEY-JONES, Beryl, 1912- . She was born in New York
City and grew up there and in Maine. She received her
education in Brooklyn at Pratt Institute and in New
York at both the Art Students League and National
Academy of Design. She has designed greeting cards
and magazines in addition to book illustration. She
married Burton J. Jones, Jr., and they have resided
in Marblehead, Massachusetts. For children she illustrated E. Eager's Mouse Manor (Pellegrini & Cudahy,
1952). ICB-2

BAKACS, George. Illustrator and book designer. He received his education at the University of Industrial Arts
in Budapest, Hungary, where he was born. He also
studed at Colgate University in Hamilton, New York.

His home has been in Flushing, New York. In addition to children's books, George Bakacs has illustrated encyclopedias and textbooks. He has also designed record covers. For boys and girls he illustrated A. Silverstein's Circulatory Systems: The Rivers Within (Prentice-Hall, 1970).

BALDRIDGE, Cyrus Le Roy, 1889- . Cartoonist, illustrator, teacher. Born in Alton, New York, he later made his home in Santa Fe, New Mexico. He received his art education at Frank Holme's School of Illustration prior to graduating from the University of Chicago. At one time he served as President of the National Association of Commercial Arts and of both the University of Chicago Club and Artists Guild in New York. Mr. Baldridge has been a lecturer and teacher of book design in addition to illustrating books. He illustrated several books written by his wife Caroline Singer. He traveled throughout the Far East and visited the places mentioned by Marco Polo in order to sketch authentic pictures for R. Walsh's Adventures and Discoveries of Marco Polo (Random, 1953). He also illustrated M. Dodge's Hans Brinker (Grosset, n.d.) ICB-1, ICB-2

BALDWIN-FORD, Pamela. She spent her childhood in Torrington, Connecticut and studied at the Paier School of Art in Hamden, Connecticut. She later taught drawing and painting at Paier. She married artist and graphic designer Woodruff Ford and has lived in New Haven, Connecticut. For young people she illustrated V. Pitt's Let's Find Out about Neighbors (Watts, 1970) and J. Bothwell's The Parsonage Parrot (a Junior Literary Guild selection; Watts, 1969).

BALL, Robert. Artist and etcher. He was born in New York City and spent his childhood there. He also lived in France, England, and Spain. He studied in Brittany and in Paris at the Académie Colarossi. The artist later made his home in New York and Massachusetts. He has had exhibitions of his work in Paris. Robert Ball has created etchings and has also worked in water color. For young people he illustrated M. Pace's Clara Barton (Scribner's, 1941). ICB-2

BALTZER, Hans, 1900- . He was born in Berlin. At the age of 24 he decided to work in commercial art and

later illustrated books. He was awarded a silver medal at Leipzig's International Book Art Exhibition. The
artist has made his home in East Germany. In color
he illustrated J. Swift's Gulliver's Travels (Duell, 1961,
originally published by Kinderbuchverlag, Berlin as
"Gullivers Reisen"). ICB-3

BARE, Arnold Edwin, 1920- . He was born in New York
City, grew up on Long Island, and later made his
home in Huntington, Long Island. He studied at the
School of Industrial Art, in New York, and at the Yale
School of Fine Arts. His early interest in historical
drawing and puppetry combined with foreign travel
helped Mr. Bare in his career as an illustrator. For
boys and girls he illustrated two books by L. Kingman, Ilenka (Houghton, 1945) and Mikko's Fortune
(Ariel, 1955). ICB-1, ICB-2

BARKER, Carol Minturn, 1938- . Born in London, she
studied at the School of Art, Chelsea, London, Central
School of Arts and Crafts, London, and at the College
of Art, Bournemouth, Hampshire. She also spent a
year of training in graphic design in her father's studio.
Her first picture book in color resulted from a 1960
visit to Greece. Her work includes H. Bates' Achilles
the Donkey (Watts, 1962) and A. Fisher's I Wonder
How, I Wonder Why (Abelard-Schuman, 1962). She also wrote and illustrated Carol Barker's Birds and
Beasts (Watts, 1972). ICB-3

BARKLEY, James. He studied at the School of Visual Arts
and has made his home in Yonkers, New York. Mr.
Barkley's work has received much recognition including: the Society of Illustrators Gold Medal in 1969 and
the Society of Illustrators Award for Excellence in
1968. In addition to books, his illustrations have appeared in such magazines as Seventeen, Playboy, and
Redbook. He illustrated the 1970 Newbery Medal award
book Sounder, by W. Armstrong (Harper, 1969).

BARNES, Catherine J., 1918- . Art teacher and illustrator born in Philadelphia, Pennsylvania. She received
her education at the Philadelphia Museum School of Industrial Art and New York City's Art Students League.
In addition to book illustration, Catherine Barnes has
also worked in advertising and taught art in various
schools including oil painting at Rosemont College.

The artist married Roger E. Sullivan and has lived in
Mantua, New Jersey. Her juvenile book illustrations
include P. Lauber's The Runaway Flea Circus (Random, 1958) and D. Fisher's Understood Betsy (Holt,
1946). ICB-2

BARNETT, Moneta. This illustrator of books for children
received her education in New York at Cooper Union
and the Brooklyn Museum. Her drawings can be found
in M. Borreson's Let's Go to an Art Museum (Putnam, 1960). She also illustrated M. Elting's A Mongo
Homecoming (M. Evans, 1969).

BARNHART, Nancy, 1889- . She was born in St. Louis,
Missouri, and later made her home in Brookline, Massachusetts. She received her education in St. Louis
at Mary Institute and in New York City at the Art Students League. She also attended Smith College and
did further study in Paris. Miss Barnhart has been
both an artist and author. She has written and illustrated articles about the Holy Land for newspapers.
Her illustrations can be found in K. Grahame's The
Wind in the Willows (Scribner's, 1913). ICB-1, ICB-2

BARRETT, Alan. Illustrator, costume and graphic designer,
he has worked in the theater as a free-lance designer.
At one time the artist was associated with the BBC
in England and was the recipient of an Arts Council
Bursary in Theatre Design. In addition to his work
in Bristol at the Theatre Royal, Alan Barrett has done
costume design for the film industry. For children he
illustrated P. Pearce's Beauty and the Beast (Crowell,
1972).

BARRETT, Ron. Art director and illustrator, Ron Barrett
spent his early years in New York City. He attended
schools in Manhattan and the Bronx and graduated from
Brooklyn's Pratt Institute. He has served in the Army,
worked in advertising, and has been an advertising art
director in addition to illustrating books for children.
Mr. Barrett has also been associated with television
as a consulting art director. His drawings can be
found in three of J. Barrett's works: Animals Should
Definitely Not Wear Clothing (Atheneum, 1970), Benjamin's 365 Birthdays (Atheneum, 1974) and Old Mac-
Donald Had an Apartment House (Atheneum, 1969).

BARRIOS, David. Artist-caricaturist. He graduated from
    Reed College in Portland, Oregon, where he studied
    Mexican-American literature. Prior to a fulltime ca-
    reer as a writer and illustrator, David Barrios was
    associated with the public schools in Portland. His
    hobbies have included fishing and swimming in addition
    to children and drawing. He illustrated C. Keller's
    Ballpoint Bananas and Other Jokes for Kids (Prentice-
    Hall, 1973).

BARRY, James E. Artist, portrait painter, native New
    Yorker. After graduating from Brooklyn's Pratt Insti-
    tute, he attended the Art Career School in New York
    City. Mr. Barry served in West Berlin in Army In-
    telligence. Following his years in service, he devoted
    his time to painting portraits and book illustration
    which includes S. Rosenfeld's Ask Me a Question About
    Rockets, Satellites, and Space Stations (Harvey, 1971),
    B. Seeman's The Story of Electricity and Magnetism
    (Harvey, 1967) and A. Witting's A Treasury of Greek
    Mythology (Harvey, 1966).

BARSS, William, 1916- . Born in Syracuse, New York, he
    grew up in Ohio where he later studied at the Columbus
    Art School. He also attended the Child-Walker School
    of Design in Boston, Massachusetts. He has lived in
    China; first, as an illustrator in the Office of War In-
    formation during World War II and later as a Cultural
    Relations Officer for the U.S. Information Service. He
    has enjoyed working in the medium of casein when il-
    lustrating books for boys and girls. He and his family
    have lived in Boston, Massachusetts. William Barss
    illustrated: B. Walker's Hilili and Dilili (Follett, 1965)
    and I. Asimov's Words of Science (Houghton, 1959).
    ICB-3

BARTSCH, Jochen, 1906- . He was born in Germany and
    later attended the School for Applied Art in Breslau,
    the Academy for Applied Art in Munich, and Berlin's
    Reimannschule. Prior to devoting his time to graphic
    arts, he worked in ceramics. During World War II,
    he was in the German Army and became a prisoner in
    France. His work has won prizes and recognition in
    Germany and Austria. Mr. Bartsch and his family
    have lived in Gauting, Germany. For boys and girls
    he illustrated J. Krüss' My Great-Grandfather and I
    (tr. from German by Edelgard von Heydekampf Brühl;
    Atheneum, 1964). ICB-3

BASILEVSKY, Helen, 1939- . She was born in Brussels,
Belgium. She came to this country in 1949 and settled
in Sea Cliff, Long Island where she has continued to
live. After receiving a B. A. degree from Pratt Institute in Brooklyn, Miss Basilevsky toured Europe and
the Middle East for six months. In 1963 she served
as an interpreter with the U. S. I. A. exhibit in Russia.
For children she illustrated M. Masey's Branislav the
Dragon (a Junior Literary Guild selection) (McKay,
1967), and S. Rosenfeld's Drop of Water (Harvey,
1970).

BATTAGLIA, Aurelius. He studied at the Corcoran School
of Art in Washington. He has painted murals for children's rooms and illustrated for both periodicals and
newspapers. He also worked and taught at the Walt
Disney Studios. During World War II, he did educational film work for the Navy. Later he made his
home in New Jersey. For young people he illustrated
The Fireside Book of Favorite American Songs, ed. by
M. Boni (Simon, 1952).

BAUERNSCHMIDT, Marjorie, 1926- . An artist who has
worked in pen and ink, she was born in Baltimore,
Maryland. She married electrical engineer Edward F.
Barnhart, and they have lived in Ellicott City, Maryland. The artist graduated cum laude from Wilson
College in Chambersburg, Pennsylvania, where she illustrated her first book. At one time she worked in
the field of advertising. Her juvenile illustrations can
be found in Lillian Morrison's books; Remember Me
When This You See (Crowell, 1961) and Yours Till
Niagara Falls (Crowell, 1950). ICB-2

BAUMHAUER, Hans, 1913- . Artist, painter, traveler.
He was born in Munich, Germany, and studied there
at the Academy of Fine Arts. He later made his home
in Freiburg in Breisgau, South Baden, Germany. He
learned the art of stained-glass windows when he was
a teenager, and in 1952 he began his career in mosa-
ics and stained-glass windows when he opened his own
studio. He did further art study during his travels
which included the Far East. His work has also included portraits, ceramics, sculpture, and Gobelin
tapestries. For young people he illustrated M. Dodge's
Hans Brinker (Dutton, 1956). ICB-2

BAYNES, Pauline Diana, 1922- . Born in Brighton, England, she spent her early years in India and later in
southern England. Pauline Baynes attended both the
Farnham and Slade Schools of Art. She married Fritz
Otto Gasch and has lived near Farnham in Surrey.
The artist has belonged to the Society of Industrial
Arts. She has always been interested in book illustration, and her drawings can be found in Uden's A Dictionary of Chivalry (Crowell, 1968). ICB-2, ICB-3

BEER, Richard. Artist, stage designer, lecturer. He was
born in London, England, where he later attended
Slade School and University College in London. He al-
so studied in Paris and at Ardengly College in Sussex.
Richard Beer has been a stage designer for the Royal
Ballet and has lectured at the Chelsea School of Art in
London. His work can be found in London's Victoria
and Albert Museum and at the Metropolitan Museum of
Art in New York. He illustrated R. Green's Tales
from Shakespeare (Atheneum, 1965). ICB-3

BEGAY, Harrison. Illustrator and painter, born in Arizona
on the Navajo reservation at White Cone. Prior to
serving in Europe and Iceland during World War II, he
attended Black Mountain College in North Carolina.
Mr. Begay has received many prizes for his work in
Indian art and was awarded the French Palme Aca-
démique medal for artistic achievement. His paintings
have been exhibited in art galleries and museums
throughout Europe and the United States. For boys
and girls he illustrated A. Crowell's A Hogan for the
Bluebird (Scribner's, 1969).

BELL, Corydon, 1894- . Born in Tiffin, Ohio, he studied
at the University of Michigan and Western Reserve University in Cleveland. Prior to his work in book design
and illustration, he worked in commercial art. He
married Thelma Harrington, a writer. The Bells have
lived near Cashiers, North Carolina. For young people
he illustrated E. Gray's I Will Adventure (Viking, 1962)
and J. Diggins' String, Straightedge, and Shadow (Viking, 1965). ICB-2, ICB-3

BELTRAN, Alberto, 1923- . Artist, illustrator, engraver,
born in Mexico City. He studied in Mexico at the
Free School of Art and Publicity (Escuela Libre de
Arte y Publicidad). He was awarded the National

Engraving Award in 1958 and placed first in the engraving section in the 1960 First Interamerican Painting and Engraving Biennial held in Mexico City. He
has become known as "the successor to the late Miguel
Covarrubias" because of his artistic abilities and deep
understanding of Mexico's ancient Indian cultures. For
boys and girls he illustrated B. Traven's Creation of
the Sun and the Moon (Hill & Wang, 1968) and V. Von
Hagen's Maya, Land of the Turkey and the Deer (World,
1960). ICB-3

BEMELMANS, Ludwig, 1898-1962. Born in Meran (then
part of Austria), the son of a Belgian painter. He
came to the United States at the age of 16. Following
his arrival in this country, he worked in several New
York hotels and studied painting. His first children's
book was Hansi (Viking, 1934). Many of the incidents
for his "Madeline" books were provided during the author's stay in France. In 1954 he was awarded the
Caldecott Medal for his book Madeline's Rescue (Viking,
1953). His other juvenile titles include: The High
World (Harper, 1954, Parsley (Harper, 1955), and
Quito Express (Viking, 1965). ICB-1, 2 & 3, ABYP-2

BENNETT, Rainey, 1907- . Born in Marion, Indiana, he
studied at the University of Chicago, Art Institute
of Chicago, the American Academy of Art, and the
George Grosz-Maurice Stern School in New York. He
later made his home in Chicago. Mr. Bennett has
been known as an outstanding watercolorist which
achievement resulted in several assignments to South
America. In addition to illustrating books, he has also done advertising for a large department store in
Chicago. He wrote and illustrated After the Sun Goes
Down (World, 1961), which was selected by the American Institute of Graphic Arts for their 1961-62 Children's Book Show. He also illustrated C. Cullen's My
Lives and How I Lost Them (Follett, 1969). ICB-3

BENNETT, Richard, 1899- . Although he was born in Ireland, Richard Bennett came to the United States at the
age of four. He has lived in both New York and Seattle, Washington. The artist attended Columbia University in New York and the University of Washington
in Seattle. He has been both a writer and artist and
has illustrated juvenile and adult books. Many of his
drawings have a western theme. He wrote and

illustrated Little Dermat and the Thirsty Stones, and
Other Irish Folk Tales (Coward-McCann, 1953). He
also illustrated W. MacKellar's Ghost in the Castle
(McKay, 1960). ICB-1, ICB-2

BENNETT, Susan. She was born in Minnesota and has made
her home in New York City. Miss Bennett studied at
St. Olaf College in Northfield, Minnesota. She later
attended art and music classes at the International Summer School in Oslo, Norway. For boys and girls she
illustrated A. Derleth's Beast in Holger's Woods (Crowell, 1968) and Y. Uchida's In-Between Miya (Scribner's, 1967).

BERELSON, Howard. He studied industrial design and sculpture at Pratt Institute in Brooklyn, New York and also
traveled in Mexico where he studied design. Mr. Berelson has made his home in Brooklyn, New York. His
work has appeared in magazines in addition to J.
May's The First Living Things (Holiday, 1970).

BERNSTEIN, Zena. She graduated from Syracuse University with a Bachelor of Fine Arts degree. Her black
and white illustrations which appeared in the 1972 Newbery Medal book, Mrs. Frisby and the Rats of NIMH,
by R. O'Brien (Atheneum, 1971), depicted birds and
animals with scientific accuracy; each feather of
the crow was meticulously drawn. Zena Bernstein's illustrations have also appeared in magazines. In addition to the Newbery Medal Book she
illustrated E. Coatsworth's Down Half the World (Macmillan, 1968).

BERSON, Harold, 1926- . Born in Los Angeles, he studied at the University of California at Los Angeles and
Grande Chaumiere Academy in Paris. In New York he
began his art career drawing for Humpty Dumpty magazine. Mr. Berson married an artist (Paula), and
they have lived in New York City. He and his wife
have enjoyed music, ballet, and travel. He illustrated
P. McGinley's Mince Pie and Mistletoe (Lippincott,
1961) and B. Lord's The Perfect Pitch (Walck, 1965).
Books which he wrote and illustrated include Pop! Goes
the Turnip (Grosset, 1966) and Why the Jackal Won't
Speak to the Hedgehog (Seabury, 1969). ICB-3

BIBLE, Charles, 1937- . He was born in Waco, Texas

and later made his home in San Francisco and New
York. Mr. Bible studied at Pratt Institute in Brooklyn. In addition to illustrating books for boys and
girls, he has been the artist for several poster series
including one on black poets. He illustrated N. Gio-
vanni's Spin a Soft Black Song (Hill, 1971).

BILECK, Marvin, 1920- . He was born in Passaic, New
Jersey, and studied at Cooper Union in New York, at
the London School of Architecture in England, and in
France on a Fulbright Grant. During World War II, he
was in the service in Europe, North Africa, and England. His pencil and water color drawings in Rain
Makes Applesauce (by J. Scheer; Holiday, 1964) received recognition not only as one of the New York
Times' "Ten Best Illustrated Children's Books" of the
year but also as runner-up for the Caldecott Medal in
1965. He later taught at the Philadelphia College of
Art. His work includes: M. Lawrence's Crissy at the
Wheel (Harcourt, n.d.), A. Colver's Nobody's Birthday
(Knopf, 1961), and J. Johnston's Sugarplum (Knopf,
1955). ICB-2, ICB-3

BINN, Mark. He received his education at the Parsons and
Phoenix Schools of Design. He also attended the Art
Students League in New York City. His work has ap-
peared in nature and science books for young readers.
He illustrated R. Kadesch's Math Menagerie (Harper,
1970).

BIRD, Alice. Artist-illustrator. Since members of her family were scientists, Alice Bird grew up learning to ap-
preciate and to observe accurately the world of nature.
As a talented craftsman, she combined her knowledge
of botany and art to portray realism in her book illustrations. Original lithographs were used in the M. Mc-
Kenny's book, Trees of the Countryside (Knopf, 1942).

BIRO, Val (Balint S.), 1921- . Born in Budapest, Hungary,
where he later studied at the Jaschnick School of Art.
He also attended the Central School of Art and Crafts in
London. Prior to becoming a free-lance artist in 1953,
he was in the publishing business. Mr. Biro has
stated that he does not specialize in illustrations for
children but does a great deal of work for magazines
and adults. His work includes: photography, gouache,
etching, and water color. He has made his home in

England. For young people he wrote and illustrated
Gumdrop (Follett, 1966). ICB-2, ICB-3

BJORKLUND, Lorence F. Artist-illustrator, born and educated in St. Paul, Minnesota. He later studied at
Pratt Institute in Brooklyn. He has worked both in
the magazine and advertising field but has preferred
illustrating books. He has been interested in American history and travel. At one time he traveled by
rowboat from St. Paul to New Orleans. Lorence
Bjorklund has made his home in Croton Falls, New
York. Juvenile books which he has illustrated include:
B. Grant's American Forts, Yesterday and Today (Dutton, 1965), M. Compton's American Indian Fairy Tales
(Dodd, n.d.), W. Hay's Pontiac: Lion in the Forest
(Houghton, 1965), M. Freeman's Stars and Stripes
(Random, 1964), and R. Montgomery's Thornbush Jun-
gle (World, 1966). ICB-2, ICB-3

BLAIR, Helen, 1910- . Born in Hibbing, Minnesota, the
artist grew up there and in Massachusetts, New York,
and New Jersey. She studied in Boston at the Museum
of Fine Arts and also attended the Massachusetts Normal Art School. Her chief interest has been in the
field of sculpture, and she has been associated with an
art firm in New York. She married Stanley Crosbie,
and they have lived in Grand Junction, Colorado. For
young people she illustrated three works by F. Means,
Assorted Sisters (a Junior Literary Guild selection;
Houghton, 1947), Great Day in the Morning (Houghton,
1946), and Moved Outers (Houghton, 1945). ICB-2

BLAISDELL, Elinore, 1904- . She was born in Brooklyn,
New York where she grew up. She also lived in Maryland and Pennsylvania, and later resided in New York.
The artist attended New York's Naum M. Los Art School.
and the Art Students League. She also studied in London at the Slade School of Fine Art. She has belonged
to both the Artists Guild and the Society of Illustrators.
In addition to book illustrating, Elinore Blaisdell has also been a writer. She was the recipient of the 1939
Julia Ellsworth Ford Foundation Prize. Juvenile books
which she has illustrated include: F. Oursler's Child's
Life of Jesus (Watts, 1951), and two by M. Hunt, Double
Birthday Present (Lippincott, 1947) and Matilda's Buttons (Lippincott, 1948). ICB-1, ICB-2

BLAKE, Quentin, 1932- . Born in Sidcup, Kent, England,
he studied at Downing College, Cambridge and in London at the University Institute of Education. He also
attended the Chelsea School of Art. In addition to
books, his illustrations have appeared in Punch magazine. Prior to being an art instructor at the Royal
College of Art in the School of Graphic Design, Quentin Blake taught English at the French Lycee in London. His home has been in South Kensington, London.
For boys and girls he illustrated J. Yeoman's Alphabet Soup (Follett, 1970); E. Rees' Pun Fun (Abelard-
Schuman, 1965), and E. Hunter's The Wonderful But-
ton (Abelard-Schuman, 1961). ICB-3

BLEGVAD, Erik, 1923- . He was born and grew up in
Copenhagen, Denmark where he later studied at the
school of Arts and Crafts (Københavns Kunsthåndvärk-
erskole). Mr. Blegvad has worked in a Copenhagen
advertising agency, as a free-lance artist in London,
and later became well-known in the United States as a
magazine and book illustrator. He married painter
Lenore Hochman and has lived in London and Westport,
Connecticut. His work includes B. Miles' Having a
Friend (Knopf, 1959) and L. Blegvad's Mr. Jensen &
Cat (Harcourt, 1965). Lenore and Erik Blegvad wrote
The Great Hamster Hunt (Harcourt, 1969). ICB-2,
ICB-3

BLOCH, Lucienne, 1909- . Born in Geneva, Switzerland,
the daughter of a composer, she studied at the École
des Beaux Arts in Paris and also in Florence and Berlin. She married artist Stephen P. Dmitroff, and they
have painted murals in Grand Rapids, Michigan and San
Jose, California. Museums in the United States and
Europe have had in their collections both her lithographs and glass sculpture. The recipient of many
awards, Lucienne Bloch has made her home in Mill
Valley, California. She illustrated E. Hurd's Sand-
pipers (Crowell, 1961) and E. Hurd's Starfish (Crowell, 1962). ICB-1, ICB-2

BLUST, Earl R. Artist, painter, printmaker. Born in Har-
risburg, Pennsylvania, he graduated from the College
of Art in Philadelphia. He has lived in Lemoyne,
Pennsylvania, where he has been an art director for
the Krone Art Service. His work has been shown in
private collections and in many exhibits. For children

he illustrated E. Wier's <u>Action at Paradise Marsh</u> (a Junior Literary Guild selection) Stackpole, 1968).

BOBRI, V.   see   BOBRITSKY, Vladimir

BOBRITSKY, Vladimir, 1898- . V. Bobri is his pseudonym. This artist and musician was born in Kharkov, Ukraine. He studied at the Kharkov Imperial Art School. Vladimir Bobri has been recognized as an authority on folk lore of different countries and on gypsy music. Before coming to America in 1921, he worked with archeologists in Turkey and the Crimea and painted icons in Greece. Mr. Bobri operated a textile firm in the United States, painted murals, and worked in advertising in addition to book illustration. He has also served as art director and editor of <u>Guitar Review</u> magazine. He has directed radio programs of chamber music. The artist has received several citations from the Art Directors Club for advertising design and numerous awards for book illustration. His work can be found in: R. Gans' <u>Icebergs</u> (Crowell, 1964) and B. Budney's <u>A Kiss Is Round</u> (a Junior Literary Guild selection; Lothrop, 1954). ICB-2, ICB-3

BOCK, Vera. Born in St. Petersburg, Russia, her mother was a Russian concert pianist and her father, an American banker. At the time of the Revolution, she came to the United States to live; however, she spent a year in England where she studied engraving. It was also at this time that she became interested in photoengraving and the printing process. She has had a one-man show in the Farnsworth Art Museum in Rockland, Maine, and her work has appeared in many exhibitions including one sponsored by the State Department which toured Burma, India, and Ceylon. Vera Bock's home has been in New York City. For young people she illustrated two works edited by A. Lang <u>Arabian Nights</u> (Longmans, 1946), and <u>Rose Fairy Book</u> (Longmans, 1948). ICB-1, ICB-2, ICB-3

BOCK, William Sauts. His Indian name is Netamuxwe. Lecturer and artist, a graduate of the Philadelphia College of Art. A Lutheran minister, he has worked with the Navaho Indians in Arizona. In order to find important Indian sites, the artist has traveled the Susquehanna River by canoe. The Oklahoma Cherokee-Lenapes adopted William Bock into their tribe and gave him an

Indian name. He illustrated for young people Alex W.
Bealer's Only the Names Remain (Little, 1972).

BODECKER, Nils Mogens, 1922- . N. M. Bodecker was
born in Copenhagen, Denmark, where he later studied
art at the School of Applied Arts (Kunsthåndvärkerskole).
He came to the United States in 1952. He has been an
editorial assistant on an art magazine, and his illustrations have appeared in newspapers and magazines. Mr.
Bodecker has also written poetry. In 1972 his book
Miss Jaster's Garden (Western, 1972) was selected as
one of "Ten Best Illustrated Books" of the year by the
New York Times. He illustrated: E. Eager's Magic
or Not? (Harcourt, 1959) and E. Eager's Seven-Day
Magic (Harcourt, 1962). ICB-2, ICB-3

BOKER, Irving. This artist and his family have made their
home on Long Island. His juvenile illustrations can be
found in E. Wuorio's The Singing Canoe (World, 1969).

BOLDEN, Joseph. Joseph Bolden has worked in both advertising and book illustration. He studied at the Philadelphia Museum School of Industrial Art. His work has
appeared in Jack and Jill and other magazines. For
young people he illustrated L. Silliman's The Purple
Tide (Winston, 1949).

BOLIAN, Polly. Prior to graduating from the Rhode Island
School of Design, the artist attended George Washing-
ton University. She also studied at New York's Art
Students League and the Corcoran Gallery of Art. Her
home has been in Easthampton, Long Island, New York.
At one time Miss Bolian was art director for CARE,
Inc. In addition to illustrating books and magazines,
she has also worked in advertising. For boys and
girls she illustrated: G. Marks' The Amazing Stetho-
scope (Messner, 1971); F. West's Getting to Know the
Two Vietnams (Coward-McCann, 1963), and I. Bowen's
The Mystery of the Talking Well (Lippincott, 1966).

BOLOGNESE, Donald Alan, 1934- . Calligrapher, illustrator, born in New York City. He studied and later
taught at Cooper Union Art School. His work has not
only appeared in books but also in the magazine sections
of newspapers. Mr. Bolognese has also taught calligraphy at Pratt Institute in Brooklyn. Books which he
has illustrated include: J. Ritchie's Apple Seeds &

Soda Straws (Walck, 1965), C. Bulla's The Ghost of
Windy Hill (Crowell, 1968), and J. Lexau's More Beautiful Than Flowers (Lippincott, 1966). ICB-3

BONE, Stephen, 1904- . English artist. Born in London,
Mr. Bone spent part of his childhood in Italy. He
studied art at the Slade School of Fine Art in London.
His father was also an artist, Sir Muirhead Bone.
Stephen Bone's work has been included in numerous
collections, and he has served as art critic of the Manchester Guardian. With his wife, Mary Adshead, he
collaborated on The Little Boy and His House (Winston,
1937). ICB-2

BONSALL, Crosby Barbara (Newell), 1921- . Born in New
York City, she later made her home in Hillsgrove,
Pennsylvania. She studied at the New York University
School of Architecture and American School of Design
in New York City. Mrs. Bonsall has worked in adver-
tising, written books, and created doll characters.
Crosby Bonsall has also illustrated books for other
writers. Some of her books have appeared under the
name of Crosby Newell. She illustrated R. Underwood's
Ask Me Another Riddle (Grosset, 1964) and J. Nodset's
Go Away Dog (Harper, 1963). Juvenile books which she
wrote and illustrated include The Case of the Dumb Bells
(Harper, 1966) and Who's a Pest? (Harper, 1962). ICB-3

BOOTH, Graham, 1935- . British artist and teacher. He
was born in London, grew up in Canada, and has lived
in Placentia and Laguna Beach, California. He attended
the University of California at Los Angeles and received
his master's degree in fine arts from the University of
Southern California. Graham Booth has been an art director, free-lance artist, and has managed an advertising agency. At one time he served on the staff of
the Vancouver School of Art but later taught art at
Fullerton Junior College. Juvenile books which he illustrated include: M. Taylor's Bobby Shafto's Gone to
Sea (Golden Gate, 1970), M. Taylor's Henry the Ex-
plorer (a Junior Literary Guild selection; Atheneum,
1966), and P. Martin's Sing, Sailor, Sing (Golden Gate,
1966). ICB-3

BORJA, Corinne and Robert. Husband-wife team who have
lived in Chicago. Both attended the Institute of Design
and the American Academy of Art. Corinne Borja has

worked as a fashion illustrator, and her husband has
been interested in wood engraving, typesetting, filmstrips, and book design. They illustrated N. Richards'
Giants in the Sky (a Junior Literary Guild selection;
Children's Press, 1967).

BORJA, Robert   see   BORJA, Corinne

BORNSCHLEGEL, Ruth. She spent her childhood in Denver,
Colorado, was graduated from Harding College in Sear-
cy, Arkansas, and did advanced study at the Kansas
City Art Institute. Her home has been in New York
City where she has been a book designer for a publish-
ing firm. Prior to her career as an illustrator, Miss
Bornschlegel was a commercial artist and worked in li-
braries. For children she illustrated P. Cohen's The
Bull in the Forest (a Junior Literary Guild selection;
Atheneum, 1969).

BOZE, Calvin. A free-lance artist, Calvin Bozé received
his art training at the Art Center College of Design in
Los Angeles. He has been both a designer and illustrator. His drawings can be found in S. Lewis' The
Tell It--Make It Book (Hawthorn Books, 1972).

BOZZO, Frank. He was born in Chicago, attended New
York's School of Visual Arts, and has made his home
in New York City. Prior to illustrating books for
young people, he illustrated for magazines and adult
books. He illustrated: A. Shulman's Awake or Asleep
(Young Scott Books, 1971) and G. McHargue's The
Beasts of Never (Bobbs, 1968).

BRAGG, Charles. He has illustrated for magazines in addition to books for young people. He has had one-man
shows, and his work has appeared on record covers.
The recipient of a Gold Medal by the Society of Illustrators, the artist has lived in California. He illustrated S. Fleischman's Longbeard the Wizard (Little,
1970).

BRANSOM, Paul, 1885- . He was born in Washington,
D.C. Paul Bransom has been called the "dean of
American animal artists." When he was 17, he was
drawing for the New York Evening Journal. Early in
his career, he also contributed illustrations to an encyclopedia. At one time he had a studio in the N.Y.

Zoological Park. Mr. Bransom has belonged to:
Audubon Artists, Society of Illustrators, Salmagundi
Club, and the American Water Color Society. He has
lived on a ranch in Jackson Hole, Wyoming, and spent
his summers at Canada Lake in the Adirondacks. He
illustrated H. McCracken's <u>Biggest Bear on Earth</u>
(Stokes, 1943), R. Perkins' <u>Marlin Perkins' Zooparade</u>
(Rand, 1954) and J. Lippincott's <u>Wahoo Bobcat</u> (Lippincott, 1950). ICB-1, ICB-2

BRENNER, Fred. Born in Newark, New Jersey, he later
made his home in West Nyack, New York. He received his education at the School of Fine Arts in Colorado Springs and the Art Students League in New York.
Mr. Brenner has been both a book and magazine illustrator. For young people he illustrated: F. Monjo's
<u>The Drinking Gourd</u> (Harper, 1970), and his wife Bar-
bara's <u>The Flying Patchwork Quilt</u> (a Junior Guild selection; Scott, 1965).

BREVANNES, Maurice, 1904- . French artist. Born in
Paris, he attended school there at the Académies Julian and Ranson. He also studied at the Ecole des Arts
Décoratifs. The artist became an American citizen after coming to the United States when he was 25 years
old. His home has been in Westport, Connecticut. Mr.
Brevannes painted murals for the New York World's
Fair in 1939. His paintings have been exhibited in
Philadelphia and New York. The artist has traveled
abroad and in Canada and the United States. For young
people he illustrated: two works by C. Bishop <u>Bern-
ard and His Dogs</u> (Houghton, 1952) and <u>Lafayette:
French-American Hero</u>, Garrard, 1960). ICB-2

BREY, Charles. He was born in Kansas City, Missouri,
and grew up in Pittsburgh, Pennsylvania, where he
later made sketches of its steel industry. Following
service in the Air Force, Mr. Brey attended the Carnegie Institute, the University of Pittsburgh, and the
Rhode Island School of Design. He has worked in advertising in New York and later was associated with an
engineering firm as a staff artist. In 1957 he became
a free-lance artist and has illustrated for monthly publications. For boys and girls he illustrated J. Mun-
ves' <u>We Were There at the Opening of the Atomic Era</u>
(Grosset, 1960).

BRIGGS, Raymond Redvers, 1934- . Born in London, England, he grew up in Wimbledon where he later attended the School of Art. He also studied at the Slade School of Fine Art in London. Mr. Briggs and his wife, a painter, have made their home near Brighton. He has worked in advertising in addition to illustrating books. He compiled and illustrated Fee Fi Fo Fum (Coward, 1964) which was the runner-up for the Kate Greenaway Medal awarded by England's Library Association for "the most distinguished work in the illustration of children's books." He received that award for his illustrations in The Mother Goose Treasury (Coward, 1966). He also illustrated I. Serraillier's Tale of Three Landlubbers (Coward, 1971). ICB-3

BRIGHAM, Grace. An artist and librarian, Miss Brigham graduated from Goddard College in Plainfield, Vermont and also attended the Boston Museum of Fine Arts. In addition to book illustrating, she has been assistant regional librarian of the Free Public Library Service, Regional Library in Rutland, Vermont, and a free-lance artist. Her home has been in Cuttingsville, Vermont. For young people she illustrated W. Osgood's Ski Touring (Tuttle, 1969).

BRIGHT, Robert, 1902- . He was born in Sandwich, Massachusetts, and spent his childhood in the town of Göttingen, Germany. Later he made his home in Santa Fe, New Mexico, and in La Jolla, California. He studied at Princeton University. He has worked in advertising in New York City and has written for the Baltimore Sun. Many children have enjoyed his "Georgie the Ghost" picture books. Mr. Bright has written his books and used acetate in two- and three-color separations in his illustrations. The Brussels World's Fair honored him with a showing of "Georgie" in 1959. He wrote and illustrated, all for Doubleday, Friendly Bear (1957), Georgie (1944), Georgie and the Magician (1966), and Georgie and the Noisy Ghost (1971). ICB-2, ICB-3

BRINCKLOE, Julie. A native of Mare Island, California, Julie Brinckloe later made her home in Pittsburgh, Pennsylvania. She attended Pittsburgh's Carnegie-Mellon University and also studied in Virginia at Sweet Briar College. Her illustrations can be found in Art Buchwald's The Bollo Caper (Doubleday, 1974).

BROMHALL, Winifred. She was born in Walsall, England, and later studied at the Walsall Art School in Birmingham. She also attended Birmingham University. After arriving in America in 1924, Winifred Bromhall worked in Boston in the Children's Art Center and in the Art Department of a New York Settlement. Her home has been in Ithaca, New York. She wrote and illustrated, all for Knopf, Bridget's Growing Day (1957), The Chipmunk That Went to Church (1952), Johanna Arrives (1941), and Mary Ann's Duck (1967). ICB-1, ICB-2

BROOKE, Leonard Leslie, 1862-1940. Born in Birkenhead, England, the illustrator attended the Royal Academy Schools. L. Leslie Brooke has been compared to Randolph Caldecott, who also had a gifted quality of illustrating a story with wit and humor. The noted illustrator married his cousin, Sybil Diana Brooke, and they lived near London at Hampstead. In addition to illustrating picture books for children, he has done portraits and watercolors. His most famous books, which he wrote and illustrated, include: Johnny Crow's Garden (1904) and Johnny Crow's Party (1907), both published by Warne.

BROOMFIELD, Robert, 1930- . He was born in Brighton, Sussex, England, and later studied at the Brighton School of Art and Crafts. He worked in advertising prior to becoming a free-lance artist. The majority of his work has been done in color. Mr. Broomfield has lived in England where he also contributed drawings to a children's television show on BBC in addition to illustrating books for children. His work includes A. Hewett's Mr. Faksimily & the Tiger (Follett, 1969). ICB-3

BROWN, Marcia Joan, 1918- . Born in Rochester, New York, she attended the State College for Teachers in Albany, Columbia University, the Woodstock School of Painting, the New School for Social Research, and the Art Students League. She later worked with children in the New York Public Library. After telling the story of Stone Soup (Scribner's, 1947), she decided to create a picture book about it. She won the Caldecott Medal in 1955 for Cinderella (Scribner's, 1954) and again in 1962 for Once a Mouse (Scribner's, 1961). Other titles include Bun: A Tale from Russia

(Harcourt, 1972) and five for Scribner's: <u>Dick Whitt</u>-<u>tington and His Cat</u> (1950), <u>Felice</u> (1958), <u>How, Hippo</u>!
(1969), <u>Little Carousel</u> (1946), and <u>The Neighbors</u>
(1967). ICB-2, ICB-3, ABYP-2

BROWN, Palmer, 1919- . Born in Chicago, Illinois, he
grew up in the suburb of Evanston and in Pennsylvania.
His home has been in Bareville, Pennsylvania. The
artist received his B.A. degree from Swarthmore College and his M.A. from the University of Pennsylvania
in Philadelphia. He served in the Air Force during
World War II. His work has been published in both
children's and adult magazines including <u>Jack and Jill</u>
and <u>Woman's Day</u>. For boys and girls he wrote and illustrated: all for Harper, <u>Beyond the Pawpaw Tree</u>
(1954), <u>Cheerful</u> (1957) and <u>Something for Christmas</u>
(1958). ICB-2, ICB-3

BRUSSEL-SMITH, Bernard, 1914- . Art director, illustrator, teacher, born in New York's Greenwich Village.
He studied at the Pennsylvania Academy of the Fine
Arts and was the recipient of the Cresson Scholarship
for foreign travel. He also attended New York's New
School for Social Research where he later became an
instructor. Besides teaching at the New School for Social Research, he has been a teacher of graphic design
and wood engraving at Cooper Union and the Philadelphia Museum School of Art. The artist has received
the Philadelphia Art Directors Club's first prize Gold
Medal. His work has appeared in numerous magazines
including <u>Newsweek</u>, <u>Time</u>, and <u>Reader's Digest</u>. B.
Brussel-Smith has also worked in advertising. He illustrated E. Weart's <u>Royal Game</u> (Vanguard, 1948).
ICB-2

BRUSTLEIN, Daniel. His pseudonym is Alain. Born in Al-
sace, France, he became an American citizen and has
lived both in Paris and in New Jersey. Alain's cartoons have appeared frequently in the <u>New Yorker</u> magazine. He married the former Janice Tworkov (see
ABYP-2). The artist illustrated his wife's picture book,
<u>Minette</u>, "by Janice" (McGraw, 1959). ICB-2

BRYSON, Bernarda, 1903- . Born in Athens, Ohio, she
studied at Ohio University, Ohio State University, Cleveland School of Art, and the New School for Social Research in New York. In addition to books, her

illustrations have appeared in many magazines. She
has also worked on newspapers and taught art. Her
husband, Ben Shahn, has also been an artist. They
have lived in Roosevelt, New Jersey. For young people
she illustrated: H. Gregory's Alphabet for Joanna
(Holt, 1963), N. Belting's Calendar Moon (Holt, 1964),
and P. Clarke's The Return of the Twelves (Coward-
McCann, 1962). ICB-3

BUBA, Joy Flinsch. She was born and grew up in Lloyd's
Neck, Huntington, Long Island. At the age of 16 she
traveled and lived abroad. Joy Buba's early interest
in birds and animals on Long Island later inspired her
work as an artist. She has studied in New York, Paris, at the Städel Kunst Institut in Frankfurt, and also
at the Munich Academy in Germany. Her work has appeared in numerous magazines, on television, and in
books for young people. The artist later made her
home in New York City. For boys and girls she illustrated H. Zim's Frogs and Toads (Morrow, 1950).
ICB-2

BURCKMYER, Elizabeth. Born in California, she studied
at Cornell University and later became an associate
professor of freehand drawing at the University. She
has also done free-lance illustrating. The book which
she illustrated for young people was M. Phillips' The
Makers of Honey (Crowell, 1956).

BURKERT, Nancy Ekholm, 1933- . Born in Sterling, Colorado, she grew up in the Midwest, and graduated from
the University of Wisconsin. She married artist Robert Burkert who has been an Associate Professor of
Art at the University of Wisconsin, and they have lived
in Milwaukee. Nancy Burkert has held watercolor exhibitions in New York and Chicago. She illustrated H.
Andersen's The Nightingale (Harper, 1965) which was
a 1965 Honor Book in the New York Herald Tribune's
Spring Book Festival. It also received the 1966 Gold
Medal awarded by the Society of Illustrators. Other
juvenile books which she illustrated include J. Up-
dike's Child's Calendar (Knopf, 1965), H. Andersen's
Fir Tree (Harper, 1970) and N. Carlson's Jean-
Claude's Island (Harper, 1963). ICB-3

BURNINGHAM, John Mackintosh, 1936- . Artist, illustrator, muralist, born in England. He attended the

Central School of Arts in Holborn, London, at the age
of 20. Mr. Burningham has resided in London where
he has designed posters, murals, and illustrated books.
His work has also appeared in magazines. He was
awarded the 1963 Kate Greenaway Medal for his first
book Borka (Random, 1963). He also wrote and illustrated: Eighty Days (Holt, 1972) and Harquin (Bobbs,
1967). He illustrated I. Fleming's Chitty Chitty Bang
Bang (Random, 1964). ICB-3

BURNS, Irene. She was born in Boston, graduated from the
Massachusetts College of Art, and has lived in Brookline. Irene Burns has taught art and painted portraits
in addition to illustrating books. Her work can be
found in V. Andrus' Black River (Little, 1967) and J.
Jackson's Missing Melinda (a Junior Literary Guild selection; Little, 1967).

BURRIS, Burmah. She graduated from college in Mississippi and continued her studies at the Art Institute in
Chicago. Prior to working as a free-lance artist, she
taught high school mathematics and science. Her work
has appeared in adult books and magazines. Her first
illustrations for young people appeared in B. Carlson's
Listen! and Help Tell the Story (Abingdon, 1965). She
also illustrated C. Shapp's Let's Find Out about Police-
men (Watts, 1962).

BURTON, Virginia Lee, 1909- . Born in Newton Centre,
Massachusetts, the artist later lived in Gloucester,
Massachusetts. She studied art and dancing at the Cali-
fornia School of Fine Arts and also attended Boston's
Demetrios School of Drawing and Sculpture. She has
taught dancing and contributed sketches to the Boston
Transcript. She won the Caldecott Medal in 1943 for
her book The Little House (Houghton, 1942). Juvenile
titles include: six works by Houghton, Calico, The
Wonder Horse (1950); Choo Choo (1937), Katy and the
Big Snow (1943), Life Story (1962), Maybelle, The
Cable Car (1952) and Mike Mulligan and His Steam
Shovel (1939). ICB-1, ICB-2, ICB-3, ABYP-2

BYFIELD, Barbara Ninde. Artist and author. She has
lived in New York in Greenwich Village. An expert in
cooking, she has also been interested in the supernatur-
al world of sorcerers, gnomes, and vampires. Barbara Byfield has been both an illustrator and author.

Her drawings can be found in S. Agnew's The Giant
Sandwich (Doubleday, 1970).

BYRD, Grady. Artist and illustrator, Mr. Byrd has been
awarded many prizes for his work. He has been associated with Keesler Air Force Base as a technical illustrator. Grady Byrd has exhibited his work in New
Orleans at the Nahan Galleries. For children he illustrated D. Titler's Unnatural Resources (Prentice-Hall,
1973).

-C-

CALDECOTT, Randolph, 1846-1886. The Caldecott Medal,
awarded to the artist of the most distinguished American picture book for children published in a given year,
was named after this English illustrator. Born in
Chester, England, he later worked in a bank and studied at the Manchester School of Art. He worked with
the distinguished engraver Edmund Evans, and together
they created many picture books. Married to Marion
Brind, he lived near London. When he was 40, Randolph Caldecott died of tuberculosis in St. Augustine,
Florida. He created Randolph Caldecott's Picture
Book (No. 1) Containing The Diverting History of John
Gilpin, The House That Jack Built, An Elegy on the
Death of a Mad Dog, The Babes in the Wood (Warne,
n. d.).

CAMPBELL, Virginia, 1914- . She was born in New Or-
leans, Louisiana and studied at Gulf Park College,
Gulfport, Mississippi, King-Smith Studio School, Lisa
Gardiner Ballet School, and New York's American
Academy of Dramatic Arts. Prior to painting, Virginia
Campbell was in the theater, where she appeared in
plays with both Judith Anderson and Eva LaGallienne.
She married John Becker and has lived in Rome. She
illustrated her husband's book, Near-Tragedy at the
Waterfall (Pantheon, 1964). ICB-2

CARIGIET, Alois, 1902- . Commercial artist and book il-
lustrator, he was born in Truns (Grisons), Switzerland.
He later made his home in Zürich. A noted muralist,
Mr. Carigiet has also been a writer. He was a 1966
recipient of the Hans Christian Andersen International
Children's Book Medal. He wrote and illustrated:

Anton and Anne (Walck, 1969), <u>The Pear Tree, the Birch Tree & the Barberry Bush</u> (Walck, 1967). He also illustrated S. Chönz's <u>The Snowstorm</u> (Walck, 1958). ICB-2, ICB-3

CARLE, Eric. Artist, art director, graphic designer. He was born in Syracuse, New York, grew up in Stuttgart, Germany, and has lived in Greenwich Village, New York City. Eric Carle has worked in advertising and for the <u>New York Times</u> in addition to illustrating books. At one time his poster designs were used in Germany by the U.S. Information Service. The artist has traveled in Europe and Mexico and has been associated with foreign publishing firms. Both the Society of Illustrators and the American Institute of Graphic Arts have exhibited his work. The International Children's Book Fair in Bologna awarded him first prize in 1970 for his work. For children he illustrated A. Fisher's <u>Feathered Ones and Furry</u> (a Junior Literary Guild selection; Crowell, 1971).

CARLONI, Giancarlo. Illustrator and cartoonist. Born in Italy, he has resided in Milan. Italian children have enjoyed his book illustrations. Mr. Carloni later became a cartoonist and with Giulio Cingoli was awarded the 1964 Prize Venezia. Mr. Carloni collaborated with Mr. Cingoli to illustrate his first book for children in America. It was G. Rocco's <u>Gaetano the Pheasant</u>, (Harper, 1966). ICB-3

CARLSON, Al. His early life was spent in Baltimore, Maryland. He graduated from the University of Virginia in Charlottesville in 1959. Mr. Carlson has been associated with publishing and educational firms and has created "Sesame Street" films. His work has been exhibited in museums, and he was the recipient of the 1970 New York Society of Illustrators Award. For boys and girls he illustrated D. Carlson's <u>The Human Apes</u> (a Junior Literary Guild selection; Atheneum, 1973).

CARRICK, Donald. He has illustrated many books written by his wife, Carol Carrick. Their small son and dog first appeared in their book, <u>The Dirt Road</u> (Macmillan, 1970). This book also had as its setting the landscape of the Carricks' Vermont summer home. During the remainder of the year they have made their home in New York City. His work with his wife includes

The Brook (Macmillan, 1967) and The Old Barn
(Bobbs-Merrill, 1966).

CARROLL, Ruth Robinson, 1899- . She was born in Lancaster, New York, and later studied at Vassar and the
Art Students League. Murals and portraits preceded
her first book for boys and girls, entitled What Whiskers Did (Walck, 1965; first published in 1932 by Macmillan), which was a story without words, only pictures. She married an author and editor named La-
trobe Carroll who later collaborated on books with her.
Ruth Carroll has received recognition for her work
since she was a junior in college, and the Pennsylvania
Academy selected one of her landscapes for exhibition
purposes. Mr. and Mrs. Carroll have lived in North
Carolina and New York. Her work includes The Chimp
and the Clown (Walck, 1968) and The Witch Kitten
(Walck, 1973). ICB-2, ICB-3

CARTY, Leo. He was born in New York City. When he
was 11 he was awarded a scholarship to the Museum
of Modern Art School for Children. Leo Carty later
studied at Cooper Union. Following service in the Air
Force, he attended Pratt Institute. Mr. Carty's greeting cards for Blacks have been created by his Anton
Studios, Inc. The Brooklyn Public Library had a one-
man show of his art work. He illustrated the following books for boys and girls: J. Griffin's Nat Turner
(Coward, 1970) W. Myers' Where Does the Day Go?
(Parents, 1969).

CARY [sic]. His books for boys and girls have been signed
by his surname. He studied at the Massachusetts
School of Art. In addition to illustrating books, he
has also worked in advertising. The artist and his
family have lived in West Barnstable, Massachusetts,
where he has served as director of the Cape Cod Art
Association and worked in the Little Theatre group.
He illustrated L. Anderson's Abe Lincoln and the River
Robbers (Garrard, 1971) and S. Russell's Wonderful
Stuff (Rand, 1963).

CATHER, Carolyn. The daughter of an army officer, she
spent her childhood in Japan and the Philippines. She
studied at Duke University in Durham, North Carolina.
Following World War II, she lived in Japan where she
worked on the newspaper Stars and Stripes. Carolyn

Cather later made her home in New York City.   Her
work includes: E. Helfman's Celebrating Nature:
Rites and Ceremonies Around the World (Seabury, 1969)
and D. Nathan's Women of Courage (Random, 1964).

CELLINI, Eva and Joseph.   Hungarian artists.   They were
born in Budapest, where they later attended the Academy of Fine Arts.   Both became American citizens after
coming to the United States in 1956.   The Cellinis have
lived in Leonia, New Jersey.   Eva Cellini has enjoyed
gardening and reading as hobbies.   For boys and girls
she illustrated: B. Glemser's All About Biology (Random, 1964), C. Shapp's Let's Find Out about New
Year's Day (Watts, 1968) and R. Dudley's Partners in
Nature (Funk & Wagnalls, 1965).   His work includes
Davy Jones' Haunted Locker, ed. by R. Arthur (Random, 1965); H. Dolson's Disaster at Johnstown (Random, 1965) and G. Conklin's Elephants of Africa (Holiday, 1972).   ICB-3

CELLINI, Joseph, 1924- .   see CELLINI, Eva

CHAPMAN, Peggy.   She was born in Newfoundland, lived in
Toronto, and later studied at the Maidstone College of
Art in Kent, England.   In addition to working as a free-
lance artist, she has been an art teacher.   She married a graphic designer and has lived near Cranbrook
in Kent, England.   Peggy Chapman has been a member
of the Society of Industrial Artists and Designers.   For
young people she illustrated B. Rinkoff's Tricksters and
Trappers (Abelard, 1971).

CHAPPELL, Warren, 1904- .   Artist and designer, born in
Richmond, Virginia.   His home has been in Norwalk,
Connecticut (in the Silvermine section).   After graduat-
ing from the University of Richmond, he studied at the
Art Students League in New York and the Colorado
Springs Fine Arts Center.   He did further study in Ger-
many.   Warren Chappell has been a typographer and
teacher in addition to illustrator.   He wrote and illus-
trated The Nutcracker, (Knopf, 1958).   He also illus-
trated G. Household's Prisoner of the Indies (a Junior
Literary Guild selection; Little, 1968).   ICB-1, ICB-2,
ICB-3

CHARLES, Donald.   Artist and cartoonist, he has lived in
Chicago with his artist wife and children.   He received

his education in California at the Art League School and
the University of California. His career began as a
feature writer and artist for the San Francisco Chron-
icle. His work also appeared in Cosmopolitan and New
Yorker magazines. Prior to devoting fulltime to book
illustration, the artist had been a newspaper editor and
a creative director of an advertising firm. He has also been a truck driver, longshoreman, and ranch hand.
Mr. Charles has been the recipient of numerous graphic societies' awards, and his work has been published
in both periodicals and textbooks. For children he has
illustrated V. Poulet's Blue Bug's Safety Book (Children's Press, 1973).

CHARLOT, Jean, 1898- . American artist and muralist,
    born in Paris, France. His home has been in Honolulu,
    Hawaii. In 1921 he began his career in art in Mexico
    where he completed many distinguished frescoes and
    murals. He also wrote on Mexican archeology and art.
    He has been the recipient of honorary degrees and has
    been on the staff at the University of Hawaii. Jean
    Charlot has made his own color separations using brush
    or pen drawings on acetate. His work includes M.
    Brown's A Child's Good Night Book (Scott, 1950) and
    M. Schlein's Kittens, Cubs & Babies (Scott, 1959). He
    also illustrated two Newbery Award winners: J. Krum-
    gold's ...And Now Miguel (Crowell, 1953) and A.
    Clark's Secret of the Andes (Viking, 1952). ICB-1,
    ICB-2, ICB-3

CHORAO, Kay. A relative newcomer to the field of chil-
    dren's book illustration (1972), she grew up in Indianap-
    olis and Cleveland. She graduated from Wheaton Col-
    lege in Norton, Massachusetts and studied at London's
    Chelsea School of Art. Her husband, Ernesto Chorao,
    has been both a painter and teacher. They have lived
    in New York City. She illustrated B. Williams' Al-
    bert's Toothache (a Junior Literary Guild selection;
    Dutton, 1974) and J. Viorst's My Mama Says There
    Aren't Any Zombies, Ghosts, Vampires, Creatures,
    Demons, Monsters, Fiends, Goblins, or Things (Athen-
    eum, 1973). She also wrote and illustrated The Repair
    of Uncle Toe (Farrar, 1972).

CHWAST, Jacqueline, 1932- , and Seymour.
    They have lived in New York City. Jacqueline Chwast
    was born in Newark, New Jersey where she later

attended the Newark School of Fine and Industrial Art.
She also studied at the Art Students League in New
York. Seymour Chwast, artist and graphic designer,
has been a partner in the Push Pin Studios. His work
has appeared in magazines and on television. With
Martin Moskof he wrote and illustrated Still Another
Alphabet Book (McGraw, 1969). Her work includes
Aunt Bella's Umbrella, ed. by W. Cole (Doubleday,
1970) and S. Warburg's I Like You (Houghton, 1965).
ICB-3

CHWAST, Seymour   see   CHWAST, Jacqueline

CINGOLI, Giulio.   Italian artist and cartoonist. He has
lived in Milan. Mr. Cingoli's work has appeared in
books published for boys and girls in Italy. He has
been interested in cartooning and, with Italian cartoonist Giancarlo Carloni, was the recipient of the Prize
Venezia in 1964. Giulio Cingoli and Mr. Carloni's
book illustrations first appeared in the United States in
G. Rocco's Gaetano the Pheasant (Harper, 1966).
ICB-3

CLAVELOUX, Nicole.   His drawings have appeared in many
books for children. The New York Times selection as
one of the "ten best illustrated books of the year" was
awarded to his illustrations in the book Alala (Harlin
Quist, 1971).

COALSON, Glo.   Her childhood was spent in Abilene, Texas.
Following graduation from Abilene Christian College,
she visited her brother and sister-in-law in Kotzebue,
an Eskimo village in Alaska. She made many drawings
of Eskimos during her stay and became interested in
Eskimo folklore. Later she made her home in New
York City. For young people she illustrated The Long
Hungry Night, by E. Foster and S. Williams (a Junior
Literary Guild selection; Atheneum, 1973).

COBER, Alan E., 1935- . He was born in New York City
and studied at the University of Vermont, School of
Visual Arts, New School for Social Research, and
Pratt Graphic Center in New York. In addition to
books he has contributed illustrations to many magazines. In 1965 the Artists Guild of New York named
Alan Cober "Artist of the Year." The Cobers have lived
in Ossining, New York. His work includes: L. Gar-

field's <u>Mister Corbett's Ghost</u> (Pantheon, 1968), R.
Smith's <u>Nothingatall, Nothingatall, Nothingatall</u> (Harper,
1965), J. Cunningham's <u>Viollet</u> (Pantheon, 1966) and
M. Polland's <u>The White Twilight</u> (Holt, 1965). ICB-3

CoCONIS, Ted. His early years were spent in Chicago
where he later studied at the Art Institute and the
Academy of Fine Arts. He also attended Knox College
at Galesburg, Illinois. The artist and his family have
resided in Weston, Connecticut. He has had exhibitions
of his work in New York City art shows, and his drawings have appeared in such magazines as <u>McCalls</u>,
<u>Ladies Home Journal</u>, and <u>Good Housekeeping.</u> Boys
and girls have enjoyed his illustrations in the 1971 Newbery Medal award book by B. Byars, <u>The Summer of</u>
<u>the Swans</u> (a Junior Literary Guild selection; Viking,
1970).

COLABELLA, Vincent. A talented artist, he graduated from
the Pratt Institute School of Fine and Applied Arts in
Brooklyn, New York. He and his family have lived in
Westchester County, New York. Mr. Colabella has illustrated both books and educational films, and in 1968
he received the International Film and Television Festival's Grand Trophy for several of his filmstrips. His
drawings can be found in R. Wood's <u>Mystery of Gold</u>
<u>Hill</u> (Harvey House, 1971).

COLLARD, Derek. English artist, designer, and teacher.
He has lived in Naphill, Buckinghamshire, England. In
1969 he began a design company in his home and later
moved it to a location in London. Derek Collard has
also taught in a college of art. He has created book
jackets in addition to illustrating children's books. His
first picture book for boys and girls was P. Pearce's
<u>The Squirrel Wife</u> (Crowell, 1971).

COMPERE, Janet. She was born in New York and later
graduated from Baylor University in Waco, Texas. Her
major was drama. Her work has been included in the
permanent collections of the Brooklyn and Whitney Museums. For young people she illustrated M. Davidson's
<u>Louis Braille</u> (Hastings House, 1972).

CONNOLLY, Jerome Patrick, 1931- . Born in Minneapolis,
he studied at the University of Minnesota. He has
painted diorama backgrounds for museums in addition to

illustrating books for boys and girls. He met his wife,
an editor, on one of his early assignments at the Illinois State Museum, and they have lived in Stamford,
Connecticut. He has been staff artist for the Natural
Science for Youth Foundation and a member of the Society of Animal Artists. For young people he illustrated F. Wood's Cat Family (Harvey, 1968) and R.
Hutchins' The Travels of Monarch X (Rand, 1966).
ICB-3

CONTRERAS, Jerry. He studied at Chouinard and has designed and illustrated for magazines and Time-Life
Books. Mr. Contreras has lived in New York City.
His black-and-white illustrations appeared in A. Orr-
mont's James Buchanan Eads, (Prentice-Hall, 1970).

COOLEY, Lydia. She attended the University of California
at Los Angeles and the Art Students League in New
York. Her paintings have been exhibited at the Santa
Barbara Museum of Art and the Whitney Museum of
American Art. Lydia Cooley has taught at the Ojai Val-
ley School and has made her home in Santa Barbara.
She illustrated J. Cunningham's Onion Journey (Panthe-
on, 1967).

COOMBS, Patricia, 1926- . She was born in Los Angeles
and later attended De Pauw University and Michigan
State. She received B.A. and M.A. degrees from the
University of Washington. She and her husband, James
Fox, have made their home in Waterford, Connecticut.
Her books about "Dorrie the witch" (pen and ink with
color separation on acetate) have been very popular with
boys and girls. These include Dorrie and the Blue
Witch (a Junior Literary Guild selection; Lothrop, 1964)
and Dorrie and the Witch Doctor (Lothrop, 1967). She
also illustrated G. Cretan's Lobo (Lothrop, 1969).
ICB-3

COONEY, Barbara, 1917- . She was born in Brooklyn, New
York and has lived in Illinois, Iowa, Massachusetts, and
New York. Barbara Cooney graduated from Smith College in Northampton, Massachusetts. She and her husband, Dr. Charles Talbot Porter, have lived in Pepper-
ell, Massachusetts. In 1959 she won the Caldecott Medal for her edition of Chaucer's Chanticleer and the Fox
(Crowell, 1958). Her illustrations also appeared in
The Little Juggler (a Junior Literary Guild selection;

Hastings House, 1961), which she adapted from an old
French legend. Other juvenile books which she illustrated include W. De La Mare's Peacock Pie (Knopf,
1961) and E. Field's Wynken, Blynken, and Nod (Hastings, 1970). ICB-1, ICB-2, ICB-3, ABYP-2

COREY, Robert. Designer and illustrator, he has lived in
Los Angeles. He has received many awards both here
and abroad for his graphic designs. Robert Corey went
to South America and visited the ancient Inca ruins of
Peru which provided background material for some of
his illustrations in J. Castellanos' Tomasito and the
Golden Llamas (Golden Gate Junior Books, 1968).

COSGRAVE, John O'Hara, II, 1908- . He was born in San
Francisco and later studied at Marin Junior College,
the University of California, the California School of
Fine Arts, and in Paris, France. From boyhood, he
has been interested in ships and seaports. Besides
book illustration, he has illustrated for magazines and
designed Christmas cards. During World War II, he
served in the infantry and in the Office of Strategic
Services. Mr. Cosgrave married editor Mary Silva
and has lived in Pocasset, Massachusetts. His work
includes America Sails the Seas (Houghton, 1962) and
Clipper Ship (Macmillan, 1963). He also illustrated
C. Carmer's Henry Hudson, Captain of Ice-Bound Seas
(Garrard, 1960). ICB-1, ICB-2, ICB-3

CRANE, Walter, 1845-1915. English illustrator, Walter
Crane was the son of an artist. Walter Crane, Kate
Greenaway and Randolph Caldecott have been known as
the three outstanding illustrators of children's books of
the 19th century. He studied with the noted wood engraver, W. J. Linton. His first work was the creation of designs for the covers of novels printed by Edmund Evans. The artist believed that text and drawings should be combined to create harmony in books.
Walter Crane used bold outlines with flat, bright colors. He has been called "the true artist of Fairyland"
by writer Gleeson White. He illustrated The Baby's
Own Aesop (Routledge, 1887) and Pan-Pipes, comp. by
T. Marzials (Warne, 1900).

CREWS, Donald. A free-lance artist, Donald Crews attended Cooper Union in New York City. He has also been
a photographer and designer. The American Institute

of Graphic Arts Children's Book Show exhibited several of his books including We Read: A to Z (Harper, 1967). His illustrations can also be found in H. Milgrom's ABC of Ecology (Macmillan, 1972).

CRICHLOW, Ernest T., 1914- . Born in Brooklyn, New York, he studied at the Commercial Illustration School of Art and the Art Students League in New York. His first one-man show was held in 1953. He has taught painting at Brighton Art Center and has made his home in Brooklyn. His work includes: M. Levy's Corrie and the Yankee (Viking, 1959), C. Bulla's Lincoln's Birthday (Crowell, 1965) and J. Griffin's Magic Mirrors (Coward, 1971). ICB-3

CROMMELYNCK, Landa. French painter and illustrator, Landa Crommelynck graduated from the renowned School of Applied Art in Paris. She has lived in Paris with her husband Piero Crommelynck, a well-known etcher. Her illustrations can be found in Charles Perrault's Fairy Tales (tr. from the French by Sasha Moorsom; Doubleday, 1972).

CROSBY, John. He was born in Toronto, Canada, and later studied at the university there. He began his career in art by drawing pictures of birds for a nature magazine. Later his work appeared in books, and he created natural history film strips for the National Film Board. Prior to becoming a museologist with the National Parks Branch of the Department of Indian Affairs and Northern Development, he worked in Ottawa as Artist-Naturalist of the Zoology Department of the National Museum. He illustrated two of C. May's works Book of American Birds (St. Martin's, 1967) and Second Book of Canadian Animals (St. Martin's, 1964).

CROWELL, Pers, 1910- . Born in Pasco, Washington, he later made his home near Portland at Beaverton. He studied in Los Angeles at Chouinard Art Institute and in New York at the Phoenix Art Institute. Prior to his career as an illustrator, Pers Crowell had been associated with the Union Pacific Railroad. For children he illustrated J. Kellogg's Hans and the Winged Horse (Reilly & Lee, 1964). ICB-2

CRUIKSHANK, George, 1792-1878. In C. Meigs' A Critical

History of Children's Literature (Macmillan, 1953) are
these words: "George Cruikshank ... made pictures
for the Grimm's 'Fairy Tales' when they were trans-
lated into English in 1823 that have never been sur-
passed in their humour, their exuberant fancy and the
way in which they are at one with the spirit of these
sturdy folk tales." Born in London, he was the son of
a political caricaturist. Cruikshank, too, was a caricaturist for over 50 years. Also an illustrator, he
created etchings for author Charles Dickens. He illustrated Grimm's Popular Stories (Oxford, 1913).

CRUZ, Ray. Designer, illustrator, native New Yorker. He
attended Pratt Institute in Brooklyn and graduated from
Cooper Union in New York. His work has included advertising illustration, textile and wallpaper design, and
package design. The artist has been interested in wildlife in addition to travel here and abroad. He has lived
near Washington Square in Greenwich Village. For
young readers he illustrated M. Craig's Where Do I Be-
long? (Four Winds, 1971) and J. Yolen's The Wizard of
Washington Square (World, 1969).

CUFFARI, Richard. Born in Brooklyn, New York, he later
graduated from Pratt Institute. His paintings have been
exhibited in many galleries of New York and were also
included in the United States Information Agency's Graphic Arts-USA Exhibit in Russia. He married an artist
and has lived in Brooklyn. The books which he illustrated for boys and girls include E. Ladd's Indians on
the Bonnet (Morrow, 1971); D. Aldis' Nothing Is Impos-
sible (a Junior Literary Guild selection; Atheneum,
1969).

CUMPSTON, Astrid Kate Oatelayé   see   WALFORD, Astrid

-D-

DANSKA, Herbert, 1927- . Artist and illustrator, he was
born in New York City. After graduating from New
York's Art Students League and Brooklyn's Pratt Institute, he studied in Paris at the Académie Julian. Pri-
or to his art career, Herbert Danska served in the
United States Air Corps during World War II. In addition to illustrating books and magazines, he has been a
filmmaker. For a great deal of his work, the artist

has often used watercolor in combination with other
materials. His book illustrations for children can be
found in V. Haviland's Favorite Fairy Tales Told in
Russia (Little, 1961). ICB-2, ICB-3

DARWIN, Beatrice. Born in Boston, she attended the Massachusetts School of Art where she later did graduate
work on a scholarship. She also studied abroad in
Sweden. She married calligrapher and graphic artist
Leonard Darwin and has lived in California. She illustrated J. Foster's Pete's Puddle, (Houghton, 1950).

DARWIN, Leonard. His early years were spent in Beverly
and Needham, Massachusetts. He attended the Massachusetts School of Art in Boston where he studied advertising and design. He married an illustrator and
has lived in Danville, California. In addition to illustrating children's books, Len Darwin has worked as an
art director, fashion and design instructor, and map
draftsman. He has also worked in advertising. For
young people he illustrated three works by S. Corbett:
What Makes a Light Go On? (Little, 1966), What Makes
a Plane Fly? (a Junior Literary Guild selection; Atlantic, 1967) and What Makes TV Work? (Little, 1965).

D'ATTILIO, Anthony. A citizen of the United States, Anthony D'Attilio was born in Italy. He has worked in
New York City at the American Museum of Natural History as an Associate in the Department of Living In-
vertebrates. In addition to a career as an artist, he
has also been a writer. His speciality has been in
writing about and drawing marine mollusks (shellfish).
The artist's work has appeared in books and scientific
papers. For young people he illustrated W. Stephens'
Octopus Lives in the Ocean (Holiday, 1968); and
Stephens' Sea Horse: A Fish in Armor (Holiday, 1969).

D'AULAIRE, Edgar Parin   see   D'AULAIRE, Ingri

D'AULAIRE, Ingri (Mortenson), 1904- ; and Edgar Parin
D'Aulaire, 1898- . Husband-wife team. Ingri Mortenson was born in Norway, and Edgar, who was the
son of an Italian portrait painter, was born in Campo
Blenio, Ticino, Switzerland. They met when both were
studying art in Paris. After their marriage, they arrived in the United States. They have achieved distinction in their early picture books by drawing directly on

lithograph stone. They have lived on a farm in Wil-
ton, Connecticut. The Caldecott Medal was awarded
to their book Abraham Lincoln, (Doubleday, 1939).
Their books include: Animals Everywhere (Doubleday,
1940), Ingri and Edgar Parin D'Aulaire's Book of
Greek Myths (Doubleday, 1962), Buffalo Bill (a Junior
Literary Guild selection; Doubleday, 1952), Ola,
Doubleday, 1932). ICB-1, ICB-2, ICB-3, ABYP-2

DAVIS, Bette. Born in Joplin, Missouri, she studied at
Pratt Institute. She was head of the art department
(Special Services) in the U.S. Marine Corps Woman's
Reserve during World War II. Her work has appeared
in both science books and encyclopedias. She has enjoyed painting the ocean near her home in New Jersey.
Her illustrations appeared in M. Butler's Twice Queen
of France: Anne of Brittany (a Junior Literary Guild
selection; Funk, 1967).

DE LARREA, Victoria. She was born in New York City, at
19 traveled around the world on a cargo ship as an of-
ficer-stewardess, and later attended Queen's College in
New York. She married a photographer and has lived
in New York. Her illustrations have appeared in many
books. These include A. Low's Herbert's Treasure
(Putnam, 1971), C. York's Miss Know It All (Watts,
1966), K. Starbird's The Pheasant on Route Seven
(Lippincott, 1968) and K. Green's Philip and the Pooka
(Lippincott, 1966).

DELESSERT, Etienne. Born in Lausanne, Switzerland, he
later lived in Paris and New York. He has worked in
graphic design, advertising, and film. In addition to
illustrating children's books, he has been vice president of a publishing firm. His work includes Kipling's
Just So Stories (Anniversary Edition; Doubleday, 1972)
and E. Ionesco's Story Number 1 (Harlin Quist, 1968)
and Story Number 2 (Harlin Quist, 1970). He wrote
and illustrated How the Mouse Was Hit on the Head by
a Stone and So Discovered the World (Doubleday, 1971).

DE LULION, John. The artist has lived in South Egremont,
Massachusetts. He has operated his own art gallery
with special emphasis on antique prints. For young
people he illustrated A. Paul's Kids Camping (Doubleday, 1973).

DE PAOLA, Tomie. Illustrator, instructor, born in Meriden, Connecticut. He graduated from Pratt Institute in Brooklyn, New York. He has taught art at Newton College of the Sacred Heart in Massachusetts and at San Francisco College for Women. He has lived in New York, Connecticut, and California. He wrote and illustrated Wonderful Dragon of Timlin (Bobbs-Merrill, 1966). He also illustrated W. Wise's Monsters of the Middle Ages (Putnam, 1971); Tricky Peik and Other Picture Tales, ed. by J. Hardendorff (Lippincott, 1967). ICB-3

DEVLIN, Harry see DEVLIN, Wende

DEVLIN, Wende and Harry. Husband-wife team. Wende Devlin has been both a portrait painter and a writer. Her husband has been a free-lance illustrator. With their seven children, the Devlins have lived in Mountainside, New Jersey. Their work includes: Aunt Agatha, There's a Lion Under the Couch! (Van Nostrand, 1968), How Fletcher Was Hatched (Parents' Magazine Press, 1969) and The Knobby Boys to the Rescue (Parents' Magazine Press, 1965).

DEWEY, Ariane. Born in Chicago, Illinois, she graduated from Sarah Lawrence College in Bronxville, New York. Following graduation from college, she has been an art editor of children's textbooks in addition to a researcher in an industrial-design firm. As a supplement to her art education, in college Ariane Dewey was a volunteer at the Museum of Modern Art in New York City and later worked in an art gallery in New York. For young people she illustrated, with Jose Aruego, R. Kraus' Herman the Helper (Windmill, 1974).

DI FIORI, Lawrence. He was born in Philadelphia, Pennsylvania. Mr. Di Fiori has been a teacher in addition to a book illustrator. His juvenile book drawings include: J. Wahl's Anna Help Ginger (Putnam, 1971), L. Untermeyer's Cat O' Nine Tales (American Heritage Press, 1971).

DI GRAZIA, Thomas. Artist and poet, he was born in New Jersey. After graduating from New York City's Cooper Union, he did further study in Rome at the Academy of Fine Arts. The artist and his family have lived in New York City. Mr. Di Grazia has been a designer and painter in addition to being a book illustrator. His drawings can be found in N. Carlson's The Half Sisters (Harper, 1970).

DILLON, Corinne Boyd. She was born in Louisville, Kentucky, and grew up in Kentucky, Minnesota, and New York. She attended Friends School in Providence, Rhode Island, and the Barnard School for Girls in New York. Corinne Dillon also studied at Académie Julian in Paris. Her home has been in New York City. She illustrated: I. McMeekin's Kentucky Derby Winner (a Junior Literary Guild selection; McKay, 1949); K. Hitte's A Letter for Cathy (Abingdon, 1953). ICB-2

DOLEZAL, Carroll. Born in New London, Connecticut, she studied at the Rhode Island School of Design and at the Kansas City Art Institute. As a member of the European Honors Program, she spent a year of study in Italy. Mrs. Dolezal has been a designer for Hallmark Cards in Kansas City, Missouri and a high school art teacher in Texas. She and her husband Dr. Charles H. Dolezal, a psychologist, have lived in Austin. She illustrated I. Chittum's Clabber Biscuits (Steck, 1972); M. Wright's A Sky Full of Dragons (a Junior Literary Guild selection; Steck, 1969).

DORE, (Paul) Gustave, 1832-1883. He was born in Alsace-Lorraine at Strasbourg. He became well-known in France as a painter and sculptor, and his imaginative illustrations gave him recognition elsewhere. With Albert Robida he illustrated Rabelais' Three Good Giants (Houghton, 1887).

DOREMUS, Robert. His paintings of New York scenes were sold in order to earn money to attend Pratt Institute in Brooklyn. Bob Doremus served overseas as a photographic technician with the Air Force during World War II. The Doremus family have lived in Union Springs, New York, where the author has enjoyed sailing as a hobby. His work for children includes: E. Myers' Frederick Douglass: Boy Champion of Human Rights, (Bobbs-Merrill, 1970); A. Stevenson's John Fitch: Steamboat Boy (Bobbs-Merrill, 1966), E. Clark's Osceola: Young Seminole Indian (Bobbs-Merrill, 1965).

DOTY, Roy. He attended the Columbus School of Art in Ohio and later made his home in Connecticut. When he

was in service, he was a cartoonist on <u>Stars & Stripes</u>.
His achievements have included being named "Illustrator
of the Year" by the National Cartoonist Society.   Mr.
Doty's work has appeared in both advertisements and
periodicals.   For boys and girls he illustrated J.
Blume's <u>Tales of a Fourth Grade Nothing</u> (Dutton,
1972).

DOTZENKO, Grisha.   His pseudonym is Grisha.   Born in the
Ukraine, he studied art in Moscow.   In 1947 he ar-
rived in America and has made his home in New York
City.   For young people he illustrated J. Gunther's
<u>Meet North Africa</u> (Harper, 1957).

DOWD, Victor.   He grew up in France and later came to
America where he made his home in Westport, Connecticut.   He studied at Pratt Institute in Brooklyn,
New York, and has been both a book illustrator and advertising artist.   Mr. Dowd has enjoyed model-rail-
roading as a hobby.   For boys and girls he illustrated
C. Joy's <u>Getting to Know England, Scotland, Ireland &</u>
<u>Wales</u> (Coward, 1966), J. Wallace's <u>Getting to Know</u>
<u>France</u> (Coward, 1962).

DOWLING, Victor J., 1906- .   Born in New York City, he
later studied at Holy Cross College in Worcester, Massachusetts, and the National Academy School of Fine
Arts in New York City.   The artist has been interested
in animals and historical subjects.   Mr. Dowling has
lived on a farm in New York state.   For young people
he wrote and illustrated <u>The Old Woman's Chickens</u>
(Aladdin, 1954); he also illustrated O. Baker's <u>Bengey</u>
<u>and the Beast</u> (Dodd, 1947).

DRESSER, Lawrence.   Illustrator, commercial artist, born
in Wisconsin.   He grew up on a South Dakota Sioux
reservation.   He later studied under Robert Henri at
the New York School of Art.   Following a stay in Paris, he returned to America where his work was included in the "Armory Show" (the first exhibition of modern art).   A gun collector, Mr. Dresser has lived in
Massachusetts.   For young people he illustrated O.
Stevenson's <u>The Talking Wire</u> (Messner, 1947).

DRUMMOND, Violet H., 1911- .   Born in London, she
studied on the coast of England at The Links in Eastbourne, at Le Chateau Vitry-Sur-Seine in Paris, and

at St. Martin's School of Art in London. Prior to
studying at St. Martin's, she lived in India. The artist
received England's Kate Greenaway Award in 1957. In
addition to illustrating books, Violet Drummond has
created cartoon films for the BBC. She and her husband, Anthony Swentenham, have lived in St. John's
Wood, London. She wrote and illustrated Mr. Finch's
Pet Shop, Oxford, 1954. ICB-2, ICB-3

DUNNINGTON, Tom. He grew up in Duluth, Minnesota, and
    Iowa City, Iowa. Following service in the Marine
    Corps, he studied art at the University of Iowa, John
    Herron School of Art in Indianapolis, and at Chicago's
    American Academy of Art. He and his wife have lived
    in Elmhurst, Illinois. He illustrated N. Richards'
    The Story of Old Ironsides (a Junior Literary Guild se-
    lection; Children's Press, 1967) and K. Richards' Story
    of the Gettysburg Address (Children's Press, 1967).

DUVOISIN, Roger Antoine, 1904- . Author-illustrator. He
    was born in Geneva, Switzerland. He received his edu-
    cation in Switzerland and France. Mr. Duvoisin worked
    in design in Geneva, Lyons, and Paris. After arriving
    in America, he has been a painter, designer, and illus-
    trator. His titles include: A for the Ark (Lothrop,
    1952), And There Was America (Knopf, 1938), Christ-
    mas Whale (Knopf, 1945), The Happy Hunter (Lothrop,
    1961), House of Four Seasons (Lothrop, 1956), Lonely
    Veronica (Knopf, 1963), Petunia, I Love You (Knopf,
    1965), Spring Snow (Knopf, 1963), What Is Right for
    Tulip (Knopf, 1969). Also he illustrated Alvin Tres-
    selt's White Snow, Bright Snow (Lothrop, 1947), which
    won the Caldecott Medal in 1948. ICB-1, ICB-2, ICB-
    3, ABYP-2

-E-

EARLE, Olive Lydia, 1888- . British artist and muralist,
    born in London. She later made her home in New York
    with her artist husband, the late Harry R. Daugherty.
    Olive Earle received her art training in New York at
    the Parsons School of Design and the National Academy
    School of Fine Arts. One of her chief interests has
    been natural history. In addition to illustrating books
    and magazines, her career has also included writing.
    Her paintings have been exhibited in various museums

in this country. For children she wrote and illustrated
Birds and Their Nests (Morrow, 1952), Peas, Beans
and Licorice, (Morrow, 1971), State Trees (Morrow,
1973). ICB-2, ICB-3

EATON, John, 1942- . Canadian artist, born in Ottawa.
He received his education in Canada and at the High
Mowing School in Wilton, New Hampshire. He has
traveled throughout several European countries and
studied marble sculpturing in Italy. At one time he
lived in Fiesole near Florence, Italy. For children
he illustrated E. Cummings' Fairy Tales (Harcourt, 1965).

EATON, Tom. He was born in Wichita, Kansas. Later he
graduated from the University of Kansas. The artist
has made his home in Woodstock, New York. For
boys and girls he illustrated W. Cromie's Steven and
the Green Turtle (Harper, 1970).

EDGUN see WULFF, Edgun Valdemar

EDWARDS, Peter, 1934- . He was born in London and
later studied art there at the Regent Street Polytechnic.
Following military service, he began his illustrating career in Sweden. Peter Edwards and his wife, also an
artist, have lived in Stansted Mountfitchet in Essex.
He illustrated C. Memling's Seals for Sale (Abelard-
Schuman, 1963).

EGGENHOFER, Nicholas. Born in Bavaria, he came to the
United States when he was 16. He later made his
home in West Milford, New Jersey. Prior to coming
to America, he enjoyed reading about the old West
which has been the subject for many of his illustrations. For young people he illustrated R. Moody's
Geronimo: Wolf of the Warpath (Random, 1958); M.
Cousins' We Were There at the Battle of the Alamo
(Grosset, 1958).

EICHENBERG, Fritz, 1901- . Born in Cologne, Germany,
he studied in Leipzig at the State Academy of Graphic
Arts. He has been a cartoonist for newspapers and
magazines in addition to a book illustrator. His engravings have appeared in many distinguished books,
and he has also written and illustrated several picture
books. Mr. Eichenberg has been on the faculty of
Pratt Institute in Brooklyn and founded the Pratt

Graphic Art Center in Manhattan. Primarily his work
has been in black-and-white. The artist's home has
been in New York City. He wrote and illustrated Ape
in a Cape (Harcourt, 1952), Dancing in the Moon (Harcourt, 1955). He illustrated M. Jagendorf's Tyll Ulen-
spiegel's Merry Pranks (Vanguard, 1938). ICB-1,
ICB-2, ICB-3

EICKE, Edna. Born in Montclair, New Jersey, she received
her education in New York City at the Parsons School of
Design. She married artist Tom Funk and has resided
in Westport, Connecticut. She has designed covers for
the New Yorker magazine and has enjoyed collecting
primitive art and antique toys as hobbies. She wrote
and illustrated The Children Who Got Married (Simon,
1969). She also illustrated R. Kraus' Tree That
Stayed Up Until Next Christmas (Windmill, 1971).

EITZEN, Allan. He was born in Minnesota and later studied
art in Minneapolis. He has worked in a Pennsylvania
religious publishing firm where he learned about printing and design. The Eitzens have lived on a farm in
Pennsylvania. He has often used his own children as
models for his book illustrations. His work includes
N. Agle's Kish's Colt (Seabury Press, 1968), E. Wies-
enthal's Let's Find out about Eskimos (Watts, 1969),
L. Kauffman's What's That Noise? (Lothrop, 1966).

ELGIN, Kathleen, 1923- . In addition to illustrating books,
she has also written them. In a series she wrote on
the "Human Body," one volume, entitled The Human
Body: the Heart (Watts, 1968), received a graphic arts award at the Bologna World Book Fair in
1969. She attended the Dayton Art Institute in Ohio
and Columbia University. Miss Elgin has made her
home in New York. For young people she wrote and
illustrated First Book of Norse Legends (Watts, 1956)
and Human Body: the Glands (Watts, 1971). With
John F. Osterritter she wrote and illustrated The Ups
and Downs of Drugs (Knopf, 1972).

EMBERLEY, Edward Randolph, 1931- . Ed Emberley
graduated from the Massachusetts School of Art and attended the Rhode Island School of Design after World
War II. He has lived in Millis and Ipswich, Massachusetts. In 1968 he was awarded the Caldecott Medal for
Drummer Hoff, adapted by B. Emberley (a Junior

Literary Guild selection; Prentice-Hall, 1967). He also illustrated F. Branley's The Big Dipper (Crowell,
1962); his Green Says Go (Little, 1968), Klippity Klop
(Little, 1974), The Parade Book (a Junior Literary
Guild selection; Little, 1962), The Wing on a Flea (Little, 1961). ICB-3, ABYP-2

ERDOES, Richard, 1912- . He was born in Vienna and
studied at the Art Academies of Berlin, Paris, and Vienna. He later became a United States citizen. His
work includes murals for the Richmond, Virginia, Museum of Fine Arts and the Grace Line ship, "Santa
Maria," and illustrations for Life magazine. His interests have been photography, camping, and skiing. For
boys and girls he illustrated J. Joyce's The Cat and the
Devil (Dodd, 1934) and H. Hoke's Jokes, Jokes, Jokes
(Watts, 1954). He also wrote and illustrated A Picture
History of Ancient Rome (Macmillan, 1967). ICB-3

ERIKSON, Mel. Free-lance illustrator. He graduated from
the State University at Farmingdale, New York. Later
he studied at Pratt Institute in Brooklyn. For young
people he illustrated three works by A. Silverstein (all
for Prentice-Hall); The Digestive System (1970), The
Endocrine System (1971) and The Nervous System (1971).

ETS, Marie Hall, 1895- . Born in Wisconsin, she studied
at the University of Chicago, the Art Institute, and Columbia University. At one time she did social work and
lived for a year in Czechoslovakia. She married Harold Ets who was on the staff of Loyola University School
of Medicine. In 1960 she was awarded the Caldecott
Medal for her illustrations in Nine Days to Christmas
(Viking, 1959) which she wrote with Aurora Labastida.
Juvenile titles include Beasts and Nonsense (a Junior
Literary Guild selection; Viking, 1952), Gilberto and
the Wind, (Viking, 1963), Just Me (Viking, 1965), Mis-
ter Penny (Viking, 1935) and Talking Without Words
(Viking, 1968). ICB-1, ICB-2, ICB-3, ABYP-2

-F-

FABRES, Oscar, 1900- . Born in Santiago, Chile, he later
studied at the Académie Julian in Paris. The artist
has traveled extensively, and his work has been exhibited in many countries throughout the world. He has

made his home in New York since 1940. Besides being a book illustrator, he has been a commercial artist.
Mr. Fabrès' lively lithographic drawings appeared in
Anne and Maryke, written by Alice Fabrès (Winston,
1947). ICB-2

FAULKNER, John. Cartoonist-illustrator. Prior to a career as an artist, John Faulkner studied to be a college professor. The Faulkner family has lived near
Chicago in Glen Ellyn, Illinois. They have enjoyed
golf, skiing, and tennis as special interests. For
boys and girls he illustrated M. Moore's The Little
Band & the Inaugural Parade (a Junior Literary Guild
selection; Whitman, 1968), and two by J. Bowman,
Seven Silly Wise Men (Whitman, 1965) and Who Was
Tricked? (Whitman, 1966).

FEASER, Daniel David, 1920- . He was born in Dauphin,
Pennsylvania, and later attended Westminster Choir
College in Princeton, New Jersey, and the Philadelphia
Museum School of Art. Following World War II, he
entered the field of commercial art. He has been an
exhibit artist and designer for the Museums Branch of
the National Park Service. His home has been in Fair-
fax County, Virginia. He has illustrated three books
by H. Peterson (all for Scribner's): Forts in America,
(1964), A History of Firearms (1961) and A History of
Knives (1966). ICB-3

FEELINGS, Tom. He grew up in Brooklyn, New York and
later studied at the School of Visual Arts. In 1964 he
served as an artist with the Ghanaian Government Publishing House in Accra, West Africa. For young people
he wrote and illustrated Black Pilgrimage (Lothrop,
1972), also, he illustrated J. Lester's To Be a Slave
(Dial, 1968).

FEGIZ, Rita Fava, 1932- . Italian artist and portrait
painter, born in Rome. Her childhood was spent in
Italy, and she came to the United States when she was
13. She attended high school in Philadelphia and later
studied at the Philadelphia Museum School of Art. She
returned to Rome and married architect Carlo Fegiz
in 1962. She has done portraits of children in addition to book illustrations. Juvenile books she has illustrated (all for Little) include G. Cretan's Gift from
the Bride (1964), P. Priolo's Piccolina and the Easter

Bells (1962), and S. Butler's Starlight in Tourone (1965). ICB-3

FERGUSON, Walter W. 1930- . He was born in New York City and has lived in Brooklyn. Prior to attending Pratt Institute, he studied art at Yale University. He has traveled throughout the United States and Canada observing and sketching birds and animals. His paintings have been exhibited in many museums. Walter Ferguson has illustrated books for both children and adults, and his work has appeared in Audubon Magazine, Life, and Sports Illustrated. He has been an artist with New York's American Museum of Natural History and a member of the Society of Animal Artists. For children he illustrated R. Mathewson's Answers about Birds & Animals (Wonder, 1970), P. Sears' Barn Swallow (Holiday, 1955), C. May's When Animals Change Clothes (Holiday, 1965). ICB-2

FETZ, Ingrid, 1915- . She was born in New York City where she later studied at Columbia University and at the Workshop School of Advertising and Editorial Art. Her father, born in Switzerland, was an engineer and photographer; and her mother, a graduate of Pratt Institute, was a children's librarian. In addition to teaching art to boys and girls, Ingrid Fetz has been Director of the Cambridge, Massachusetts, Art Center for Children. She has lived in Ossining, New York. Her work includes E. Clymer's The Adventure of Walter (Atheneum, 1965), P. Showers' Before You Were a Baby (Crowell, 1968), and S. Brewton's Laughable Limericks (Crowell, 1965).

FIAMMENGHI, Gioia, 1929- . She was born in New York City where she later studied at the Art Students League and Parsons School of Design. While she was a student at Parsons, she traveled in France and Italy. She also spent several summers painting and drawing in Colombia, South America. She married Guido Caputo and has lived in Monte Carlo, Monaco. Several of her paintings have been exhibited in the American Consulate in Nice. Her work includes R. Froman's Bigger & Smaller (Crowell, 1971), S. Bartlett's A Book to Begin on Libraries (Holt, 1964), L. Gaeddert's Noisy Nancy Norris (Doubleday, 1965), and L. Moore's Papa Albert (Atheneum, 1964). ICB-2, ICB-3

FISCHER, Ann A. She was born in Peoria, Illinois. At
one time she lived in Italy where she was an art instructor and designed covers for magazines. Miss
Fischer has also worked in advertising and public re-
lations. Her paintings have been included in many private collections. For children she illustrated B.
Kohn's The Bat Book (Hawthorn Books, 1967).

FISCHER, Hans Erich, 1909-1958. The son of school teachers, Hans Fischer was born in Berne, Switzerland.
He attended schools in Berne and Zürich, and he also
studied in Geneva at École des Beaux Arts et Arts Décoratifs. He has worked in advertising in addition to
illustrating books for both adults and children. His
drawings have also appeared in magazines, and his
lithographs and pictures have been exhibited in several
countries. He has also become a well-known muralist. His children provided the inspiration for many of
his stories and illustrations. These include J. Grimm's
Traveling Musicians (Harcourt, 1955). ICB-1, ICB-2

FISK, Nicholas. This illustrator has also been an author of
fact and fiction for boys and girls (including Richthofen,
The Red Baron, Coward, 1968). He served in the
British Royal Air Force during World War II. For
young people he illustrated G. Morgan's Tea With Mr.
Timothy (Little, 1966).

FLEISHMAN, Seymour, 1918- . He has always lived in or
near Chicago where he was born. He received his education at the Art Institute in Chicago. In addition to
illustrating books, he has worked in advertising. Seymour Fleishman served in Australia and New Guinea
during World War II. He illustrated C. Woolley's
Bunny in the Honeysuckle Patch (Morrow, 1965), C.
Wooley's Cat That Joined the Club (Morrow, 1967), and
M. Jones' Know Your Bible (Rand, 1965). ICB-2,
ICB-3

FLEUR, Anne. Her pseudonym is Sari. Born in Lancaster,
Pennsylvania, she later made her home in Mount Vernon, New York. She studied at St. Joseph's School and
the Business College in Lancaster. She also attended
the Art Students League in New York. She has written
and illustrated books. Her drawings can also be found
in text books. For boys and girls she illustrated B.
White's A Bear Named Grumms (Houghton, 1953), J.

Corcoran's <u>Elias Howe, Inventive Boy</u> (Bobbs-Merrill, 1962) and A. Stevenson's <u>Virginia Dare, Mystery Girl</u> (Bobbs-Merrill, 1959). ICB-2

FLORA, James, 1914- . He was born in Bellefontaine, Ohio, and later attended Urbana College, in Urbana, Ohio. He also studied at Cincinnati's Art Academy. He later made his home in Rowayton, Connecticut. Prior to becoming associated with a record company, Mr. Flora was one of the founders of a company that published pamphlets and books. There are illustrations in his books which have reflected his two years of study and travel in Mexico. His first book for boys and girls, <u>The Fabulous Firework Family</u> (Harcourt, 1955), was a result of his Mexican travels. He also wrote and illustrated (for Harcourt) <u>Fishing With Dad</u> (1967), <u>Grandpa's Farm</u> (1965) and <u>The Joking Man</u> (1968). ICB-2, ICB-3

FLORENCE see WABBES, Maria

FLOYD, Gareth. He was born in Lancashire, England, and studied art at Lowestoft, Guilford and Brighton Colleges of Art. Mr. Floyd has done both book and magazine illustrations and in addition has taught at Leicester College of Art in England. His work includes R. Pope's <u>Desperate Breakaway</u> (Children's Press, 1970), B. Willard's <u>Flight to the Forest</u> (Doubleday, 1967) and R. Parker's <u>Second-Hand Family</u> (Bobbs-Merrill, 1967).

FORTNUM, Peggy, 1919- . Born in Harrow-on-the-Hill, England she grew up in Harrow, England; Equien, France; and Crowborough, England. She studied at the Tunbridge Wells School of Arts and Crafts in Kent and the Central School of Arts and Crafts in London. Peggy Fortnum served in the Auxiliary Territorial Service during World War II. She has been a textile designer and art teacher. She and her husband Ralph Nuttall-Smith have lived in Swinview, West Mersea, Essex, England. The many books which she has illustrated for young people include M. Bond's <u>Paddington at Large</u> (Houghton, 1963) and N. Streatfield's <u>Thursday's Child</u> (a Junior Literary Guild selection; Random, 1971). ICB-2, ICB-3

FRACE, Charles. He grew up in Pennsylvania's Bear Mountain region. As a boy he was very interested in

wildlife and made many sketches and photographs of the
different species. Later his paintings appeared in
books and magazines. In 1967 and 1971 he created the
Christmas stamps for the National Wildlife Federation.
He and his family have made their home near Matti-
tuck, Long Island. For young people he illustrated G.
Bancroft's The White Cardinal (Coward, 1973) and M.
Fox's The Wolf (Coward, 1973).

FRAME, Paul, 1913- . He was born in Riderwood, Maryland and later studied at Columbia University and the
National Academy of Design in New York City. He has
been an artist for a large department store and has
worked at Friends Seminary. His work includes W.
Wise's Booker T. Washington (Putnam, 1968), E. Thay-
er's Casey at the Bat (Prentice-Hall, 1964) and M.
Calhoun's Katie John (Harper, 1960). ICB-3

FRANÇOIS, André, 1915- . He was born in Rumania and
studied in Paris at the École des Beaux-Arts. He also attended Cassandre's School of Fine Arts and Poster
Design. In addition to his work as a painter, he has
designed sets and costumes for the theatre and illustrated for magazines. André François has received a
Gold Medal from the Art Directors' Club of New York.
He and his family have made their home near Paris.
Books which he has illustrated for young people include I. Harris' Little Boy Brown (Lippincott, 1949).
ICB-2, ICB-3

FRANÇOISE see SEIGNOBOSC, Françoise

FRANKENBERG, Robert Clinton, 1911- . Artist and teacher, born in Mount Vernon, New York. He studied at
the Art Students League and has lived in New York City.
He served in the Army during World War II. The artist has been an instructor at the School of Visual Arts
and later was in charge of the school's Illustration Department. His work has appeared in both books and
magazines. Juvenile illustrations include P. Martin's
Chicanos (Parents Magazine, 1971) and H. Miller's
The Lucky Laceys (a Junior Literary Guild selection;
Doubleday, 1962). ICB-2, ICB-3

FRASCINO, Edward. Born in New York, as a student he
spent several months in Mexico. He has also traveled
throughout the Orient. His cartoons and drawings have

appeared in the New York Times, Saturday Review, and the New Yorker magazine. Mr. Frascino has also been a painter and has done figurative work in oils or acrylic. The first children's book which he illustrated was M. Stolz's Say Something (Harper, 1968). He also illustrated (for Harper) M. Stolz's Dragons of the Queen (1969) and M. Sharmat's Gladys Told Me to Meet Her Here (1970).

FRASER, Betty M., 1928- . Elizabeth M. Fraser was born in Massachusetts, attended the Rhode Island School of Design, and has lived in New York City. Prior to being a fulltime illustrator, Miss Fraser worked several years in advertising. She has preferred pen and ink media. For young readers she illustrated M. Sanger's Checkerback's Journey (World, 1969) and H. Read's The Spell of Chuchuchan (World, 1967). ICB-3

FREAS, Lenwood. He graduated from Pratt Institute in Brooklyn, New York, and later taught design and painting at Pratt. He has had his work exhibited in many galleries both in this country and abroad. The artist's home has been in San Pedro, California. Len Freas was a former player in the Little League and later served as a New Jersey recreation counselor. He illustrated A. Bunting's book on baseball for boys and girls, entitled Pitcher to Center Field (Children's Press, 1974).

FREUND, Rudolf, 1915- . He was born in Philadelphia where he later studied at the Museum School of Industrial Art and the Graphic Sketch Club. He also attended Pennsylvania's Academy of the Fine Arts and the Art Students League in New York. His home has been in East Haddam, Connecticut. He has illustrated books for both adults and children and has become well-known for his painting and illustration in the field of natural history. Mr. Freund's work has also appeared in Life magazine ("The World We Live In"). For boys and girls he illustrated D. Peattie's Rainbow Book of Nature (World, 1957). ICB-1, ICB-2

FRITH, Michael. Illustrator, author, editor. This artist has illustrated books for the first grade child i.e., the beginning reader. Illustrator of all the nature books in the "Step-Up" series, he has also drawn the pictures for a "Sesame Street" book. Calley Frith was the photographer for the picture of Michael Frith on the book jacket. He illustrated The Perils of Penelope, by N. Stiles and D. Wilcox (Random, 1973).

FROMM, Lilo. She was born in Berlin and received her art training in Germany. An avid traveler, Lilo Fromm has made her home in Berlin and France. Her picture book illustrations first appeared in 1957 in Germany. She received the German Children's Book Prize (Deutsche Jugendbuchpreis) for the best picture book of the year in 1967. Her illustrations can be found in G. Schneider's Uncle Harry (Macmillan, 1972).

FUJIKAWA, Gyo. She was born in Berkeley, California, studied at Chouinard Art Institute in Los Angeles, and later made her home in New York City. At one time she was associated with the Walt Disney Studios. In addition to book and magazine illustration, her career has included postage stamp design and advertising. For young people she illustrated R. Stevenson's A Child's Garden of Verses (Grosset, 1957). ICB-3

FUNK, Tom. Born in Brooklyn, New York, he later graduated from Amherst College. He also studied at the Beaux Arts Institute of Design and the Art Students League in New York City. Prior to being a free-lance artist, Mr. Funk designed displays for studios and department stores. He married artist Edna Eicke (The Children Who Got Married, by E. Eicke, Windmill, 1969), and they have lived in Westport, Connecticut. In addition to books, his work has appeared in Life, New Yorker, and Fortune magazines. He has been interested in playing the guitar and banjo and taking photographs. For boys and girls he illustrated E. Battle's The Terrible Terrier (a Junior Literary Guild selection; Young Scott, 1972).

-G-

GALSTER, Robert, 1928- . He was born in Dollville, Illinois, spent his childhood in Mansville, Ohio, and later made his home in New York City. Mr. Galster studied at the Parsons School of Design. When he was in the Army Engineers in Europe, he became interested

in poster design and later worked in poster design for
the theater on Broadway. He has also painted murals
in various hotels. He illustrated P. Showers' Find
Out By Touching (Crowell, 1961) and F. Branley's
Floating and Sinking (Crowell, 1967). ICB-3

GEARY, Clifford N., 1916- . Born in Somerville, Massachusetts, he studied at Rindge Technical High School in
Cambridge, the Massachusetts School of Art in Boston,
Pratt Institute in Brooklyn, and the Art Students League
in New York. He has been interested in camping, photography, and American history. Mr. Geary has lived
in Brooklyn and Astoria, New York. He illustrated D.
Heiderstadt's Frontier Leaders and Pioneers (McKay,
1962) and M. Grant's Wonder World of Microbes, 2d.
ed. (McGraw, 1964). ICB-2

GEER, Charles, 1922- . Born on Long Island, New York,
he studied at Dartmouth College in Hanover, New Hamp-
shire and at Pratt Institute in Brooklyn, New York.
During World War II, he served on a Navy destroyer.
In 1952 he traveled throughout Europe. Mr. Geer and
his family have lived near Lebanon, New Jersey. His
work includes H. Sandburg's Gingerbread (Dial, 1964),
E. MacGregor's Miss Pickerell Goes on a Dig (Mc-
Graw, 1966) and B. Bradbury's Sam and the Colonels
(Macrae Smith, 1966). ICB-2, ICB-3

GEKIERE, Madeleine, 1919- . She was born in Zürich,
Switzerland, and later studied at the Sorbonne in Paris
and at the Art Students League in New York. She
came to the United States in 1940 and decided to become an artist. Her home has been in New York City
where she has taught art at New York University.
Books which she illustrated included two by J. Ciardi,
John J. Plenty and Fiddler Dan (Lippincott, 1963) and
Reason for the Pelican (Lippincott, 1959). She wrote
and illustrated Who Gave Us ... Peacocks? Planes?
& Ferris Wheels? (Pantheon, 1953). ICB-2, ICB-3

GENIA see WENNERSTROM, Genia Katherine

GENTLEMAN, David. Painter, illustrator, designer, he
was born in London. Later he and his family made
their home in Camden Town, London. Mr. Gentleman
has worked in watercolor and has engraved in wood.
He studied at the School of Graphic Design of the Royal

College of Art where he later taught for several years
(1953-55). He has designed wallpaper, fabrics, stamps,
and the British Steel symbol. For boys and girls he illustrated J. Langstaff's The Golden Vanity (Harcourt,
1972).

GERGELY, Tibor, 1900- . Illustrator, painter, born in
Budapest, Hungary. He has also lived in Austria and
Czechoslovakia. Mr. Gergely later made his home in
New York City. His work has been exhibited both here
and in Europe. His cartoons, portraits, and drawings
have appeared in numerous magazines and newspapers.
In addition to illustrating books, Tibor Gergely has de-
signed for the stage and painted murals. His drawings
for young people can be found in M. Brown's Wheel on
the Chimney (Lippincott, 1954) and N. Turner's When
It Rained Cats and Dogs (Lippincott), 1956). ICB-1,
ICB-2

GILL, Margery Jean, 1925- . Born in Scotland, she grew
up in Middlesex, England. She attended the Harrow
School of Art and the Royal College of Art where she
studied engraving and etching. She has taught art in
addition to her work in book illustration. Her books
for young people include S. Cooper's Dawn of Fear
(Harcourt, 1970) and R. Arthur's Requiem for a Princess (a Junior Literary Guild selection; Atheneum,
1967). ICB-3

GIOVANOPOULOS, Paul. He has lived in New York City
where he has been a painter. The first children's
book that he illustrated was written about a boy who
lived in Brooklyn. It was P. Fox's How Many Miles
to Babylon? (David White, 1967). He also illustrated
E. Hodges' Free As a Frog (Addison, 1969).

GLANZMAN, Louis S., 1922- . He was born in Baltimore,
Maryland, grew up in Virginia, and has lived in Say-
ville, Long Island, New York. He has created comic
strips and magazine covers. His portraits have appeared on the cover of Time magazine and in the Ford
Theater Museum in Washington, D.C. Mr. Glanzman
was chosen by the Society of Illustrators to tour the
Far East for the USAF in 1954, and his paintings have
been exhibited in the Pentagon. For children he illustrated J. Latham's The Chagres (Garrard, 1964), A.
Lindgren's Pippi Longstocking (Viking, 1950) and L.

Hayman's Road to Fort Sumter (Crowell, 1972). ICB-3

GLASER, Milton, 1929- . He was born in New York City, grew up in the Bronx, and graduated from Cooper Union. He studied in Italy at the Bologna Academy of Fine Arts on a Fulbright grant. With Seymour Chwast he founded the Push Pin Studios. Mr. Glaser has been an instructor at New York City's School of Visual Arts. He has designed book jackets, illustrated books, and worked in advertising. He has been the recipient of the Gold Medal of the Art Directors Club and the Society of Illustrators. For children he illustrated C. Aiken's Cats and Bats and Things With Wings (Atheneum, 1965), G. Menotti's Help, Help, the Globolinks! (McGraw, 1970), A. Tresselt's Smallest Elephant in the World (Knopf, 1959). With his wife Shirley Glaser he wrote and illustrated If Apples Had Teeth (Knopf, 1960). ICB-3

GLATTAUER, Ned. Art director, illustrator, book designer. He studied at the Academy of Art, Vienna and graduated from the University of Vienna. Mr. Glattauer has had his own graphic arts studio for illustration and design. He and his wife have made their home in New York City. For young people he illustrated M. Embry's My Name Is Lion (Holiday House, 1970).

GOBBATO, Imero, 1923- . Born in Milan, Italy, he studied at Liceo Artistico and the Academy of Fine Arts in Milan and graduated from Venice's Institute of Fine Arts. He has been a naval architect and set designer for the motion picture industry in addition to his work as an illustrator of books for young people. He and his wife have lived in Camden, Maine. His books for young people include C. Panter's Beany and His New Recorder (Four Winds, 1972), J. Curry's Beneath the Hill (Harcourt, 1967) and J. Williams' The King With Six Friends (Parents Magazine, 1968). ICB-3

GOLDSTEIN, Nathan. He grew up in Chicago and studied at the Chicago Art Institute. Later he lived in the East and taught painting and drawing at the New England School of Art and Boston University. He married a painter, and they have lived in Waban, Massachusetts. His work includes B. Bailey's Abraham Lincoln: Man of Courage (Houghton, 1960), M. Ward's Adlai Stevenson:

Young Ambassador (Bobbs-Merrill, 1967), R. Radford's Colony Leader: James Edward Oglethorpe (Garrard, 1968), and P. Dickinson's Heartsease (a Junior Literary Guild selection; Atlantic-Little, Brown, 1969).

GONZALEZ, Xavier. He was born in Almeria, Spain, and came to the United States in 1921. His sculpture and paintings are in the collections of the Whitney and Metropolitan Museums in New York, and Delgado Museum in New Orleans, and the Museum of Fine Arts in Seattle. Mr. González has taught in universities and has received awards from the National Academy of Arts and the American Academy of Arts and Letters. He married painter Ethel Edwards and has lived in New York City. His work includes He Who Saw Everything: the Epic of Gilgamesh, ed. by A. Feagles (Scott, 1966).

GOODENOW, Girard, 1912- . He was born in Chicago and later studied at the Art Institute of Chicago and the Art Students League in New York. His illustrations have appeared in Woman's Day, and the Saturday Evening Post. He also has done advertising art. His work for young people includes G. Conklin's The Bug Club Book (Holiday, 1966) and How Insects Grow (Holiday, 1969); M. DeJong's Smoke Above the Lane (Harper, 1951). ICB-2

GOODWIN, Harold. The artist's illustrations which appear in A Singing Wind, ed. by Q. Hawkins (Macmillan, 1968) are delicate line drawings which have a majestic quality particularly appropriate for this book of poetry. He has made his home in Old Lyme, Connecticut. He also illustrated B. Baker's Do Not Annoy the Indians (Macmillan, 1968).

GORDON, Margaret Anna, 1939- . She was born and grew up in London, England. She studied in London at St. Martin's School of Art, Central School of Arts and Crafts, and Chamberwell School of Arts and Crafts. She married a publisher who encouraged her career in art. The artist has used ink and gouache in her color illustrations. For children she illustrated G. Macbeth's Jonah and the Lord (Holt, 1970). ICB-3

GOREY, Edward St. John, 1925- . Artist and writer, born in Chicago, Illinois. He received his B.A. degree from Harvard. In addition to illustrating books

by different authors, Edward Gorey has also written
and illustrated his own books for children which include The Bug Book (Random, 1960). He also illustrated J. Ciardi's The King Who Saved Himself from
Being Saved (Lippincott, 1965), E. Fenton's Penny
Candy (Holt, 1972) and R. Levine's Three Ladies Be-
side the Sea (Atheneum, 1963). ICB-3

GORMAN, Terry   see   POWERS, Richard M.

GORSLINE, Douglas Warner, 1913- . Illustrator, writer,
he was born in Rochester, New York, and has lived
in New York City. He attended the Yale School of
Fine Arts and the Art Students League in New York.
Mr. Gorsline has done both book and magazine illustration, worked in advertising art, and written books. He
has been the recipient of many art awards and has won
national recognition for his "Portrait of Thomas Wolfe."
His work has appeared in many galleries and museums.
For young people he illustrated P. Horgan's Citizen of
New Salem (Ariel, 1962) A. Malkus' Story of Good
Queen Bess (Grosset, 1953) and J. Wood's Trust Thy-
self (Pantheon, 1964). ICB-2, ICB-3

GRABIANSKI, Janusz, 1929- . He was born in Szamotuly,
Poland and studied at the Academy of Art in Cracow
and Warsaw. His likes have been listed as: children,
flowers, animals, birds, and fast cars. He has designed two series of stamps which have been issued
in Poland. The Gold Medal of the 1960 Milan Trien-
nale was awarded to Mr. Grabianski. For young
people he illustrated The Big Book of Animal Stories
(Watts, 1961) and The Big Book of Wild Animals
(Watts, 1964), both comp. and ed. by M. Green;
Perrault's Classic French Fairy Tales (Hawthorn,
1967). He also wrote and illustrated Birds and Dogs
(both Watts, 1968). ICB-3

GRABOFF, Abner, 1919- . He was born in New York City
and grew up in East Orange, New Jersey. He studied
at Brooklyn Museum Art School. In addition to illustrating books for boys and girls, he has been a commercial artist. He has lived near New York City.
The first book he illustrated for young people was M.
Schlein's The Sun Looks Down (Abelard, 1954), which
was selected as one of the ten best illustrated books
of 1954 by the New York Times. He also illustrated

E. David's Crystal Magic (Prentice, 1965); H. Liss'
Heat (Coward-McCann, 1965) and A. Hall's Mrs. Mc-
Garrity's Peppermint Sweater (a Junior Literary Guild
selection; Lothrop, 1966). He wrote and illustrated
Do Catbirds Wear Whiskers? (Putnam, 1967). ICB-3

GRAHAM, Margaret Bloy, 1920- . She was born in Toronto, Canada, and later graduated from the University
of Toronto. She also studied at New York University
and the New School for Social Research. She has illustrated for magazines in addition to books. Married
to author Gene Zion, she has illustrated many of the
books which her husband has written. Several of her
books have been Caldecott Medal honor books, and G.
Zion's The Meanest Squirrel I Ever Met (Scribner's,
1962), which she illustrated, was included in the Children's Book Show of the American Institute of Graphic
Arts. Her home has been in Cambridge, Massachusetts. Her books include two by G. Zion, All Falling
Down (Harper, 1951) and Harry by the Sea (Harper,
1965), and C. Zolotow's Storm Book (Harper, 1952).
ICB-2, ICB-3

GRANDA, Julio. Art director and illustrator, born in New
York City. He was the recipient of several awards
during service aboard an aircraft carrier in the Korean
War. Prior to free-lance book illustration, the artist
was associated with a publishing firm as a director of
art. Julio Granda has lived in Becket, Massachusetts,
with his family. His drawings for juveniles include
Experiments with Electric Currents (Norton, 1969) and
Experiments with Magnetism (Norton, 1968), both by
H. Sootin.

GRANT, Leigh. Art director and illustrator, Leigh Grant
spent her early years in Greenwich, Connecticut. She
received a degree in art history from Hollins College
in Roanoke, Virginia. After graduating with honors
in 1971 from Brooklyn's Pratt Institute, the artist
worked as a free-lance artist in London. She also did
further study in Europe at the École du Louvre, Institut Britannique, and the Sorbonne, sponsored by the
Hollins Abroad program. In addition to book illustration, Leigh Grant has created book jackets and served
as a magazine art director. Her hobbies have included
sailing and horseback riding. For children she illustrated J. Nixon's The Secret Box Mystery (Putnam,
1974).

GRAZIA, Thomas di. He was born in New Jersey, graduated from New York's Cooper Union and the Academy of Fine Arts in Rome, and has lived in New York City. In addition to illustrating books, Thomas di Grazia has also been a painter and a poet. For boys and girls he illustrated C. Zolotow's Hold My Hand (Harper, 1972).

GREENWALD, Sheila, 1934- . She was born in New York City and graduated from Sarah Lawrence College. She has written for adults, and her work has appeared in Harper's magazine. She married surgeon George Green, and they have lived in New York City. Her work includes H. Colman's The Boy Who Couldn't Make Up His Mind (Macmillan, 1965), E. Worstell's Jump the Rope Jingles (Macmillan, 1972), and B. Rinkoff's The Remarkable Ramsey (Morrow, 1965). ICB-3

GRETZER, John. He spent his early years in Council Bluffs, Iowa. He received his education at the University of Omaha and the Kansas City Art Institute. The artist served as a combat artist with the U.S. Coast Guard during World War II. Mr. Gretzer has been an art director for a publishing firm in Philadelphia. His favorite hobby has been woodcarving. For young people he illustrated G. Sentman's Drummer of Vincennes (Winston, 1952), S. Garst's Hans Christian Andersen: Fairy Tale Author (Houghton, 1965), E. Lampman's Once Upon the Little Big Horn (Crowell, 1971), and M. Cone's The Other Side of the Fence (Houghton, 1967).

GRIFALCONI, Ann, 1929- . Native New Yorker, illustrator, and art instructor. A graduate of Cooper Union, she also studied at Hunter College, New York University, and the University of Cincinnati in Ohio. In addition to teaching art, she has illustrated books and magazines. Miss Grifalconi was the 1966 Newbery Medal runner-up for her woodcuts in M. Weik's The Jazz Man (Atheneum, 1966). She also illustrated B. Byars' Midnight Fox (Viking, 1968) and wrote and illustrated City Rhythms, (Bobbs-Merrill, 1965). ICB-3

GRISHA see DOTZENKO, Grisha

GROSSMAN, Nancy S., 1940- . Born in New York City, she grew up on a farm in Oneonta, New York, and later spent a year in Puerto Rico. She attended the University of Arizona in Tucson and graduated from

Pratt Institute. She was the recipient of both the Contemporary Achievement Award in Fine Arts and a foreign travel scholarship from Pratt. Miss Grossman studied in Italy and Spain and was awarded a Guggenheim Fellowship in 1965. Her paintings have been exhibited in several one-man shows. For boys and girls she illustrated R. Caudill's Did You Carry the Flag Today, Charley? (Holt, 1966) E. Hill's Evan's Corner (Holt, 1967) and B. Baum's Patricia Crosses Town (Knopf, 1965). ICB-3

GWYNNE, Fred. Born in New York City, Mr. Gwynne was graduated from Harvard. In addition to being an artist, he has also been an actor and was in the television series "Car 54--Where Are You?" He has lived in Bedford Hills, New York. For boys and girls he illustrated G. Martin's The Battle of the Frogs and the Mice (Dodd, 1962). He wrote and illustrated Story of Ick (Windmill, 1971).

-H-

HAAS, Irene, 1929- . She was born and grew up in New York City. She attended college in North Carolina, Pratt Institute in Brooklyn, and the Art Students League in New York City. She has designed china and wallpaper and has also worked in advertising. Her home has been in Jamaica, New York. For children she illustrated E. Smith's Emily's Voyage (Harcourt, 1966) and two by E. Enright, Tatsinda (Harcourt, 1963) and Zeee (Harcourt, 1965). ICB-2, ICB-3

HADER, Berta (Hoerner); and Elmer Hader, 1889-1973. Husband-wife team, authors, illustrators. Born in Mexico, Berta Hoerner studied journalism at the University of Washington and attended the California School of Design. Mr. Hader, born in Pajaro, California, studied in Paris, France. After service in World War I, he married Berta Hoerner. The Haders have lived in Nyack, New York. In 1949 Mr. and Mrs. Hader won the Caldecott Medal for their book The Big Snow (Macmillan, 1948). Other titles, all for Macmillan include Big City (1947), Friendly Phoebe (1953), Little Antelope (1962), Midget and Bridget (1934) and Wish on the Moon (1954). ICB-1, ICB-2, ICB-3, ABYP-2

HADER, Elmer   see   HADER, Berta

HAFNER, Marilyn. Born in Brooklyn, she graduated from
    Pratt Institute and also studied at the School of Visual
    Arts in New York, Connecticut's Silvermine School of
    Art, and the Slade School in London. In addition to
    her illustrations that appear in books, her work has al-
    so been published in Good Housekeeping, McCall's, and
    Humpty Dumpty magazines. She has created designs
    for letterheads and packaging. She married author-
    artist Rudolf de Reyna and has lived in New Canaan,
    Connecticut. She illustrated E. Felder's X Marks the
    Spot (a Junior Literary Guild selection; Coward, 1972).

HALE, Kathleen, 1898- . Born in Scotland, she attended
    schools in Manchester and London. She later made her
    home in Oxford, England. The artist has been made a
    Fellow of the Society of Industrial Arts. She has de-
    signed posters and book jackets, and her children in-
    spired her to write and illustrate the "Orlando" books
    which include Orlando (The Marmalade Cat) Becomes a
    Doctor (Transatlantic Arts, 1944). ICB-2, ICB-3

HALEY, Gail. She was born in Charlotte, North Carolina,
    and studied at the Richmond Professional Institute and
    the University of Virginia. In addition to being an art-
    ist, Mrs. Haley has been an art director and an ap-
    prentice in a print shop. She has lived in New York
    City. In 1971 she won the Caldecott Medal for her
    book A Story, A Story, (Atheneum, 1970). For boys
    and girls she illustrated B. Kohn's Koalas (Prentice-
    Hall, 1965) and wrote and illustrated Noah's Ark (Ath-
    eneum, 1971).

HAMBERGER, John F. 1934- . He was born in Jamaica,
    Queens, New York, and studied at New York City's
    School of Visual Arts. His interest in nature and wild-
    life later led to his work in the Museum of Natural His-
    tory Nature and Science publication. His work has al-
    so appeared in Boys' Life magazine. Mr. Hamberger
    has belonged to the Society of Animal Illustrators, the
    Zoological Society, and the Museum of Natural History.
    For children he illustrated P. Martin's Navajo Pet
    (Putnam, 1970) and B. Kohn's Raccoons (Prentice-Hall,
    1968). He also wrote and illustrated The Day the Sun
    Disappeared (Norton, 1964). ICB-3

HAMPSHIRE, Michael Allen. He spent his boyhood in York-
    shire, England, and later studied at the University of
    Leeds.   After coming to the United States, he taught
    stage design at Marymount College in Tarrytown, New
    York.   Mr. Hampshire has traveled extensively in Eu-
    rope, the Sudan, Egypt, Ethiopia, India and Ceylon.
    He has also been interested in archaeology.   He illus-
    trated E. Grant's A Cow for Jaya (Coward, 1973), J.
    Krumgold's The Most Terrible Turk (Crowell, 1969),
    and H. Daringer's Yesterday's Daughter (Harcourt,
    1964).

HANDFORTH, Thomas Schofield, 1897-1948.   Born in Ta-
    coma, Washington, he studied art in New York and Par-
    is.   He was awarded the Caldecott Medal in 1939 for
    his book Mei Li (Doubleday, 1938), which was created
    when Mr. Handforth lived in Peking, China.   Before
    his death in 1948, Mr. Handforth resided in California.
    His work has been exhibited in many museums includ-
    ing the Metropolitan Museum of Art in New York, the
    Chicago Art Institute, and the Fogg Art Museum in Cam-
    bridge, Massachusetts.   ICB-1, ICB-2, ABYP-2

HAWKINS, Arthur.   A graduate of the University of Virginia,
    he was born in Maryland.   Later he studied art at the
    Art Students League.   Mr. Hawkins has written many
    cook books including one he wrote with his wife.   He
    has been a designer, painter, and a consulting art di-
    rector.   The Hawkinses have lived in Leonia, New Jer-
    sey.   For young people he illustrated A. Paul's Kids
    Cooking (Doubleday, 1970) and Kids Gardening (Double-
    day, 1972).

HAYNES, Robert.   He was born in Colorado and at one time
    lived in London, England.   After graduating from Colo-
    rado College he did graduate work at Columbia and Lon-
    don universities.   He married writer Nanda Weedon
    Ward, and together they wrote and he illustrated Beau
    (Ariel, 1957), Wellington and the Witch (Hastings House,
    1959).   Bob Haynes also illustrated N. Ward's Mister
    Mergatroid (Hastings House, 1960).

HEINLY, John.   The artist has made his home in Alexandria,
    Virginia.   He has served as art director for the Sunday
    magazine supplement of the Washington Evening Star.
    His books for young people include L. Foley's Some-
    body Stole Second (Delacorte, 1972) and E. Horwitz's

The Strange Story of the Frog Who Became a Prince
(Delacorte, 1971).

HELMER, Jean Cassels. Artist-illustrator. Born in Nash-
ville, Tennessee, she later made her home in Evanston, Illinois with her husband and children. She received her education in Ypsilanti, Michigan, at Eastern
Michigan University and in Chicago at the Art Institute.
Her hobbies have included weaving and ceramics, and
much of her work has been exhibited in the Midwest.
She illustrated M. Edsall's Battle on the Rosebush (Fol-
let, 1972).

HENDRICK, Joe. Artist, designer, sculptor. Mr. Hendrick
and his family have lived in Rochester, New York.
His drawings have appeared in magazines and books.
He has also worked in sculpture and designed stained
glass windows in a church. For children he illustrated
G. McHargue's The Wonderful Wings of Harold Harra-
bescu (Delacorte, 1971).

HENNEBERGER, Robert G., 1921- . He grew up in Baltimore, Maryland, where he was born. The artist
served as a medical illustrator at Bethesda Hospital
with the U.S. Navy during World War II and also was
stationed in the South Pacific. After the war, Mr.
Henneberger graduated from the Rhode Island School of
Design and later made his home in East Providence,
Rhode Island. His book illustrations include M. Christopher's Baseball Pals (Little, 1956), J. Stuart's Beat-
inest Boy (McGraw, 1953), J. Stuart's A Ride With Hu-
ey the Engineer (McGraw, 1966) and E. Cameron's
Stowaway to the Mushroom Planet (Little, 1956). ICB-
2

HENSTRA, Friso. This noted sculptor and illustrator was
born in Holland. In 1969 at Bratislava, Czechoslovakia
he was the recipient of a Golden Apple Award for his
illustrations in J. Williams' The Practical Princess
(Parents' magazine, 1969). He also illustrated Williams' The Silver Whistle (Parents' magazine, 1971).

HEUCK, Sigrid. She was born in Cologne and at one time
thought she would like to have a fashion career. She
studied at the Academy of Illustrative Art in Munich
where she illustrated her first children's book. For
young people she created the illustrations in G.

Ruck-Pauquêt's The Most Beautiful Place, (Dutton, 1965).

HIDA, Keiko, 1913-   . Japanese artist and photographer, born in Osaka. Her career began as an instructor of classical Japanese dance, and she later founded her own art school in Tokyo. She has become well-known for her exquisite calligraphy in addition to her essays and poetry. She has also designed kimonos. Keiko Hida has traveled and lectured throughout America and Europe. For boys and girls she illustrated The Prancing Pony, adapted by C. DeForest (Walker, 1967).

HIMLER, Ronald. He was born in Cleveland, Ohio. Mr. Himler later studied at the Cleveland Institute of Art. His delicate drawings which evoke the essence of childhood can be found in C. Zolotow's Janey, (Harper, 1973).

HINES, Bob. He has been an artist with the United States Fish and Wildlife Service and has designed several wildlife postage stamps for the U.S. government. He has also illustrated adult books in addition to children's books. His juvenile titles include two by R. McClung, Honker (Morrow, 1965) and Lost Wild America: The Story of Our Extinct & Vanishing Wildlife (Morrow, 1969).

HNIZDOVSKY, Jacques. He was born in the Ukraine and later came to the United States, where he became an American citizen in 1954. He received his art education in Warsaw and in Zagreb. Well-known as a graphic artist, his work has been exhibited in museums throughout this country and in international traveling exhibitions. For children he illustrated R. Silverberg's The Auk, the Dodo, and the Oryx (Crowell, 1967) and Poems of John Keats, ed. by S. Kunitz (Crowell, 1964).

HODGES, David. Born in Brooklyn, New York, he studied at the Leonardo da Vinci School of Fine Arts and the Art Students League in New York. Mr. Hodges has contributed cartoons to both the Saturday Evening Post and New Yorker magazines. He has also worked in advertising agencies. His home has been in Jamaica, Queens. For young people he illustrated M. King's Mary Baker Eddy: Child of Promise (Prentice-Hall, 1968) and H. Felton's Nat Love, Negro Cowboy (Dodd, 1969).

HOFFMANN, Christine. The artist spent her early years in
Lübeck, Germany and attended schools in Hamburg,
Paris, and Switzerland. She lived in California and
New York prior to her return to Germany. She and
her husband Gerhard Hoffmann (Doctor of Economics)
have two children. Mrs. Hoffmann illustrated D. Se-
ligman's The Trouble with Horses (a Junior Literary
Guild selection; Golden Gate, 1972).

HOFFMANN, Felix, 1911- . Born in Aarau, Switzerland,
he later studied art in Karlsruhe and Berlin, Germany.
He has continued to make his home in Aarau where he
has worked in lithography, completed etchings, draw-
ings, and woodcuts. Mr. Hoffmann also has designed
stained glass windows for churches and other buildings.
He has been the recipient of the Swiss Children's Book
Award (1957) and the New York Herald Tribune Chil-
dren's Spring Book Festival Picture Book Award (1963).
His work includes: V. Haviland's Favorite Fairy Tales
Told in Poland (Little, 1963) and the Grimm brothers'
Seven Ravens (Harcourt, 1963). ICB-2, ICB-3

HOFFMANN, Hilde. Artist, writer, traveler. She was
born in Germany and later made her home in New
York City. Several of her books were selected by the
German Ministry of Family and Youth Affairs for in-
clusion in their annual lists of best picture books.
Hilde Hoffmann wrote and illustrated: The City and
Country Mother Goose, (American Heritage, 1969) and
Green Grass Grows All Around (Macmillan, 1968).

HOGROGIAN, Nonny, 1932- . She has lived in New York
City where she was born. She graduated from Hunter
College and also studied at the New School for Social
Research in New York City. She has been married
to poet David Kherdian. She was awarded two Calde-
cott Medals, one in 1966 for L. Alger's Always Room
for One More (Holt, 1965) and in 1972 for One Fine
Day (Macmillan, 1971). She also illustrated L. Al-
ger's Gaelic Ghosts (a Junior Literary Guild selection;
Holt, 1964) and R. Burns' Hand in Hand We'll Go
(Crowell, 1965). She wrote and illustrated Apples
(Macmillan, 1972) and Billy Goat and His Well-Fed
Friends (Harper, 1972). ICB-3

HOLDSWORTH, William Curtis. He was born in Stoughton,
Massachusetts, and later lived in New York City. He

graduated from Amherst College and the Yale School of
Fine Arts. His work has appeared in galleries in Palm
Springs, New York City, and through the auspices of
the Cape Cod Art Association. He has been director
of the Allen-Stevenson School's Art program in New
York City. For young people he adapted and illustrated The Little Red Hen (Farrar, 1969).

HOLLAND, Janice, 1913-1962. A native of Washington,
D.C., she attended the Corcoran School of Art there.
She also studied in New York at Brooklyn's Pratt Institute. She painted figures and landscapes prior to illustrating books for children. Janice Holland believed in
combining realism with beauty in her drawings for young
people which included C. Coblentz's Blue Cat of Castle
Town (Longmans, 1949). ICB-2, ICB-3

HOLLING, Clancy see HOLLING, Lucille

HOLLING, Lucille (Webster), 1900- ; and Clancy Holling,
1900- . A husband-and-wife team. She was born in
Valparaiso, Indiana, and he was born in Holling Cor-
ners, Michigan. Both artists studied at the Chicago
Art Institute and later lived in Pasadena, California.
Mrs. Holling has designed costumes, illustrated for fashion publications, and has also been a ceramics instructor for the Red Cross. He wrote, and they illustrated The Book of Cowboys (Platt, 1936), The Book of
Indians (Platt, 1935) and Pagoo (Houghton, 1957). ICB-
1, ICB-2, ICB-3

HOLLINGSWORTH, Alvin. He graduated from City College in
New York, where he was Phi Beta Kappa. His home
has been in New York City and he has taught there at
the Art Students League and in the High School of Art
and Design. His work has been in both the African Museum in Washington, D.C., and the Brooklyn Museum.
The awards which his paintings have received include a
Whitney Fellowship and an Emily Lowe Award. His
drawings appeared in Black Out Loud, comp. by A.
Adoff (Macmillan, 1970).

HOUSER, Allan C., 1914- . Artist, painter, sculptor. He
was born in Apache, Oklahoma, and was given the Indian name Haozous which means "Pulling Roots." He attended Indian schools and in 1935 studied in Santa Fe at
the Indian Art School. It was here that he received

recognition for his art, and he later was awarded a
Guggenheim scholarship. His work has been exhibited
in this country and in Europe, and his murals can be
found in Indian schools in Oklahoma and New Mexico.
His father (who was chief interpreter for the famed
Indian Chief Geronimo) was the artist's best critic.
Allan Houser has worked in frescoes, secco and egg
tempera, and carved in marble. He has lived in Los
Angeles, California. For young people he illustrated
A. Clark's The Desert People (Viking, 1962) and E.
Wyatt's Geronimo, the Last Apache War Chief (Mc-
Graw, 1952). ICB-1, ICB-2, ICB-3

HOWARD, Alan, 1922- . He was born in England where he
later studied at the School of Oriental and African Studies. He was also a student at Cambridge and at the
Nottingham College of Art and Crafts. He has been interested in the art work of children and primitive people
in addition to the work of great masters. Mr. Howard
and his family have lived in Preston, England. For
young people he illustrated W. De La Mare's Tales Told
Again (Knopf, 1959). ICB-2, ICB-3

HOWARD, Rob. The artist and his wife Veronica have resided in New York's East Village. The recipient of
many awards, Rob Howard has been commended for his
illustrations in H. Buckley's The Little Pig in the Cup-
board (Lothrop, 1968). He also illustrated E. Evans'
Beginning of Life (Crowell-Collier, 1969).

HUTCHINS, Pat. Born in Yorkshire, England, she studied
at Leeds College of Art. She illustrated her first book
for children on a visit to New York. She began drawing at the age of seven when she was encouraged by a
couple "who gave her a bar of chocolate for each picture." She wrote and illustrated Changes, Changes,
(Macmillan, 1971) and Rosie's Walk (Macmillan, 1968).

HUTCHINSON, William M., 1916- . He was born in Nor-
folk, Virginia, and spent his childhood in Virginia and
West Virginia. During World War II, he served in the
Pacific. Mr. Hutchinson studied at Cleveland Art Institute in Ohio and has been a free-lance artist. He has
made his home in Westport, Connecticut. For young
people he illustred G. Barlow's Latin American Tales;
From the Pampas to the Pyramids of Mexico (Rand,
1967) and Y. Uchida's The Promised Year (Harcourt,
1959). ICB-3

HUTCHISON, Paul A., 1905- . Born in Helena, Montana,
    she grew up in the Pacific Northwest. She attended
    the University of Washington in Seattle and Pratt Insti-
    tute in Brooklyn, New York. She also studied design
    in Florence, London, and Paris. She and her husband
    have lived near Matawan, New Jersey. For young
    people she illustrated F. Cavanah's Abe Lincoln Gets His
    Chance (Rand, 1959), A. Sutton's Animals on the Move
    (Rand, 1965) and E. Hall's Hong Kong (Rand, 1967).
    ICB-2

HYMAN, Trina Schart, 1939- . She was born in Philadel-
    phia, Pennsylvania, and attended the College of Art
    there. She also studied in Boston at the Museum
    School and in Sweden at Stockholm's Konstfackskolan.
    After her marriage in 1959 to engineer and mathema-
    tician Harris Hyman, she lived in Sweden and Boston,
    Massachusetts before moving to New York. Juvenile
    stories which she illustrated include E. Johnson's All
    in Free But Janey (Little, 1968), C. Brink's The Bad
    Times of Irma Baumlein (Macmillan, 1972), A. Turn-
    bull's George (Houghton, 1965) and R. Sawyer's Joy to
    the World (Little, 1966). ICB-3

-I-J-

ILSLEY, Velma Elizabeth, 1918- . She was born in Ed-
    monton, Alberta, Canada and later made her home in
    New York City. At various times she has lived in
    California, Florida, New Jersey, and Nova Scotia. She
    received her education at Douglass College in New
    Brunswick, New Jersey, and at the Moore Institute of
    Art, Science and Industry in Philadelphia. She also
    studied at the Art Students League in New York. Vel-
    ma Ilsley has been a fashion illustrator and portrait
    painter in addition to book illustrator. Her work in-
    cludes A. Huston's Cat Across the Way (Seabury, 1968),
    and N. Agle's Kate and the Apple Tree (Seabury, 1965).
    She also wrote and illustrated Busy Day for Chris,
    (Lippincott, 1957), and The Long Stocking (Lippincott,
    1959). ICB-2

JACQUES, Faith. British artist and lecturer, born in Lei-
    cester, England. She completed her education at Lon-
    don's Central School of Arts and Crafts after serving
    with the Women's Royal Naval Service during World War

II. Miss Jacques has lectured at art schools in Surrey and London where she has made her home. She illustrated E. Mathieson's The True Story of Jumbo the Elephant (Coward, 1964) and H. Treece's The Windswept City (a Junior Literary Guild selection; Meredith, 1968).

JACQUES, Robin, 1920- . Born in Chelsea, London, he has traveled and lived in Africa, Mexico, and the United States. The Jacques family later moved to the south of France. In addition to book illustration, Robin Jacques has worked in advertising and was the Art Editor of a magazine. He served in the British Army during World War II and has been a Fellow of the British Society of Industrial Artists. For boys and girls he illustrated J. Aiken's Black Hearts in Battersea (a Junior Literary Guild selection; Doubleday, 1964), H. Burton's The Flood at Reedsmere (World, 1968), J. Aiken's Nightbirds on Nantucket (a Junior Literary Guild selection; Doubleday, 1966) and M. Bacon's Third Road, (Little, 1971). ICB-2, ICB-3

JAKUBOWSKI, Charles. This illustrator graduated from the Hussian School of Art in Philadelphia. Later he taught art in the Hussian School. His detailed black and white illustrations appear in S. Simon's Science Projects in Ecology and Science Projects in Pollution (both for Holiday House, 1972).

JAMES, Harold. He was born in Fayetteville, North Carolina, and later attended North Carolina A. & T. College. He had his own design studio (Jango Inc.) and afterwards became associated ("a founding partner") with the advertising agency Jones, James & Jameson, Inc. The artist and his family have lived in Queens Village, New York. He has illustrated several of Rose Blue's books, including Bed-Stuy Beat (Watts, 1970) and How Many Blocks Is the World? (Watts, 1970).

JANOSCH, 1931- . Born in Poland, he later studied art at the Munich Academy. In addition to illustrating books for young people, he has been an industrial designer. He has lived near Munich where he also has a studio. His vivid illustrations, which have a childlike simplicity, can be found in his book Dear Snowman (World, 1970).

JEFFERS, Susan. The artist has lived in Brooklyn, New

York where she graduated from Pratt Institute. In 1969 the American Institute of Graphic Arts included one of her books in their book exhibit. A noted graphic artist, Susan Jeffers designed (and Rosemary Wells illustrated) R. Service's The Shooting of Dan McGrew & The Cremation of Sam McGee (Young Scott, 1969).

JEFFERSON, Robert Louis, 1929- . A native Pennsylvanian, he has made his home in Philadelphia. He also lived in Morocco for two years. The artist studied in Paris at the Académie de la Grande Chaumiére and the Sorbonne after attending Philadelphia's Museum College of Art. For boys and girls he illustrated H. Foreman's Awk (Westminster, 1970), G. Cretan's Run Away Habeeb! (Abingdon Press, 1968) and M. Self's Susan and Jane Learn to Ride (Macrae Smith, 1965).

JENKYNS, Chris, 1924- . He was born in North Hollywood, California. Following his discharge from the Navy, he studied at Los Angeles City College, Chouinard Art Institute, and the Art Students League in New York. He also studied on the "G.I. Bill" at the Académie Julian, in Paris. Later he made his home in California where he worked in films in addition to illustrating books. In Paris he met Pat Diska and illustrated her book, Andy Says Bonjour (Vanguard, 1954). ICB-2

JOERNS, Consuelo. She spent her childhood in Chicago where she later attended the Art Institute. She also studied at California's Mills College and in New York at Columbia University and the School of Visual Arts. She has painted in Guatemala and on the Ile Saint-Louis in Paris. She later worked at Sneden's Landing near the Hudson River. She illustrated W. Corbin's The Everywhere Cat (a Junior Literary Guild selection; Coward-McCann, 1970).

JOHNSON, Eugene Harper. Artist and musician, Eugene Johnson was born in Birmingham, Alabama. He received his education in Paris at the Académie Julian and in Chicago at the Art Institute. He also studied in New York at the National Academy School of Fine Arts and in Brooklyn at Pratt Institute. Harper Johnson has written poetry and has been interested in both singing and painting. After a fall from a horse which broke his wrist, Eugene Johnson gave up his career

as a violinist. He has done murals and portraits, and
his work has been exhibited in private collections and
art galleries. His drawings have been published in
both books and magazines. For children he illustrated
B. Ives' Albad the Oaf (Abelard, 1965) and M. Rose's
Clara Barton: Soldier of Mercy (Garrard, 1960). ICB-
2, ICB-3

JOHNSON, John E., 1929- . Born in Worcester, Massa-
chusetts, he studied at the Philadelphia College of Art.
Following service in the army, he worked for a greet-
ing card company in New York. In addition to illus-
trating books, he has drawn for magazines and worked
in advertising. He married an artist and has lived in
New York City. His work includes B. Brenner's Beef
Stew (Knopf, 1965), I. Hodgson's Bernadette's Busy
Morning (Parents' magazine, 1968), and L. Jacobs'
Just Around the Corner (Holt, 1964). ICB-3

JOHNSTONE, Anne; and Janet Grahame Johnstone. Born in
London, the daughters of theatrical designer Doris
Zinkeisen. They have lived in Suffolk and attended St.
Martin's School of Art in London. Their book illustra-
tions have appeared in folk and fairy tale collections.
Other drawings can be found in N. Lofts' Maude Reed
Tale (Nelson, 1972) and Rupert Hatton's Story (Nelson,
1973).

JOHNSTONE, Janet see JOHNSTONE, Anne

JONES, Elizabeth Orton, 1910- . Author-illustrator, born
in Highland Park, Illinois. She studied art at the University of Chicago, and has studied painting at Fontaine-
bleau and in Paris. Elizabeth Orton Jones has illustrated many books for various authors. In 1945 she received the Caldecott Medal for Prayer for a Child (Macmillan, 1944), written by Rachel Field. She has had a
studio in Highland Park, Illinois, and has lived in Mason, New Hampshire. She has illustrated some books
written by her mother, Jessie Mae (Orton) Jones including Secrets (Viking, 1945) and This Is the Way (Viking,
1951). She also illustrated Song of the Sun (Macmillan,
1952). ICB-1, ICB-2

JONES, Harold, 1904- . He was born in London and studied at St. Dunstan's College and at the Royal College of
Art. During World War II, he served with the Royal

Engineers. He collaborated with Walter de la Mare
on his first book for children. Works of his have been
acquired by the Victoria and Albert Museum and the
Tate Gallery. The artist has made his home in Putney, London. He illustrated Bless This Day, comp by
E. Vipont (Harcourt, 1958) and Lavender's Blue, ed.
by K. Lines (Watts, 1954). ICB-1, ICB-2, ICB-3

JOYNER, Jerry. Prior to receiving his degree in illustration from the California College of Arts and Crafts, the
artist attended Oregon State University at Eugene. His
home has been in Paris. His professional career has
included being a magazine artist, designer, and illustrator. Mr. Joyner's drawings can be found in M.
Hoberman's The Looking Book (a Junior Literary Guild
selection; Knopf, 1973).

JUCKER, Sita. She has been an illustrator for Elle (the
French fashion magazine) and illustrated textbooks for
boys and girls in Switzerland. Mrs. Jucker has also
illustrated book jackets and books in Geneva, Basel,
and Paris. For young people she illustrated U. Zieg-
ler's Squaps (Atheneum, 1969).

-K-

KALMENOFF, Matthew. Born in New York City, he has
been on the staff of the American Museum of Natural
History in New York. His work has appeared in many
magazines including Natural History and Audubon Magazine. He has also painted backgrounds for habitat
groups in many museums throughout the United States.
The artist and his family have lived in Scarsdale, New
York. For young people he illustrated D. Shuttles-
worth's Animal Camouflage (Natural History Press,
1966) and G. Conklin's Chimpanzee Roams the Forest
(Holiday, 1970).

KAMEN, Gloria. Native of New York, she graduated from
Pratt Institute in Brooklyn and also studied at the Art
Students League. The artist and her husband, Elliot
Charney, a research chemist at the National Institute
of Health, have made their home in Bethesda, Mary-
land. The Charneys once lived for a year in Oxford,
England. She illustrated the following books for young
people: Betty Crocker's New Boys and Girls Cook

Book (Golden Press, 1965) and R. Friedman's Paddy McGuire and the Patriotic Squirrel (Abingdon, 1963).

KAMPEN, Owen. Illustrator and teacher, born in Madison, Wisconsin. He received his education at New York's Art Students League and the University of Wisconsin. The artist served in Italy as a B-24 pilot in World War II. He has been a college professor and portrait painter in addition to illustrating books. His drawings can be found in Jay Williams' books entitled Danny Dunn and the Automatic House (McGraw, 1965) and Danny Dunn, Time Traveler (McGraw, 1963).

KAPLAN, Boche. Artist and lecturer, Mrs. Kaplan has made her home in Oceanside, Long Island. She graduated from New York's Cooper Union School of Art and Architecture and has conducted art lectures at the Solomon Guggenheim Foundation. In addition to book illustration, the artist has been interested in textile designing, printmaking, and painting. For boys and girls she illustrated R. Abisch's Open Your Eyes (Parents' magazine, 1964) and 'Twas in the Moon of Wintertime (Prentice-Hall, 1969).

KARASZ, Ilonka, 1896- . She was born in Hungary and studied at the Royal School of Arts and Crafts in Budapest. In 1913 she came to the United States where she has made her home with the exception of several years spent in Java, the Dutch East Indies and Europe. Miss Karasz has designed covers for the New Yorker magazine, and textiles, china, and wallpaper. Her home has been in Brewster, New York. In 1949 the American Institute of Graphic Arts selected her book, The Twelve Days of Christmas (Harper, 1949), as one of the "Fifty Books of the Year." She also illustrated W. Maxwell's The Heavenly Tenants (Harper, 1946). ICB-2

KARLIN, Eugene, 1918- . He was born in Kenosha, Wisconsin, and later studied at the Chicago Art Institute, New York's Art Students League and at the Arts Center in Colorado Springs. He studied art at an early age in Chicago and received scholarships to further his education. An instructor in several distinguished art schools, Mr. Karlin has taught at Pratt Institute and the School of Visual Arts. He has worked in the advertising field and contributed illustrations to

magazines in addition to books. The Karlins have made
their home in Sunnyside, New York. His work in-
cludes: A. Church's The Aeneid for Boys and Girls
(Macmillan, 1962) and M. Moore's Puss in Boots, The
Sleeping Beauty & Cinderella... (Macmillan, 1963).
ICB-3

KASHIWAGI, Isami, 1925- . He was born in Onomea, Hawaii, and attended the University of Hawaii, Pennsylvania Academy of the Fine Arts, and studied in Europe
on a Cresson Traveling Scholarship. His home has
been in New York City. Isami (Sam) Kashiwagi served
as an interpreter with the occupation forces in Japan.
For young people he illustrated W. Ley's Engineer's
Dreams (Viking, 1954) and V. Oakes' Hawaiian Treasure (Messner, 1957). ICB-2

KAUFMANN, John, 1931- . A native of New York, the
artist has lived on Long Island. He received his education in Philadelphia at the Pennsylvania Academy of
Fine Arts and in New York at the Art Students League.
He also studied in Florence, Italy at the Istituto Statale
d'Arte. At one time he worked in an aircraft factory
and also did technical illustration. Mr. Kaufmann has
enjoyed bird watching as a hobby and has painted watercolors of shore birds. He and his family have lived in
Fresh Meadows, New York. For boys and girls he illustrated M. Selsam's Animals as Parents (Morrow,
1965), A. Norton's Fur Magic (World, 1968), and P.
Young's Old Abe: The Eagle Hero (a Junior Literary
Guild selection; Prentice-Hall, 1965). ICB-3

KEATS, Ezra Jack, 1916- . Illustrator-author, born in
Brooklyn, New York where he has continued to make
his home. During World War II, he was a camouflage
expert in the United States Air Corps. At one time he
lived in Paris. He has illustrated many books for children, but The Snowy Day (Viking, 1962) was the first
book which Mr. Keats wrote and illustrated. It was
this book which won the Caldecott Medal in 1963. With
Pat Cherr he wrote My Dog Is Lost! (Crowell, 1960),
and he wrote and illustrated Apt. 3 (Macmillan, 1971),
Over in the Meadow (Four Winds, 1972) and Peter's
Chair (Harper, 1967). ICB-2, ICB-3, ABYP-2

KEEPING, Charles William James, 1924- . Born in London, he later studied art there at the Polytechnic. He

married painter Renate Meyer and has made his home
in Bromley, South London. Charles Keeping served as
a telegraph operator with the Royal Navy during World
War II. Following the war, he did further study in
art on a fulltime grant. His work has been exhibited
in Australia, England, Italy, and the United States.
Mr. Keeping has been on the staff at Croydon College
of Art and the Polytechnic. His illustrations have appeared in N. Gray's The Apple Stone (a Junior Literary
Guild selection; Meredith, 1969), R. Sutcliff's Beowulf
(Dutton, 1962), and N. Gray's Mainly in Moonlight (a
Junior Literary Guild selection; Duell, 1967). ICB-3

KEITH, Eros. A resident of New York City, he studied at
the University of Chicago and the Chicago Art Institute.
Mr. Keith has worked in advertising, drawn covers for
records and jackets for books, and his illustrations
have also appeared in magazines. For young people he
illustrated S. Kafka's I Need a Friend (Putnam, 1971)
and E. Janeway's Ivanov Seven (Harper, 1967).

KELLOGG, Steven. He grew up in the northern part of the
state of New York and later attended the Rhode Island
School of Design. After receiving a scholarship, he
studied for a year in Florence, Italy. He also studied
in Washington, D.C. Steven Kellogg and his family
have made their home in Sandy Hook, Connecticut. He
wrote and illustrated: Can I Keep Him? (Dial, 1971),
The Wicked Kings of Bloon (Prentice-Hall, 1970). He
also illustrated J. Wahl's Crabapple Night (Holt, 1971).

KELLY, Walt, 1913-1973. Cartoonist Walter Crawford Kelly
was born in Philadelphia. He originated the character
"Pogo" which has appeared in many newspapers. In
1951 he received the "Reuben" award from the National
Cartoonists Society as "Cartoonist of the Year." Prior
to being an editorial cartoonist on the New York Star,
he was an animator in Walt Disney Studios. His work
includes: Complete Nursery Song Book, ed. by I. Ber-
tail (Lothrop, 1947) and J. O'Reilly's The Glob (Viking, 1952).

KENELSKI, Maurice. He was born in Switzerland and studied art in Zürich and at Cooper Union in New York
City. Mr. Kenelski also lived and pursued his interest in art in Copenhagen, London, and Brussels. His
home has been in Switzerland where he has been a

magazine free-lance artist. For boys and girls he illustrated M. Damjan's The Little Green Man (English
version by A. Tresselt; Parents' magazine, 1972).

KENNEDY, Richard, 1910- . Born in England, he later
studied at London's Central School of Arts and Crafts.
His career began in a publishing firm, and he then
held jobs on a newspaper and in an advertising agency.
The artist's home has been in Maidenhead, Berkshire,
England. For young people he illustrated three works
of E. Dillon's: Cruise of the Santa Maria (Funk,
(1967), Seals (Funk, 1969) and Under the Orange Grove
(Meredith, 1969). ICB-2, ICB-3

KENT, Rockwell, 1882- . He was born in Tarrytown
Heights, New York and later studied at Columbia University. He has created lithographs and wood engravings in addition to painting and drawing pictures. Mr.
Kent has also been a dairy farmer in New York state.
At one time he lived in Ireland, Alaska, Greenland,
and Newfoundland. His work has been included in the
collections at the Metropolitan Museum of Art in New
York City and the Chicago Art Institute. He illustrated
the Cambridge Edition of Shakespeare's Complete Works
(Doubleday, 1936) and E. Shepard's Paul Bunyan (Harcourt, 1952). He wrote and illustrated Wilderness
(Halcyon, 1937). ICB-1

KIDDELL-MONROE, Joan, 1908- . Born in England, she
studied at Willesden and Chelsea School of Art. Prior
to becoming a free-lance artist, she worked in advertising. She married Canadian artist Webster Murray
who died in 1951. In addition to illustrating books, the
artist has painted both landscapes and portraits. She
has lived in Mallorca. She illustrated Longfellow's
Song of Hiawatha (Dutton, 1959) and Welsh Legends and
Folk-Tales. Retold by G. Jones (Oxford, 1955). ICB-
2, ICB-3

KIDWELL, Carl. Born in Washington, Indiana, he later
made his home in New York City. He has also written books in addition to illustrating them. As a young
man he worked in a variety of jobs including bellhop,
railway coach painter, and drug store clerk. During
World War II, he served in the Navy as a radioman.
It was during this time that he decided upon art as his
future career. For young people he illustrated J.

Randall's Island Ghost (a Junior Literary Guild selection; McKay, 1971).

KIPNISS, Robert. He has made his home in New York City with his wife and children. Robert Kipniss studied in Ohio at Wittenberg University and graduated from the State University of Iowa with a Master of Fine Arts degree in history and painting. His work has been exhibited throughout this country in galleries and museums. For children he used black and white drawings to illustrate Poems of Emily Dickinson, selected by H. Plotz (Crowell, 1964).

KIRMSE, Marguerite, 1885-1954. Born in Bournemouth, England, she attended London's Royal Academy School of Music, the Polytechnic School of Art, and Frank Calderon's School of Animal Painting. She came to the United States in 1910 as a harpist in an orchestra. She married George W. Cole and lived on a farm in Bridgewater, Connecticut, where she and her husband kept dog kennels and raised blue-ribbon winners. For young readers she illustrated two books by D. L'Hommedieu, Nipper, the Little Bull Pup (Lippincott, 1943), and Togo, the Little Husky (Lippincott, 1951). ICB-1, ICB-2

KOCSIS, James C., 1936- . His pseudonym is James Paul. Born in Buffalo, New York, he grew up in Bethlehem, Pennsylvania, and later made his home in Philadelphia. He studied at the Fleisher Art Memorial School and attended the Philadelphia College of Art on a scholarship. He has been a member of the Philadelphia College of Art faculty since 1965. His career as a painter and illustrator began at the age of 14 when he held his first one-man show. Following his discharge from the Army, James Kocsis has been both a magazine and book illustrator. His work for children includes W. Jones' Edge of Two Worlds (Dial, 1968), G. Boldrini's Etruscan Leopards (Pantheon, 1968) and E. Ladd's Trouble on Heron's Neck (Morrow, 1966). ICB-3

KOERING, Ursula, 1921- . Born in Vineland, New Jersey, she spent part of her childhood in Indiana and New Jersey. She studied at the Philadelphia Museum School of Art. In addition to illustrating books, she has enjoyed sculpturing and working in pottery. Her work includes W. Hayes' Mystery at Squaw Peak (Atheneum, 1965),

E. Pedersen's Mystery of the Alaska Queen (Washburn,
1969), two works by H. O'Neill, Picture Story of Denmark (McKay, 1952) and Picture Story of Norway (Mc-
Kay, 1951). ICB-2

KRAUSS, Oscar. New York art director. He has been associated with the National Society of Art Directors and
the Art Directors Club. Prior to studying art and design at Pratt Institute, he was interested in architecture. He designed S. Glubok's The Art of Ancient
Greece (Atheneum, 1963) and The Art of Ancient Rome
(Harper, 1965).

KREDEL, Fritz, 1900- . Artist and teacher, born in Mi-
chelstadt, Odenwald, Germany. He attended art school
in Offenbach-am-Main at Kunstgewerbeschule. He became an American citizen after coming to the United
States in 1938 and has lived in New York City. At one
time Mr. Kredel taught art in Germany and later served
on the staff at Cooper Union Art School in New York.
He has received many honors for his work including
the 1938 Golden Medal for Book Illustration in Paris,
and the 1960 Goethe Plaquette in Germany. He was also awarded the Silver Jubilee Citation of the Limited
Editions Club in 1954. For children he illustrated J.
Ruskin's The King of the Golden River (World, 1946),
H. Pauli's Little Town of Bethlehem (Duell, 1963) and
M. Brown's Silent Storm: Sullivan (Abingdon, 1963).
ICB-1, ICB-2, ICB-3

KRUSH, Beth see KRUSH, Joe

KRUSH, Joe, 1918- ; and Beth Krush, 1918- . Husband-
wife team. He was born in Camden, New Jersey, and
she was born in Washington, D.C. Both attended the
Museum School of Art in Philadelphia, and both have
been art instructors. He served with the Office of
Strategic Services during World War II. The Krushs
have lived in Wayne, Pennsylvania, and have enjoyed
model airplanes and tennis as special interests. They
have been the recipients of many awards for drawing
and watercolor. Together they illustrated J. Fritz's
Magic to Burn (Coward, 1964) and J. Langstaff's The
Swapping Boy (Harcourt, 1960). ICB-2, ICB-3

KUBINYI, Laszlo. The artist grew up in Massachusetts on
Cape Ann. He has traveled in the Middle East and

throughout the world. His home has been in New York
City. Mr. Kubinyi received his education in Massachusetts at the Boston Museum School and in New York at
the Art Students League. He also attended the School
of Visual Arts. In addition to book illustration, he
has played the dumbek (a Middle Eastern drum) in an
Armenian orchestra. For boys and girls he illustrated M. Gardner's Perplexing Puzzles and Tantaliz-
ing Teasers (Simon, 1969) and B. Lifton's Silver Crane
(Seabury, 1971).

-L-

LAITE, Gordon, 1925- . He was born in New York City
and studied at Beloit College in Beloit, Wisconsin, and
the Chicago Art Institute. He was raised by Charles
and Blanche Fisher Laite who illustrated The Real
Mother Goose (Rand, 1916) under the name of Blanche
Fisher Wright. Gordon Laite and his wife Jeanne and
two children have lived in Gallup, New Mexico, since
1962. His work includes V. Voight's Adventures of
Hiawatha (Garrard, 1969), N. Belting's ...Elves and
Ellefolk (Holt, 1961), L. Wolcott's Religions Around
the World (Abingdon, 1967), and E. Dolch's Stories
from India (Garrard, 1961). ICB-3

LAMB, Lynton, 1907- . Born in India, Lynton Lamb grew
up in England and attended British schools. He later
made his home in Essex at Sandon. In addition to
drawing and writing, he has done lithography, painting,
and engraving. His work has been exhibited at the
Royal Academy, and he has belonged to The London
Group. Mr. Lamb has also taught at the Slade School
of Fine Art. He has designed British postage stamps
and written textbooks. The artist served with the Royal Engineers during World War II. For young people
he illustrated W. Mayne's A Grass Rope (Dutton, 1962).
ICB-2, ICB-3

LAMBERT, Saul. This artist has made his home in Princeton, New Jersey. He has illustrated book covers and
magazine stories in addition to books. His drawings
can be found in P. Fox's Portrait of Ivan (Bradbury,
1969).

LAMBO, Don. A graduate of Princeton University, he

studied art at Pratt Institute. He has worked in advertising in addition to illustrating books for young people.
Mr. Lambo's interests have included photography and
woodworking. On his travels around the world he took
many photographs which helped him illustrate J. Breet-
veld's Getting to Know Brazil (Coward, 1958), J. Wallace's Getting to Know the Soviet Union (Coward,
1964) and Getting to Know the U.S.S.R. (Coward, 1959).
He also illustrated M. Crary's Jared and the Yankee
Genius (McKay, 1965).

LANDAU, Jacob, 1917- . Artist, photographer, teacher.
Born in Philadelphia, Pennsylvania, he has lived in
Roosevelt, New Jersey. He studied at Philadelphia's
Museum School of Art, New York's New School for Research, and France's Académie de la Grande Chaumière in Paris. He served with the Special Services,
Engineer Command, during World War II. In addition
to illustrating books, Mr. Landau has worked in adver-
tising and produced film strips for the United Nations
Secretariat. He has also been a photographer and edi-
tor and has been on the staff at the Philadelphia Museum School of Art and Pratt Institute in Brooklyn.
His work has been exhibited both here and abroad. He
has received many honors including the 1967 National
Arts Endowment Grant. He illustrated J. Kjelgaard's
Snow Dog (Holiday, 1948) and Q. Reynolds' The Wright
Brothers, Pioneers of American Aviation (Random,
1950). ICB-2, ICB-3

LANGNER, Nola, 1930- . Born in New York City, she at-
tended Bennington College and also studied art at the
Yale School of Fine Arts. She began her career work-
ing for a magazine and in a television art studio. Mar-
ried to a sociologist, she has lived in New York City.
A great deal of her work has been in black-and-white.
Her work for young people includes R. Pack's How to
Catch a Crocodile (Knopf, 1964), H. Longman's Kitch-
en-Window Squirrel (Parents' magazine, 1969), and A.
McGovern's Who Has a Secret? (Houghton, 1964). ICB-3

LARRECQ, John M. Born in Santa Rosa, California, he
grew up in Santa Cruz and later graduated from the
College of Arts and Crafts in Oakland. Following service in the United States Air Force, he continued his
career in graphic arts. His illustrations have received awards in Art Directors' and Society of

Illustrators' shows in both Los Angeles and San Francisco. His book illustrations have appeared in ALA
Notable Book lists and the Horn Book's Honor List.
The Larrecqs have lived in Mill Valley, California.
His illustrations have appeared in the following books
by E. Ormondroyd for boys and girls: Theodore (Parnassus, 1966) and Theodore's Rival (Parnassus, 1971).

LASKER, Joseph Leon (Joe), 1919- . Artist and teacher,
Joe Lasker was born in Brooklyn, New York, and later
made his home in South Norwalk, Connecticut, where
he has been an art instructor at the Famous Artists
School. He has also taught in New York at City College and at the University of Illinois. The artist received his early education at Cooper Union Art School
in New York City. He has been the recipient of: the
Prix de Rome, a Guggenheim Fellowship, and the Edwin Austin Abbey Memorial Fellowship. His work can
be found in the Philadelphia and Whitney Museums and
the Joseph Hirshhorn Collection. It has been said that
Joe Lasker has changed from "semi-decorative" to an
"outright realistic" style in his work. He illustrated
C. Zolotow's The Man with the Purple Eyes (Abelard,
1961), and two by M. Schlein: Snow Time (Whitman,
1962) and The Way Mothers Are (Whitman, 1963).
ICB-3

LATHROP, Dorothy Pulis, 1891- . Illustrator, author,
teacher, born in Albany, New York. She attended
Teachers College, Columbia University, Pennsylvania
Academy of Fine Arts, and the Art Students League.
Mrs. Lathrop has illustrated many books by different
authors and in 1938 she received the first Caldecott
Medal for the illustrations in Animals of the Bible
(Stokes, 1937). She made her home in Albany, New
York, prior to living in Falls Village, Connecticut.
Other titles include W. De La Mare's Bells and Grass
(Viking, 1964), and seven books for Macmillan: Angel
in the Woods (1947), Follow the Brook (1960), Let
Them Live (1951), Littlest Mouse (1955), Presents for
Lupe (1940), Puppies for Keeps (1943), and Who Goes
There? (1935). ICB-1, ICB-2, ICB-3, ABYP-2

LAURENCE. Designer and illustrator. This French artist
began her career in Paris where she also attended
school. She was awarded a French government cultur-
al fellowship for her work in 1964. The artist lived

in New York City while her husband attended Columbia
University. She wrote and illustrated Seymourina
(Bobbs-Merrill, 1970) and A Village in Normandy
(Bobbs-Merrill, 1968).

LAWRENCE, Jacob. Born in Atlantic City, New Jersey, he
studied at the Harlem Workshop and the American Artists School. Recipient of both the Rosenwald and Guggenheim fellowships, Mr. Lawrence has been Artist in
Residence at Brandeis University. He has also served
on the staff of Pratt Institute, the Art Students League,
and the New School for Social Research. His work was
represented in many permanent museum collections, including the Metropolitan Museum of Art, the Whitney
Museum, and the Museum of Modern Art. For boys
and girls he wrote and illustrated Harriet and the
Promised Land (Simon, 1968).

LAWSON, Robert, 1892-1957. A native New Yorker, he attended school in Montclair, New Jersey, and received
training in art at the New York School of Fine and Ap-
plied Art. During World War I, he served in the
Camouflage Section of the United States Army in France.
He has lived near Westport, Connecticut, in a house
called "Rabbit Hill." He was awarded the Newbery
Medal in 1945 for his book, Rabbit Hill (Viking, 1944).
Juvenile contributions include: Ben and Me (Little,
(1939), Fabulous Flight (Little, 1949), Great Wheel,
(Viking, 1957), I Discover Columbus (Little, 1941), Mr.
Revere and I (Little, 1953), and Watchwords of Liberty
(Little, 1957). In 1941 he was awarded the Caldecott
Medal for They Were Strong and Good (Viking, 1940).
ICB-1, ICB-2, ABYP-2

LAZARE, Gerald John, 1927- . Jerry Lazare was born in
Toronto, Ontario, Canada. He studied at Oakwood Col-
legiate and took Famous Artists Course. During World
War II, he did comic strips. Following the war, he
studied in Paris and London. He has worked in adver-
tising and has illustrated for magazines. His home has
been in Toronto. For young people he illustrated J.
Little's Home from Far (1965), R. Burch's Queenie
Peavy (Viking, 1966), and J. Little's Take Wing (a
Junior Literary Guild selection; Little, 1968). ICB-3

LEE, Manning De Villeneuve, 1894- . Artist, illustrator,
art instructor, born in Summerville, South Carolina.

He grew up in South Carolina and Georgia. He later
made his home in Ambler, Pennsylvania. He received
his education at the Porter Military Academy, Pennsylvania Academy of the Fine Arts and the Fine Arts
School in Saumur, France. After serving as an artillery officer in World War I, he continued his studies
in Europe on an Academy Traveling Scholarship. The
recipient of many awards, Manning Lee has belonged
to the Philadelphia Art Alliance, Southern States Art
League, and was elected a Fellow of London's Royal
Society of Arts. Mr. Lee has conducted art classes,
designed postage stamps, and religious film strips.
His book illustrations include: M. Jones' Bible Stories (Rand, 1952), E. Ball's George Washington, First
President (Abingdon, 1954), and T. Lee's Things to Do
(Doubleday, 1965). ICB-1, ICB-2

LEE, Robert J. Illustrator, teacher. In addition to illustrating books, the artist has created illustrations for
magazines. His work has been displayed in many museums and homes throughout America. Mr. Lee has
taught painting in Tarrytown, New York at Marymount
College. He illustrated M. Komroff's Heroes of the
Bible (Golden Press, 1966).

LEICHMAN, Seymour. A native of New York, he studied at
New York's Cooper Union. Prior to a career as a
painter, Mr. Leichman worked in the advertising field.
His paintings have been exhibited in this country and
Mexico. He has also been interested in murals (a 30-
foot outdoor mural in Kingston, Jamaica) and motion
pictures. For young people he wrote and illustrated
The Boy Who Could Sing Pictures (a Junior Literary
Guild selection; Doubleday, 1968) and Wicked Wizard
& The Wicked Witch (Harcourt, 1972).

LEIGHT, Edward. After graduating from the Parsons
School of Design, Edward Leight taught painting to children. He has also designed theater sets, wallpaper,
and textiles. He served with the Armed Forces during World War II and after the war exhibited his overseas paintings in this country. Mr. Leight has enjoyed cooking and the theater as special interests. He
collaborated with Nancy Moore to write Miss Harriet
Hippopotamus and the Most Wonderful (Vanguard, 1963).
He also illustrated Nancy Moore's book Ermintrude
(Vanguard, 1960).

LEIGHTON, Clare Veronica Hope, 1901- . Born in England, she later studied at the Slade School of Fine Art,
University of London, and at the London County Council Central School of Art and Crafts. She has had
many distinguished awards, which include membership
in the Society of Wood Engravers, and honorary degree
from Colby College, and first prize at the International Engravers Exhibition at the Chicago Art Institute.
An American citizen, she has made her home in Wood-
bury, Connecticut. Her talents have ranged from illustrating books to designing stained glass windows.
Her wood engravings appeared in two compilations by
H. Plotz, The Earth Is the Lord's (Crowell, 1965) and
Imagination's Other Place (Crowell, 1955). ICB-2,
ICB-3

LEMKE, Horst, 1922- . Artist, cartoonist, painter. Born
in Berlin, he studied there at the Staatliche Hocheschule
für Bildende Künste. He also attended the High School
of Plastic Arts. He moved to Heidelberg after World
War II. Since 1955, he has lived in Switzerland. For
boys and girls he illustrated H. Denneborg's Jan and the
Wild Horse (McKay, 1958) and Johnny and the Jester
(Watts, 1970). ICB-3

LEMOINE, Georges. A noted European graphic designer,
Georges Lemoine has also been an illustrator. He has
geared his work toward engraving and drawing. His
pictures can be found in G. Charlton-Perrin's Little
Lord Blink and His Ice Cream Castle (McCall, 1971).

LENT, Blair, 1930- . He was born in Boston, Massachusetts, and attended the Boston Museum School and also
studied in Europe on a Cummings Traveling Scholarship. He illustrated M. Hodges' The Wave (Houghton,
1964), which was runner-up for the Caldecott Medal in
1965, and he won the Caldecott Medal in 1973 for A.
Mosel's The Funny Little Woman (Dutton, 1972). He
has made his home in Cambridge, Massachusetts. He
also illustrated W. Sleator's The Angry Moon (Little,
1970) and F. Branley's The Christmas Sky (Crowell,
1966). ICB-3

LEWIN, Ted. He was born in Buffalo, New York and later
made his home in Brooklyn. In 1956 he was awarded
the Dean's Medal when he graduated from Pratt Institute. The artist has been a professional wrestler and

skin diver. His great interest in animals and conservation resulted in a trip to East Africa where he sketched and studied the animals in game reserves. For boys and girls he illustrated B. Horvath's Not Enough Indians (Watts, 1971).

LEWIS, Anne. Artist, designer, writer. She was born in Boston, attended the Boston Museum of Fine Arts, and graduated from the Massachusetts College of Art. She has been both an illustrator and writer of books. Mrs. Lewis and her family have lived in New York City. For boys and girls she illustrated C. Greene's Let's Learn about the Orchestra (Harvey House, 1967).

LILLY, Charles. Born in New York, his childhood was spent in Queens. Later he and his wife, who has also been his agent, made their home in the Bronx. Prior to becoming a free-lance illustrator, he has been a postal clerk and assistant to a photographer. For boys and girls he illustrated B. Greene's Philip Hall Likes Me. I Reckon Maybe (a Junior Literary Guild selection; Dial, 1974).

LIPPMAN, Peter J., 1936- . He was born in Flushing, Queens, New York, and graduated from Columbia College and the Columbia School of Architecture. He also studied at the Art Students League. Following army service, he worked for an architect prior to becoming an illustrator of children's books. His drawings have appeared in Holiday magazine, and he has written articles on the history of architecture. He wrote and illustrated Plunkety Plunk (Ariel, 1963). He also illustrated V. Cobb's Science Experiments You Can Eat (Lippincott, 1972) and G. Selden's Sparrow Socks (Harper, 1965). ICB-3

LISOWSKI, Gabriel. Commercial artist, illustrator, born in Jerusalem. Mr. Lisowski spent his early years in Warsaw and Vienna. Prior to becoming interested in graphic design, he studied architecture in Vienna. His first book for American boys and girls was M. Levoy's The Witch of Fourth Street and Other Stories (Harper, 1972).

LOBEL, Anita, 1934- . Artist and textile designer. Born in Cracow, Poland, she grew up in Poland and Sweden and later studied at Pratt Institute in Brooklyn, New

York. Her husband Arnold Lobel has also been an illustrator and author of books for boys and girls. They
have lived in Brooklyn. She wrote and illustrated Potatoes, Potatoes (1967) and Under a Mushroom (1970);
she also illustrated F. Monjo's Indian Summer (1968)
and M. DeJong's Puppy Summer (1966), all for Harper.
ICB-3

LOCKE, Margo; and Vance Locke. She graduated from Texas Women's University in Denton, Texas, and also
studied at the Art Students League in New York City.
Her experience has included portrait painting, cartoons,
and fashion advertising. Her husband, Vance Locke,
is also an illustrator--C. Graves' Paul Revere, Rider
for Liberty (Garrard, 1964). They have lived in Los
Altos, California. She illustrated C. Wolcott's I Can
See What God Does (Abingdon, 1969) and T. Tichenor's
Smart Bear (Abingdon, 1970).

LOCKE, Vance see LOCKE, Margo

LOEWENSTEIN, Bernice. She was born in New York City,
attended the Art Students League, and graduated from
Bryn Mawr College in Pennsylvania. Mrs. Loewenstein and her family have made their home in Bingham-
ton, New York. At one time the illustrator was associated with publishing firms where she worked in the
children's book departments. For young readers she
illustrated E. Coatsworth's Bess and the Sphinx (Macmillan, 1967) and B. Wells' Horse on the Roof (Lippincott, 1970).

LONETTE, Reisie Dominee, 1924- . Born in New York,
she has been associated with a publishing firm in addition to being an illustrator and book jacket designer.
A graduate of Pratt Institute in Brooklyn, Reisie Lonette studied in New York at the School of Interior Design and The New School for Social Research. She also attended the Art Students League. Her artist husband Vincent Nucera died at the age of 37 in 1964.
Her drawings for children can be found in M. Vance's
Jared's Gift (Dutton, 1965) and C. Snedeker's Lysis
Goes to the Play (Lothrop, 1962). ICB-2, ICB-3

LORD, John Vernon, 1939- . British artist and teacher.
He was born in Glossop, Derby, England, and later
became associated with the Brighton College of Art as

an instructor. His drawings can be found in both
books and magazines. For children he illustrated J.
Burroway's The Truck on the Track (Bobbs-Merrill,
1970).

LORENTOWICZ, Irena, 1910- . Born in Warsaw, Poland,
her educational background includes study at the Sorbonne and the Academy of Arts, and International Institute of Theatrical Lyceum in Warsaw. She has designed for the theatre and ballet. In 1937 she received a Gold Medal at the Paris Exposition. Prior to
making her home on Long Island, the artist lived in
Spain and Portugal. She illustrated E. Kelly's Hand
in the Picture (a Junior Literary Guild selection; Lippincott, 1947). ICB-1, ICB-2

LORRAINE, Walter Henry, 1929- . Born in Worcester,
Massachusetts, he later made his home in Newton.
Walter Lorraine graduated from the Rhode Island
School of Design in Providence after two years spent
in the Navy. He worked as a book designer and pro-
duction head in a publishing firm before he became an
illustrator of books. He has also been on the staff at
the Museum of Fine Arts School and Boston University.
His illustrations in Alastair Reid's I Will Tell You of
a Town (Houghton, 1956) and in Julia Cunningham's
Dear Rat (Houghton, 1961) were among the "Ten Best
Illustrated Children's Books" in 1956 and 1961, as se-
lected by the New York Times. He also illustrated
C. Annett's The Dog Who Thought He Was a Boy
(Houghton, 1965), S. Warburg's From Ambledee to
Zumbledee (Houghton, 1968) and J. Hawes' My Daddy
Longlegs (Crowell, 1972). ICB-2, ICB-3

LUDWIG, Helen. She studied at the Hartford (Connecticut)
Art School and the Art Students League in New York.
Later she and her husband, a philosophy professor,
made their home in San Francisco. Her work has ap-
peared in galleries, and she has had one-man shows.
For young people she illustrated M. Selsam's All about
Eggs (Scott, 1952) and M. Selsam's Microbes at Work
(Morrow, 1953).

LUFKIN, Raymond H., 1897- . At one time a free-lance
commercial artist, Raymond Lufkin was born in Salem,
Massachusetts, and later made his home in Tenafly,
New Jersey. He studied in Boston at the New School

of Design. He designed maps and war bond posters
during World War II and later created colored drawings of special events that took place on some of the
American rivers. His illustrations for children can
be found in A. Bontemps' Story of the Negro (3rd. ed. ,
Knopf, 1958). ICB-1, ICB-2

LYALL, Dennis. He graduated from the University of Kansas in Lawrence. Later he and his family lived in
Houston, Texas. His work in book illustration has
been said to be a combination of "witty style, brilliant
color, and imaginative perspective." For boys and
girls he illustrated N. Zimelman's So You Shouldn't
Waste a Rhinoceros (Steck, 1970).

-M-

MAAS, Julie. A native New Yorker, she has lived on New
York's Lower East Side since her marriage to photog-
rapher Michael Shields. She received her early educa-
tion in art from her parents who were both artists.
Julie Maas began her career as a book illustrator after
graduating from high school. Juvenile books which she
has illustrated include E. Cooper's And Everything
Nice (Harcourt, 1966), P. Hubbell's Apple Vendor's
Fair (Atheneum, 1963), P. Hubbell's 8 A. M. Shadows
(Atheneum, 1965), and J. Blos' "It's Spring," She Said
(Knopf, 1968).

McCAFFERY, Janet. She graduated from the Philadelphia
College of Art. Prior to her marriage, she worked at
Street and Smith Publications. Later she worked as a
free-lance artist in advertising and in both book and
magazine illustration. She has lived in New York City.
Her work includes three books by M. Calhoun, Flower
Mother (1972), The Goblin Under the Stairs (1968), and
The Last Two Elves in Denmark (1968), and D. Ever-
son's Mrs. Popover Goes to the Zoo (1963), all for
Morrow.

McCANN, Gerald, 1916- . He was born in Brooklyn, New
York, where he later attended Pratt Institute. During
World War II, he was in the service in North Africa.
Mr. McCann has created book covers and contributed
illustrations to magazines in addition to illustrating
books for young people. His work includes S. Meek's

Bellfarm Star (Dodd, 1955), and A. Colver's Florence
Nightingale: War Nurse (Garrard, 1961). ICB-2

MacCLAIN, George. A newcomer to the field of children's
literature, the artist spent his early childhood in Philadelphia. He later graduated from the College of Art
in that city. Mr. MacClain has enjoyed the hobby of
collecting and refinishing old furniture. He has lived
on Long Island with his family. For young readers he
illustrated I. Elmer's Anthony's Father (Putnam, 1972).

McCLOSKEY, Robert, 1914- . Born in Hamilton, Ohio, he
studied at the National Academy of Design in New York.
During World War II, he was in the Army where he
drew training pictures. He has been the recipient of
several awards including the Prix de Rome in 1939,
and the Caldecott Medal in 1942 and again in 1958. The
award in 1942 was given to him for his book Make Way
for Ducklings (Viking, 1941) and in 1958 for his book
Time of Wonder (Viking, 1957). The McCloskeys have
lived in New York and spent summers on their island
off the coast of Maine. His titles include Blueberries
for Sal (1948), Centerburg Tales (1951), K. Robertson's Henry Reed, Inc. (1960), Homer Price (1943),
Lentil (1940), and One Morning in Maine (1952), all for
Viking. ICB-1, ICB-2, ICB-3, ABYP-2

McCULLY, Emily Arnold, 1939- . Born in Galesburg, Illinois, she graduated from Brown University and received an M.A. degree in Art History from Columbia.
At one time she lived in Brussels and New York but
later made her home in Swarthmore, Pennsylvania,
where her husband has been a professor of Renaissance
and Reformation history at Swarthmore College. Mrs.
McCully has designed book jackets in addition to book
illustrations. Her work has also appeared in magazines.
For young readers she illustrated L. Schoettle's Grand-
pa's Long Red Underwear (Lothrop, 1972), N. Carlson's Luigi of the Streets (Harper, 1967) G. Panetta's
Sea Beach Express (Harper, 1966), and E. Neville's
The Seventeenth-Street Gang (Harper, 1966). ICB-3

McDANIEL, J. W. Illustrator, commercial artist. He
graduated from the Columbus College of Art and Design in Columbus, Ohio. He has lived in Logan, Ohio
and later made his home in New York City. For young
people he illustrated D. Wood's This Nation (World,
1967).

McDERMOTT, Gerald. A filmmaker and artist, he was
   born in Detroit, Michigan. Mr. McDermott and his
   artist wife have lived in France. He was the recipient of the Blue Ribbon at the American Film Festival
   for the film version of his book Anansi the Spider,
   adapt. and illus. by G. McDermott (Holt, 1972).

MacDONALD, James. Born in Scotland, he later lived in
   Roslyn, New York. He studied art in both Scotland
   and the United States. He has worked in advertising
   in addition to illustrating books and book jackets,
   maps, and title pages. Mr. MacDonald has enjoyed
   travel and painting (watercolors) in Maine. For young
   people he illustrated C. Rourke's Davy Crockett (Harcourt, 1934) and O. Hall-Quest's Jamestown Adventure
   (Dutton, 1950).

McDONALD, Ralph J. Naturalist-painter. He has made his
   home in Madison, Tennessee. In addition to illustrating books for boys and girls, he has also painted portraits including one for a state governor. His work includes B. Carlson's Let's Pretend It Happened to You
   (1973), M. Ward's Ollie, Ollie Oxen-Free (1969), and
   Spooky Tales about Witches, Ghosts, Goblins, Demons,
   and Such, comp. by M. Luckhardt (1972), all for Abingdon.

McENTEE, Dorothy, 1902- . She was born in Brooklyn,
   New York where she later attended Pratt Institute.
   She also studied in Chester Springs at the Pennsylvania Academy of the Fine Arts. Ms. McEntee has taught
   in a Brooklyn high school in addition to creating watercolors which have been exhibited. She also has done
   wood engraving. For boys and girls she illustrated
   her sister, Fran Martin's books, Nine Tales of Raven
   (Harper, 1951) and Pirate Island (Harper, 1955).
   ICB-2

MACHETANZ, Frederick, 1908- . Artist-writer, he was
   born in Kenton, Ohio. He and his wife, author Sara
   Dunn Machetanz have lived in Alaska and Ohio. Frederick Machetanz studied at Ohio State University and at
   the American Academy of Arts and the Art Institute in
   Chicago. He served with Naval Intelligence during
   World War II. He has been a filmmaker and lecturer
   in addition to a book illustrator. For children he
   wrote and illustrated On Arctic Ice (Scribner's, 1940),

Panuck, Eskimo Sled Dog (Scribner's, 1939). He and
his wife wrote Robbie and the Sled Dog Race (Scribner's, 1964). ICB-1, ICB-2

MacINTYRE, Elizabeth. Born in Sydney, Australia, she
later lived in North Narrabeen, New South Wales. Married to artist John Eldershaw, she has worked in advertising, created a comic strip, and illustrated children's books. She wrote and illustrated Ambrose Kangaroo (Scribner's, 1942). ICB-1, ICB-2

McINTYRE, Kevin. Born in New York City, he graduated
from Syracuse University. In 1969-70 he was awarded
a Fine Arts Fellowship to study in Florence, Italy.
When he was 21 he illustrated his first book, and his
fourth one was T. Devlin's The Wild and Free (Scribner's, 1969). He also illustrated G. Eckstein's Every-
day Miracle (Harper, 1965).

MACK, Stanley. Art director and illustrator. His early
years were spent in Providence, and he later received
his education at the Rhode Island School of Design.
Stanley Mack has been associated with the New York
Times Book Review and the New York Herald Tribune
Book Week as an art director. He has also worked in
advertising, and his drawings can be found in several
magazines and books. The artist has been honored by
the American Institute of Graphic Arts, the Society of
Illustrators, and the Art Directors Club. For children
he illustrated G. Keenen's The Preposterous Week (Dial, 1971).

MacKAY, Donald A. Artist, illustrator, painter. His home
has been in Ossining, New York. The American Watercolor Society and the Society of Illustrators have exhibited his pictures. His work has also appeared in such
magazines as Harper's, Life, and Newsweek. For boys
and girls he illustrated P. Fox's The Stone-Faced Boy
(Bradbury Press, 1969), and S. Kelley's Summer Growing Time (Viking, 1971).

McKEE, David. Born in England, he studied at Plymouth
College of Art and continued his studies in London.
His work has appeared in Punch magazine. Mr. Mc-
Kee and his family have made their home in London,
England. For boys and girls he illustrated K. Bau-
man's Joseph, the Border Guard (Parents' magazine,
1972).

MacKENZIE, Garry, 1921- . Born in Manitoba, Canada,
   he studied in Los Angeles at Chouinard Art Institute.
   In 1945 he went to New York City and began illustrating children's books. Following a stay in Cambridge,
   England, he lived on Staten Island, New York. His
   work includes C. Bailey's Flickertail (Walck, 1962),
   A. Goudey's Here Come the Cottontails! (Scribner's,
   1965), and Read to Me Again, by Child Study Association of America (Crowell, 1961).   ICB-2, ICB-3

MacKNIGHT, Ninon, 1908- . Ninon is her pseudonym.
   She was born and raised in Sydney, Australia. Later
   she came to the United States and began illustrating
   books for boys and girls. She married Wilbur Jordan
   Smith and has lived in Woodland Hills, California. Her
   work includes E. Meadowcroft's By Wagon and Flatboat
   (Crowell, 1938); For a Child, ed. by W. McFarland
   (a Junior Literary Guild selection; Westminster, 1947),
   and P. Krasilovsky's Scaredy Cat (Macmillan, 1959).
   ICB-2

McLACHLIN, Steve. Illustrator-painter. Mr. McLachlin
   and his family have made their home in Ormand Beach,
   Florida. He combined his work as an artist with his
   love of animals to illustrate P. Fox's book for boys
   and girls entitled Dear Prosper (David White, 1968).

McMULLAN, James, 1934- . He was born in Tsingtao,
   North China, grew up in China, Canada, and India,
   and came to the United States in 1951. His home has
   been in New York City since 1959 when he became an
   American citizen. He studied art in Seattle and at
   Pratt Institute in Brooklyn. Jim McMullan has been
   honored by the American Institute of Graphic Arts and
   the Society of Illustrators. He also received recognition from Print magazine. The artist has been associated with the Push Pin Studios since 1964. In addition
   to book illustration, he has worked in advertising and
   designed book jackets. For boys and girls he illustrated J. Williamson's And Forever Free (Knopf, 1966);
   K. Braun's Kangaroo & Kangaroo (Doubleday, 1965),
   and M. De Jong's The Last Little Cat (Harper, 1961).
   ICB-3

McNAUGHT, Harry. Born in Scotland, he grew up in Philadelphia. He studied at the Philadelphia Museum School
   of Art. He later lived with his wife and four children

in Carversville, Pennsylvania. He illustrated M.
Keene's Beginner's Story of Minerals & Rocks (Harper,
1966), and P. Farb's The Land, Wildlife, and Peoples
of the Bible (Harper, 1967).

MADDEN, Don. Artist and teacher, he was born in Cleveland, Ohio. He spent his childhood in New York City
and Atlantic City. After his marriage, the artist
made his home in New York City and maintained a
summer home in upper New York near Ballston Spa.
Following graduation, for two years he was an art instructor at the Philadelphia Museum College of Art.
His work has appeared in Parents' Magazine, Good
Housekeeping, Harper's Bazaar, and Seventeen publications in addition to reproductions in Graphis and the
New York Art Director's Annual. His work has also
been exhibited abroad, and he has been awarded gold
and silver medals by the Philadelphia Art Director's
Club. He illustrated P. Showers' A Drop of Blood
(Crowell, 1967). He also wrote and illustrated Lem-
onade Serenade; or, The Thing in the Garden (a Junior Literary Guild selection; Whitman, 1966).

MADISON, Steve. He was born in Brooklyn, New York, and
later graduated from New York City Community College. Mr. Madison has been interested in photography, design, and illustration. His home has been in
New York City. For young people he illustrated F.
Temko's Papercutting (Doubleday, 1973).

MAESTRO, Giulio. Born in New York City, he lived in
Greenwich Village. He studied at Cooper Union Art
School and at Pratt Graphic Center. Prior to doing
free-lance work, he worked in all aspects of the advertising field. Mr. Maestro retold and illustrated
The Tortoise's Tug of War (Bradbury, 1971) of which
the Horn Book magazine said, "...his retelling is less
significant than his full-color paintings, which are lively and distinctive in composition and color." He also
illustrated E. Sommer's The Bread Dough Craft Book
(Lothrop, 1972) and J. Delton's Two Good Friends
(Crown, 1974).

MAITLAND, Antony Jasper, 1935- . British artist, born
in Andover. He grew up in England, Germany, and
the Far East. He later made his home in London.
The artist attended Bristol's West of England College

of Art.   He also studied abroad.   He has designed
book jackets and created murals in addition to writing
and illustrating books.   Mr. Maitland was the 1961 recipient of the Kate Greenaway Award for his drawings
in A. Pearce's Mrs. Cockle's Cat (Lippincott, 1961).
He also illustrated A. Molloy's A Proper Place for
Chip (Hastings House, 1963) and P. Lively's The Ghost
of Thomas Kempe (a Junior Literary Guild selection;
Dutton, 1973).   ICB-3

MALVERN, Corinne.   Sister of author Gladys Malvern, she
studied for four years at the Art Students League in
New York.   She later lived in Los Angeles where she
drew fashion advertisements and continued her art studies at night.   She has had one-man shows, and for
boys and girls she illustrated R. Baker's First Woman
Doctor (Messner, 1944) and three works by G. Malvern, Eric's Girls (Messner, 1949), The Foreigner
(a Junior Literary Guild selection; Longmans, 1954),
and Your Kind Indulgence (Messner, 1948).

MAROKVIA, Artur, 1909- .   He was born in Stuttgart, Germany; he later studied painting there at the Akademie,
and also at the Académie de la Grande Chaumière in
Paris.   He received a diploma from the School of Music in Dresden.   He has painted in Greece, Austria,
Mexico, Yugoslavia, Finland, Russia, and Spain.   His
favorite hobby has been playing the piano.   He and his
wife have lived in New York City and Cuernavaca, Mexico.   He illustrated in four colors G. Conklin's When
Insects Are Babies (a Junior Literary Guild selection;
Holiday, 1969).   His illustrations also appeared in V.
Haviland's Favorite Fairy Tales Told in Ireland (Little,
1961).   ICB-2, ICB-3

MARS, Witold T., 1908- .   He was born and grew up in
Poland and received his early education in the schools
of Cracow.   After graduating from the Academy of Fine
Arts in Warsaw, Poland, he continued to study art in
Italy, France, and Germany.   He served with the Pol-
ish Forces in Great Britain during World War II.   Af-
ter the war, Mr. Mars exhibited his paintings in many
galleries throughout England and also did book illustra-
tions for several British publishers.   He came to the
United States in 1951 and has lived in Forest Hills,
Long Island.   He has been a member of New York's
Polish Institute of Art and Science since 1965.   For

boys and girls he illustrated L. Shotwell's <u>Adam Book-out</u> (Viking, 1967); C. Brink's <u>Andy Buckram's Tin Men</u> (a Junior Literary Guild selection; Viking, 1966), and <u>Fairy Tales from Viet Nam,</u> retold by D. Robertson (Dodd, 1968). ICB-2, ICB-3

MARSH, Reginald, 1898-1954. Born in Paris, France, he came to America at an early age and grew up in New Jersey. A Yale University graduate, he also studied at New York's Art Students League and in Europe. His illustrations and sketches have appeared in magazines and newspapers. Mr. Marsh has been an art instructor at Moore Institute and the Art Students League and has also designed for the theater. His paintings can be found in the permanent collections of the Library of Congress, Metropolitan Museum of Art, and Whitney Museum. He has been the recipient of many art awards. For boys and girls he illustrated T. Aldrich's <u>The Story of a Bad Boy</u>, (Pantheon, 1951). ICB-2

MARSHALL, Constance Kay, 1918- . Born in Waterford, Ireland (Eire), the artist grew up in Cheshire, England and later made her home in Hitchin, Hertfordshire, England. She studied in Staffordshire and London at the Burslem Art School and the Royal College of Art. Constance Marshall has worked in advertising in addition to illustrating books. Her drawings for children can be found in R. Manning's <u>Green Smoke</u> (Doubleday, 1958). ICB-2

MARSHALL, Daniel. English illustrator and graphic artist, he was born in London and attended the Brighton Art School. Prior to living in New York City, the artist had resided in Brazil and Chile. His drawings and paintings have been exhibited in England, New York, and South America. For boys and girls he illustrated B. Levine's <u>Hex House</u> (Harper & Row, 1973).

MARTIN, David Stone, 1913- . He was born in Chicago, the son of a Presbyterian minister. He later lived in California and New York. He studied at the Chicago Art Institute. He began his career as an artist at the Chicago World's Fair in 1933 when he served as an architect's assistant. He later became head of the Federal Arts Project in Chicago and was artist correspondent for <u>Life</u> magazine during World War II. In addition to book and magazine illustration, Mr. Martin has

designed jazz album covers and worked in commercial
advertising. He has also been an art director. His
work has been exhibited at galleries and museums
throughout this country. David Martin has been honored many times by the Art Directors Club of New
York and the Society of Illustrators. For young people
he illustrated N. Hentoff's Journey into Jazz (Coward,
1968). ICB-2

MARTIN, René. He was born in Paris, the son of an engraver and artist. He studied art in Switzerland and
received several fine arts grants from the Swiss government. At one time Mr. Martin lived and painted
in Morocco. He became an American citizen and made
his home in Key Largo, Florida. His work includes
I. Tannehill's All about the Weather (Random, 1953),
H. Zim's Blood (Morrow, 1968) and W. Stephens' Sea
Turtle Swims the Ocean (Holiday, 1971).

MARTIN, Stefan, 1936- . Artist and wood engraver, born
in Elgin, Illinois. He grew up in New York and New
Jersey and studied at Chicago's Art Institute. He has
been on the staff of the Art Center in Summit, New
Jersey and has resided in Roosevelt, New Jersey. Mr.
Martin's work can be found in private collections, and
he was awarded the Tiffany Grant in print-making. He
has also been honored for his book illustrations for
children. His work includes R. Lockard's Glaciers
(Coward, 1970) and E. Coatsworth's They Walk in the
Night (Norton, 1969). ICB-3

MARTINEZ, John. He was born in New York City and studied at the Art Students League and the School of Visual Arts. In addition to illustrating books, he has also
been a painter. Mr. Martinez has lived in Leonard-
town, Maryland. For boys and girls he illustrated
M. Vroman's Harlem Summer (Putnam, 1967) and L.
Muehl's Hidden Year of Devlin Bates (Holiday, 1967).

MASTERMAN, Dodie, 1918- . Born in Brixham, Devon-
shire, England, she studied at the University of Lon-
don and the Slade School of Fine Art. She has been
an instructor in addition to a painter. She married
Standish Masterman, and they have lived in London.
The Mastermans at one time lived in Washington,
D.C. For boys and girls she illustrated E. Farjeon's
Perkin the Pedlar (Oxford, 1956). ICB-2

MATHIESEN, Egon, 1907- . Born in Esbjerg, Denmark, he later made his home in Copenhagen. The artist never attended art school. He has written and designed books in addition to illustrating them. Egon Mathiesen has been a recipient of the Danish government prize for children's books and the Royal Academy of Denmark awarded him the Eckersberg Medal for his abstract painting "Children Play." He has also created murals for several public buildings. Juvenile books which he wrote and illustrated include: Blue-Eyed Pussy (Doubleday, 1951), Jungle in the Wheat Field (McDowell, 1960) and Oswald the Monkey (McDowell, 1959). ICB-2, ICB-3

MATULAY, Laszlo, 1912- . Born in Vienna, Austria, where he attended the Academy of Applied Arts. He also studied in New York at the New School for Social Research after coming to the United States in 1935. He has lived in Hampton and Flemington, New Jersey. Mr. Matulay served in the U.S. Army during World War II. In addition to books, he has illustrated for magazines and has been an art director. For children he illustrated M. Batten's Discovery By Chance (Funk, 1968) and F. Sutton's We Were There at the First Airplane Flight (Grosset, 1959). ICB-2

MAURER, Werner. Mr. Maurer has been a commercial artist in addition to his work as an illustrator of children's books. He has lived in a farmhouse near Berne, Switzerland. He illustrated E. Borchers' The Old Car (Bobbs-Merrill, 1971).

MAUZEY, Merritt, 1898- . Born in Clifton, Texas, he attended art school in Dallas. His work has been exhibited in one-man shows and at both universities and museums. Mr. Mauzey has been the recipient of numerous awards, and in 1946 he was awarded the Guggenheim Memorial Fellowship in Creative Lithography. For young people he wrote and illustrated Cotton-Farm Boy (Abelard, 1953) and Texas Ranch Boy (Abelard, 1955). ICB-2

MAX, Peter. A young artist who has won numerous awards for excellence in advertising art has had reproductions of his work appear throughout this country. Peter Max grew up in China, Tibet, and Israel and studied astronomy and art. He also received his education

in Paris and Rome and studied at New York City's Art
Students League.   For young people he illustrated A.
Kirsch's Teen Cuisine (Parents' magazine, 1969).

MAXEY, Betty.   She spent her childhood in Chicago where
she attended the Chicago Art Institute and the American Academy of Art.   Mrs. Maxey has worked in advertising in New York, Chicago, and London.   She has
also created book jackets and illustrations for magazines.   Her husband Dale has been both an author and
illustrator.   Her work includes N. Streatfeild's The
Family at Caldicott Place (a Junior Literary Guild selection; Random, 1968).

MAYER, Mercer, 1943- .   He was born in Little Rock,
Arkansas, spent his childhood in Hawaii, and later
lived in Sea Cliff, Long Island.   Prior to devoting fulltime to book illustration, he was an art director in an
advertising agency.   He wrote and illustrated: Frog,
Where Are You? (Dial, 1969) and There's a Nightmare
in My Closet (Dial, 1968).   He also illustrated G.
Mendoza's The Gillygoofang (Dial, 1968).

MAYS, Lewis Victor, 1927- .   Lewis Victor Mays, Jr.,
was born in New York City and later graduated from
Yale University.   He attended college following service
as a navy officer during World War II.   Mr. Mays also served in the navy during the Korean War.   His illustrations have appeared in books and magazines.   His
home has been in Clinton, Connecticut.   Victor Mays'
work includes I. Asimov's The Kite That Won the Revolution (Houghton, 1963), and S. Corbett's One By Sea
(Little, 1965).   ICB-2, ICB-3

MEANS, Elliott.   A Texan by birth, Elliott Means later
made his home in New York City.   His speciality in
the art world has been horses and Westerns.   For
children he illustrated M. Leighton's Comanche of the
Seventh (Ariel Books, 1957).

MERIDA, Carlos, 1891- .   Artist, instructor.   Born in
Guatemala, he later studied in Paris at the Van Don-
gen Art School.   He created many murals in Mexico
and also made one for the Municipal Palace in Guatemala.   He has taught in Mexico and in Texas.   The
artist's home has been in Mexico City.   His work has
been included in the Dallas and San Francisco

Museums and in New York's Museum of Modern Art.
He illustrated P. Ross' ... Made in Mexico (Knopf,
1952). ICB-2

MERKLING, Erica.   Artist-teacher.   Born in Vienna, she
later made her home in New York City with her husband
and children.   Prior to book illustration, Erica Merkling was a fashion designer and art instructor at Parsons School of Design.   For children she illustrated
M. Schlein's The Best Place (Whitman, 1968), and
J. Udry's If You're a Bear (Whitman, 1967).

MERWIN, Decie, 1894- .   Born in Middlesboro, Kentucky,
she grew up in Tennessee and later lived in New York
City following her marriage to writer Jack Bechdolt.
She attended boarding school in Cincinnati, Ohio, and
art school in Boston, Massachusetts.   Her work has
appeared in the Christian Science Monitor.   For young
readers she illustrated I. Eastwick's Fairies and Such-
like (Dutton, 1946), R. Caudill's Up and Down the River (Holt, 1964), and R. Palmer's Wise House (Harper,
1951).   ICB-2

MEYERS, Robert W., 1919- .   He was born in New York
City and later made his home in Bogota, New Jersey.
He received his education in New York at the Art Stu-
dents League, National Academy of Design, Traphagen
School of Design, and the Grand Central School of Art.
Mr. Meyers served as a navigator with the U.S. Air
Force during World War II.   He has worked in adver-
tising, and his illustrations have been published in mag-
azines and books.   For children Bob Meyers illustrated
C. Hoff's Johnny Texas (Wilcox & Follett, 1950).
ICB-2

MICOLEAU, Tyler.   Artist, professional ski instructor,
graduate of the Rhode Island School of Design.   He has
been a commercial artist and an art instructor at
Brown University.   He has also taught skiing in Jackson, New Hampshire and at Squaw Valley, California.
He designed and illustrated W. Mace's Tennis Techniques Illustrated (Barnes, 1952).

MIKOLAYCAK, Charles.   Mr. Mikolaycak has been an art
director and designer in addition to illustrating books.
He has been the recipient of a Gold Medal for art direction and was awarded numerous honors by the

Society of Illustrators. In 1967 and 1968 his illustrations appeared in one of the "Fifty Best Books of the
Year" selected by the American Institute of Graphic
Arts. His colored illustrations appeared in B. Rinkoff's The Pretzel Hero (Parents' magazine, 1970).

MILHOUS, Katherine, 1894- . Illustrator, author, native
of Philadelphia. She attended the Pennsylvania Museum's
School of Industrial Art and the Academy of Fine Arts.
She was the recipient of a Cresson traveling scholarship and studied abroad. Miss Milhous has served as
supervisor on a Federal Art Project. Many of her stories have had a Pennsylvania Dutch background. She
received the Caldecott Medal in 1951 for The Egg Tree
(Scribner's, 1950). Other titles include Appolon-
ia's Valentine (1954), First Christmas Crib (1944),
Herodia, the Lovely Puppet (1942), Patrick and
the Golden Slippers (1951), and With Bells On
(a Junior Literary Guild selection; 1955), all
for Scribners. ICB-1, ICB-2, ICB-3, ABYP-
2

MILL, Eleanor. She was born in Detroit, Michigan, and
studied at the Corcoran School of Art in Washington,
D.C. Both her mother and her husband have been art-
ists. She has made her home in Rhinebeck, New York.
Her illustrations for young people include C. Joy's
Getting to Know Costa Rica, El Salvador and Nicaragua
(Coward, 1964), C. Taylor's Getting to Know Indonesia
(Coward, 1961), and J. Udry's What Mary Jo Shared
(Whitman, 1966).

MILLER, Grambs. Artist, lithographer. She was born in
Peking, China, grew up in Tientsin, and also lived in
France and Mexico. The illustrator and her husband
later made their home in New York City. She has
spent summers on Martha's Vineyard in Massachusetts
where she and her husband have continued their interest in and enjoyment of nature. Her beautiful and delicate pictures can be found in many books, including P.
Ladyman's Learning about Flowering Plants (Scott,
1970).

MILLER, Mitchell. The artist's first pictures in Jack Sendak's book Martze (Farrar, 1968) were chosen for the
AIGA Children's Book Show for 1967-1968. It was
these illustrations that won recognition for him

from Publishers Weekly, which stated, "Write down
his name so that when he becomes a Great Big Name
among illustrators, you can say, 'I knew he'd be a
Great Big Name the minute I saw his illustrations for
Martze!' " Mr. Miller also illustrated J. Wahl's How
the Children Stopped the Wars (Farrar, 1969).

MINALE, Marcello, 1938- . Born in Tripoli, Libya, Africa, he studied art in Naples, Italy. At one time he
lived in Scandinavia and Finland and later worked in
graphic design. In 1964 he became partners with Brian Tattersfield and formed a company called Minale,
Tattersfield, Ltd. which has specialized in design (both
industrial and book design). The artist has lived in
London. For children he illustrated M. Flanders'
Creatures Great and Small (Holt, 1965). ICB-3

MINJA, Park. Book illustrator, painter, textile designer.
A native of Korea, she later made her home in New
York City. Miss Minja graduated with honors from
Seoul National University College of Fine Arts. Her
juvenile book illustrations include K. Ik's Love in
Winter (1969) and The Shoes from Yang San Valley
(1970), both for Doubleday.

MITSUHASHI, Yoko. Illustrator and designer, born in Tokyo,
Japan. After graduating from the Women's College of
Fine Arts in Tokyo, she became associated with Japan's leading studio of design, the Nippon Design Center. She was one of the few women chosen for membership in the Japan Advertising Artists Club. Her
work has appeared in national magazines, and she has
worked in New York since 1962. For boys and girls
she illustrated C. Zolotow's I Have a Horse of My
Own (Abelard-Schuman, 1964) and M. Leister's Silent
Concert (Bobbs-Merrill, 1970).

MITSUI, Eiichi. This Japanese artist has illustrated several of Betty Jean Lifton's books for boys and girls, including Joji and the Fog (Morrow, 1959), Kap the
Kappa (Morrow, 1960), and The Rice-Cake Rabbit,
(Norton, 1966). With Yoshinobu Sakakura the artist
illustrated Y. Yasuda's Old Tales of Japan (Tuttle,
n.d.). ICB-3

MIZUMURA, Kazue. Artist-author, born in Kamakura, Japan. She studied at Tokyo's Women's Art Institute and

Pratt Institute in Brooklyn, New York. Her husband
Claus Stamm has also been a writer. In addition to
book illustration, she has worked in advertising and
textile design. Her home has been in Stamford, Connecticut. She wrote and illustrated I See the Winds
(Crowell, 1966). She also illustrated V. Plasmati's
Algernon and the Pigeons (Viking, 1963), M. Matsuno's
Chie and the Sports Day (World, 1965), and B. Freschet's Jumping Mouse (Crowell, 1971). ICB-3

MOCNIAK, George. He was born in Greensboro, Pennsylvania, and studied at the School of Industrial Art and
the School of Visual Arts in New York City. At one
time Mr. Mocniak lived in Hamburg, Germany. He
later made his home in New York City. His work for
young people includes painting book jackets for S.
Hample's Blood for Holly Warner (Harper, 1967) and
R. Lipsyte's The Contender (Harper, 1967). He also
illustrated S. Abbott's Old Dog (Coward, 1972), and
E. Neville's Traveler from a Small Kingdom (Harper,
1968).

MOFSIE, Louis. He has taught art in Meadowbrook High
School on Long Island. Mr. Mofsie has also been the
leader of a dance group of American Indians. He was
not only the illustrator but also the hero of a book for
young people by M. Elting called The Hopi Way (Lippincott, 1969).

MOMMENS, Norman, 1922- . Born in Belgium, he attended school in Holland and studied the art of mural painting. Mr. Mommens later made his home in Sussex,
England. Some of his pottery has been placed in the
Brighton Museum. In addition to his work in mural
painting and sculpturing, he illustrated for boys and
girls Dib Dib and the Red Indians (Faber, 1955).
ICB-2

MONK, Marvin Randolph, 1921- . Artist and designer,
born in Moultrie, Georgia. He studied in New York at
the Parsons School of Design. Mr. Monk has toured
in Italy and France and has lived in the southeastern
United States. He has been both a fabric and fashion
designer in addition to a book and magazine illustrator.
His drawings can be found in Joseph Gaer's books for
children, which include Adventures of Rama (Little,
1954) and Fables of India (Little, 1955). ICB-2

MONTRESOR, Beni, 1926- . Designer, illustrator, born
in Verona, Italy, he later made his home in New York.
He attended Verona Art School, the Academy of Fine
Arts in Venice, and was awarded a two-year scholarship to the Centro Sperimentale di Cinematografia in
Rome. After his arrival in the United States, he illustrated and wrote picture books. Also he designed the
sets and costumes for the Broadway musical "Do I
Hear a Waltz?" and the Metropolitan Opera productions
of "The Last Savage" and "Centerentola." In 1965 he
was awarded the Caldecott Medal for his illustrations
in B. De Regniers' May I Bring a Friend? (a Junior
Literary Guild selection; Atheneum, 1964). He wrote
and illustrated: A for Angel (Knopf, 1969), House of
Flowers, House of Stars (Knopf, 1962), and Witches
of Venice (Knopf, 1963). ICB-3, ABYP-2

MOORE, Janet Gaylord. Artist, painter, teacher. Miss
Moore has lived in Cleveland, Ohio where she has been
an associate curator at the Cleveland Museum of Art.
Her summers have been spent on Deer Isle, Maine.
She has been a teacher and lecturer on art. For young
readers she wrote and illustrated The Many Ways of
Seeing (World, 1968).

MORAN, Connie. Mrs. Moran has lived in a studio apartment on Chicago's North Side. Her fondness for both
dogs and cats resulted in her animal illustrations for
books. Her work includes E. Meeks' Bow Wow! Said
the Kittens (Wilcox, 1952) and I. Eberle's Steam Shovel
Family (McKay, 1948).

MORDVINOFF, Nicolas, 1911- . His pseudonym is Nicolas.
Author, artist, born in Petrograd (now known as Lenin-
grad). He graduated from the University of Paris. He
began drawing at an early age and continued to do so
when he lived in the South Pacific. In Tahiti writer
William Stone asked him to illustrate a book which
later influenced his coming to America. Bear's Land
(Coward, 1955) was the first book written by Nicolas
Mordvinoff. He collaborated with William Lipkind to
write books for children. In 1952 this team, known as
Will and Nicolas, won the Caldecott Medal for Finders
Keepers (illustrated by Mr. Mordvinoff; Harcourt, 1951).
They also created Magic Feather Duster (Harcourt,
1958). ICB-1, ICB-2, ICB-3, ABYP-2

MORGAN, Ava. Artist, illustrator, designer. She attended New York's Cooper Union where she studied art. She did extensive travel both here and abroad after her marriage to chemical engineer Alfred Weiss. The artist and her family have resided in New Jersey. For boys and girls she illustrated E. Hautzig's Let's Make Presents (Crowell, 1962).

MORGAN, Roy, 1928- . Born in Wales, he later studied at the Cardiff College of Art and London's Royal College of Art. Following service in the Royal Navy, he began his art career. Mr. Morgan's work has included lithography and wood engraving. His home has been in Aberystwyth, Wales. He illustrated B. Picard's Stories of King Arthur and His Knights (Oxford, 1955). ICB-2

MORRILL, Leslie. An artist, traveler, teacher, Leslie Morrill has held national exhibits of his work. He graduated from the Cranbrook Academy of Art and Boston's School of the Museum of Fine Arts. He has been a college art instructor. His drawings can be found in magazines, films, and filmstrips. For children he illustrated P. Buck's Mrs. Starling's Problem (Day, 1973).

MORROW, Barbara. She grew up in Cleveland Heights, Ohio. Her father used to operate a print and antiques gallery in a Cleveland bookstore. Mrs. Morrow studied mural painting at the Cleveland Institute of Art. She has worked in an art library and has also been a college art instructor. Her husband Robert has taught at Kent State University in Kent, Ohio. The first children's book she illustrated was J. Jackson's Chicken Ten Thousand (a Junior Literary Guild selection; Little, 1968). She also illustrated D. Spicer's Kneeling Tree (Coward, 1971).

MORSE, Dorothy (Bayley), 1906- . She was born in New York City and has lived there and in Bedford Village with her husband Harry D. Morse. She received her education at Connecticut College for Women in New London and the New York-Phoenix School of Design. She has studied with both Thomas Fogarty and Norman Rockwell. For children she illustrated M. Vance's Leave It to Linda (Dutton, 1958) and F. Cavanah's The Secret of Madame Doll (Vanguard, 1965). ICB-2

MORTON, Marian.   Her husband has also been an artist,
     and they have lived in Mamaroneck, New York.   She
     has worked in graphics and ceramic sculpture in addi-
     tion to magazine and advertising illustration.   Marian
     Morton studied art in South America and Europe.   She
     has illustrated adult books, and for your people illus-
     trated H. Sandburg's Bo and the Old Donkey (Dial,
     1965), and M. Bourne's Raccoons Are for Loving (Ran-
     dom, 1968).

MORTON-SALE, Isobel, 1904-   ; and John Morton-Sale,
     1901-   .   Husband-wife team, both born in London.
     Mrs. Morton-Sale studied at Ramsgate School of Art
     in Margate and London's Central School of Arts where
     her husband also attended.   Mr. Morton-Sale also
     studied at the Putney School of Art.   The Morton-Sales
     have made their home in Edgemoor, Mortonhampstead,
     Devon, England.   John Morton-Sale has enjoyed paint-
     ing landscapes, and his wife has been interested in
     painting children.   This team created the illustrations
     for E. Farjeen's Martin Pippin in the Daisy Field
     (Stokes, 1937).   ICB-1, ICB-2

MORTON-SALE, John   see   MORTON-SALE, Isobel

MOY, Seong, 1921-   .   Artist and teacher, born in Canton,
     China.   His early years were spent in China and the
     United States.   He received his education in Minnesota
     at St. Paul School of Art.   He also studied in New
     York at the Art Students League and Hans Hofmann
     Art School.   His home has been in New York City.
     Mr. Seong Moy has been the recipient of numerous
     awards for his work which has been exhibited both here
     and abroad.   For children he illustrated M. Bro's
     Animal Friends of Peng-U (Doubleday, 1965).   ICB-3

MOYERS, William, 1916-   .   Artist, cowboy, teacher.
     Born in Atlanta, Georgia, he grew up on a ranch in
     Colorado.   After graduating from Colorado's Adams
     State College in Alamosa he studied at the Los Angeles
     Art Institute.   When he was a young man, Mr. Moyers
     rode in rodeos.   He later became a cartoonist at the
     Walt Disney Studio and was a high school teacher.   He
     served in the Army Signal Corps during World War II.
     The Moyers family has lived in New Mexico and Geor-
     gia.   He illustrated Famous Indian Tribes (Random
     House, 1954), which he co-authored with D. C. Cooke.

Juvenile books which he illustrated include N. Peale's
Coming of the King (Prentice-Hall, 1956), W. Heuman's
Little League Hotshots (Dodd, 1972), and S. Garst's
Ten Gallon Hat (Ariel Books, 1953). ICB-2

MUELLER, Hans Alexander, 1888- . Artist, author,
    teacher. He was born in Nordhausen, Germany, stud-
    ied in Leipzig at the State Academy of Graphic Arts
    and Bookcrafts, and later made his home in New York
    City after coming to the United States in 1937. Hans
    Mueller has taught both here and in Germany. He has
    illustrated books for various publishing firms in addi-
    tion to books for children which include D. Humphreys'
    Verdi (Holt, 1948). ICB-2

MULLINS, Edward S. He studied in Boston at the New Eng-
    land School of Art and graduated from Boston Univer-
    sity. He has lived in Connecticut where he has been
    an art instructor at Milford Academy. Mr. Mullins
    has also conducted art classes in his studio and de-
    signed greeting cards in addition to book illustrations.
    He has also done portrait painting. He wrote and il-
    lustrated Animal Limericks (Follett, 1966), and The
    Big Book of Limericks (Platt, 1969).

MUSSINO, Attilio, 1878-1954. He was born in Turin, Italy,
    attended the Accademia Albertina, and became a well-
    known cartoonist, book illustrator, and painter. He
    died at Vernante, Italy in 1954. In 1908 Attilio Mus-
    sino was awarded a gold medal at the International Ex-
    position for his drawings of Pinocchio which later ap-
    peared in The Adventures of Pinocchio, by "C. Collodi"
    --(Macmillan, 1926).

MYERS, Bernice. She married an artist, and they have
    lived in various countries throughout the world. Later
    she and her husband made their home in New York
    City. She wrote and illustrated in three colors Not
    This Bear! (Four Winds, 1968). In two colors she il-
    lustrated John Peterson's How to Write Codes and Send
    Secret Messages (Four Winds, 1970).

                              -N-

NADLER, Robert. Architect and artist, born in Alexandria,
    Egypt. He received a degree in architecture from the

University of Pennsylvania in Philadelphia. He married an architect and has lived in New York. Mr.
Nadler has belonged to the American Institute of Architects. For young readers he illustrated T. Hughes'
The Iron Giant (Harper, 1968), and J. Wood's Mam-
moth Parade (Pantheon, 1969).

NAGY, Al. Designer-illustrator, born in New York City.
He studied art at New York's Cooper Union. Mr. Nagy
has been a commercial artist in addition to illustrating
books. For boys and girls he illustrated J. Navarra's
Clocks, Calendars & Carousels (Doubleday, 1967), and
M. O'Neill's Take a Number (Doubleday, 1968)

NAKATANI, Chiyoko. Native of Japan, she attended Japa-
nese art schools and later studied in Switzerland and
France. In addition to her own country, her work has
been published in the United States, England, and many
European countries. The artist has made her home in
Tokyo. Her work includes the 1968 Children's Spring
Book Festival Honor Book (among picture books), The
Brave Little Goat of Monsieur Séguin, adapted by A.
Daudet (World, 1968). She also illustrated E. Kishida's
Hippo Boat (World, 1968).

NANKIVEL, Claudine. She grew up in Englewood, New Jersey. Claudine Nankivel attended the Art Students League
in New York and also studied in France. For children
she illustrated A. Deming's Getting to Know Algeria
(1963), and C. Joy's Getting to Know Hong Kong (1962),
both for Coward.

NAVARRA, Toby. Teacher, illustrator. She studied at Up-
sala College in East Orange, New Jersey and at Jersey
City State. In addition to teaching second grade, Mrs.
Navarra has taught art and guitar at Seton Hall. Her
work has received recognition at various art shows.
Her father-in-law, Professor John Gabriel Navarra,
wrote the book she illustrated, Drugs and Man (Doubleday, 1973).

NAYLOR, Penelope. Artist, painter, traveler. She received
her education at Smith College in Northampton, Massachusetts. Prior to living in New York City, Miss Naylor traveled and lived in Africa and Europe. Her work
has been exhibited in the United States and Europe including one-man shows in New York and Lisbon. For

young people she illustrated A. Silverstein's Bionics
(McCall, 1970), and F. Warren's Music of Africa
(Prentice-Hall, 1970).

NEBEL, Gustave.   He was born in France. His work
    has been exhibited in both America and Europe,
    and he has designed scenery for the ballet in Paris.
    Many of his frescoes and murals have been purchased
    by private collectors in America.   He wrote and illus-
    trated Happy Old Engine (Funk, 1968).   He also illus-
    trated J. Mahon's Creative Writing (Watts, 1968).

NEGRI, Rocco.   Born in Italy, he grew up in Argentina.   He
    studied at the Art Students League and the School of Vis-
    ual Arts in New York.   Many of his books have been il-
    lustrated with woodcuts and include D. Manuel's Tales
    from Count Lucanor (adapted from Spanish by T. Tal-
    bot; Dial, 1970).

NESS, Evaline (Michelow), 1911- .   Illustrator-author, born
    in Union City, Ohio, she grew up in Pontiac, Michigan.
    Prior to attending art school she studied library science
    and took courses in education.   She attended the Art
    Students League in New York, the Art Institute in Chi-
    cago, and the Accademia di Belle Arti in Rome.   She
    has created illustrations for magazines.   In addition to
    living in Rome, Evaline Ness has also visited Bangkok
    and traveled throughout the Orient.   Several of her book
    illustrations have been runners-up for the Caldecott
    Medal.   In 1967 she received the Caldecott Medal for
    her book Sam, Bangs and Moonshine (Holt, 1966).   She
    also wrote and illustrated A Double Discovery (Scrib-
    ner's, 1965), Do You Have the Time, Lydia? (Dutton,
    1971), Long, Broad & Quickeye (Scribner's, 1969), Mr.
    Miacca (Holt, 1967), and Pavo and the Princess (Scrib-
    ner's, 1964).   ICB-3, ABYP-2

NETAMUXWE see BOCK, William Sauts

NEWELL, Crosby see BONSALL, Crosby

NICHOLS, Marie C., 1905- .   Born in Brooklyn, New York,
    she later studied at Boston's Museum of Fine Arts and
    the School of Practical Art.   Due to her children's in-
    terest in animals, Marie Nichols began pet portrait
    painting.   Others requested her work.   Her home has
    been in Weston, Massachusetts.   For boys and girls

she illustrated M. Mason's Mr. Meadowlark (Hastings House, 1959). ICB-2

NICKLAUS, Carol. Her childhood was spent in Columbus, Ohio where she later graduated from Ohio State University. As an undergraduate, she was a guest editor on Mademoiselle magazine. Following graduation, she worked for this same magazine and later as a free-lance artist in New York City. In her first endeavor, F. Heide's Look! Look! A Story Book (McCall, 1971), she used a watercolor wash technique. Carol Nicklaus also illustrated D. Carlson's Girls Are Equal Too (a Junior Literary Guild selection; Atheneum, 1973).

NICOLAS see MORDVINOFF, Nicolas

NINON see MacKNIGHT, Ninon

NISENSON, Samuel. Designer and illustrator. His drawings can be found in books about sports, nature, music, and biography. Mr. Nisenson also created the "Minute Bi-ographies" series. For young people he illustrated M. Davis' The Giant Book of Sports (Grosset, 1967) and W. DeWitt's History's Hundred Greatest Events (Grosset, 1970).

NIVOLA, Claire. Painter and sculptor, the artist was born in New York City and later made her home in Cam-bridge, Massachusetts. She graduated from Radcliffe College and traveled in Europe where she spent a great deal of time in Italy. She illustrated M. Cimino's The Disobedient Eels and Other Italian Tales (Pantheon, 1970).

NONNAST, Marie, 1924- . Born on the Fourth of July in Jenkintown, Pennsylvania, she studied at the Moore In-stitute of Art in Philadelphia. She and her husband, a consulting engineer, have made their home in New Hope, Pennsylvania. Her work has appeared in many maga-zines including Woman's Day in which she made sever-al hundred paintings of birds in full color. She illus-trated A. Goudey's Graywings (Scribner's 1964) and Red Legs (Scribner's, 1966). ICB-2, ICB-3

NOONAN, Julia. Born in Naugatuck, Connecticut, she later made her home in Brooklyn, New York. She gradu-ated from Pratt Institute. Her work has appeared in

Redbook and McCall's magazines. For boys and girls
she illustrated J. Langstaff's Gather My Gold Together
(Doubleday, 1971).

NURA see ULREICH, Nura

NYMAN, Ingrid Vang, 1916- . Artist and sculptor, she
was born in Copenhagen, Denmark. She received her
education at the Royal Danish Academy of Art. After
her marriage to artist and author Arne Nyman, she
lived in Stockholm and Copenhagen. At one time she
illustrated books for a Swedish publishing firm. Her
chief speciality has been in animal drawings. She
gained recognition in the United States for her illustrations in P. Freuchen's Eskimo Boy (Lothrop, 1951).
ICB-2

-O-

OBRANT, Susan. She spent her early years in Old West-
bury, New York and Philadelphia, Pennsylvania. Pri-
or to attending New York City's Parsons School of Design, she studied psychology at the University of Buffalo. Her work has been honored by the Society of Illustrators and Art Direction. She married attorney
Steven Meier and has lived in Rego Park, New York.
For boys and girls she illustrated J. Aiken's The
Cuckoo Tree (a Junior Literary Guild selection; Doubleday, 1972).

OECHSLI, Kelly, 1918- . He was born in Butte, Montana,
and grew up in Seattle, Washington, where he later
studied at the Cornish School of Art. He has worked
in both black-and-white and color. Mr. Oechsli, his
wife, and four children have made their home in Haw-
thorne, New York. He illustrated M. Ward's The Bug
Man (Abingdon, 1972), M. Craig's The Dragon in the
Clock Box (Norton, 1962), and Piper, Pipe That Song
Again!, ed. by N. Larrick (Random, 1965). ICB-3

OHLSSON, Ib, 1935- . He was born in Copenhagen where
he attended the School of Decorative and Applied Arts.
He also studied at Randersgade Skole. He spent two
years in the Danish Civil Defense program and later
traveled throughout Europe. In addition to his work in
advertising and graphic design, Ib Ohlsson has also illustrated textbooks. The artist first came to America

on a student grant in 1950 and returned to live in Kew
Gardens, New York in 1960. His work for children
includes E. Fenton's <u>Big Yellow Balloon</u> (Doubleday,
1967), M. Craig's <u>The Long and Dangerous Journey</u>
(Norton, 1965) and J. Williams' <u>Philbert the Fearful</u>
(Norton, 1966). ICB-3

OLDDEN, Richard. His work has been published in such
magazines as the <u>Saturday Review</u> and <u>New Yorker</u>.
The artist has been interested in fencing and has become well-known as a swordsman both in this country
and abroad. His first illustrated book for boys and
girls was entitled <u>Pip Squeak, Mouse in Shining Armor</u>,
by R. Kraus (Windmill, 1971).

OLUGEBEFOLA, Ademola. An educator, artist, and designer, he was born in St. Thomas, Virgin Islands,
and later made his home in New York City. The artist
received a Doctorate of Fine Art Development from the
Wensi Nyumba Ya Sanaa Academy of African Arts and
Studies. He illustrated A. Fuja's <u>Fourteen Hundred
Cowries</u> (Lothrop, 1971).

ORBAAN, Albert F., 1913- . He was born in Rome, Italy
and came to the United States at 18. His father was
an art historian in the Netherlands. During World War
II, he served in Army Military Intelligence. Following
the war, he studied at the Art Students League. Before he became an artist, he was a reporter on a newspaper. His home has been in New York City. His
work includes O. Burt's <u>John Charles Fremont</u> (Messner, 1955), M. Holland's <u>No Room for a Dog</u> (Random,
1959), and F. Smith's <u>The Sound of Axes</u> (Rand, 1965).
ICB-2

ORR, William A. He acquired a great interest in the American Indian when he lived in Arizona near the Gila
River Apache Reservation. He later made his home
in Florida. In order to gain authenticity in his drawings, the artist did extensive research in Washington,
D.C. at both the Smithsonian Institution and the Library
of Congress. His book illustrations can be found in V.
Carlson's <u>Cochise</u> (Harvey House, 1973).

OSBORN, Robert Chesley, 1904- . He was born in Osh-
kosh, Wisconsin, and later made his home in Salisbury,
Connecticut. He attended Yale University and the British Academy in Rome. He also studied in Paris at

the Académie Scandinav. Mr. Osborn has written and
illustrated books for adults in addition to illustrating
books for children. His drawings have appeared in
such magazines as Harper's and Life. For boys and
girls he illustrated J. Ciardi's I Met a Man (Houghton,
1961) and E. Rees' The Song of Paul Bunyan and Tony
Beaver (Pantheon, 1964). ICB-3

OXENBURY, Helen. She was born in Ipswich, Suffolk, England. After studying for two years at the Ipswich School
of Art, she continued her art studies at London's Central School of Art. She has been a theatrical designer
in Israel and England and once served as art director on
a biblical film. Following her marriage to artist and
writer John Burningham, she has been a free-lance designer. Her book for young people was Number of
Things (Watts, 1968). She also illustrated M. Mahy's
Dragon of an Ordinary Family (Watts, 1969).

-P-

PAGET-FREDERICKS, Joseph Edward Paget Rous-Marten,
1908- . Born in San Francisco, he grew up in California and also spent periods of his childhood abroad.
He studied at the University of California, the California College of Arts and Crafts, the Munich Academy of
Fine Arts, and the École des Beaux Arts. A friend of
his family, the distinguished Anna Pavlova, was re-
sponsible for the artist's first exhibition in London. He
illustrated M. Anderson's A Gift for Merimond (Oxford, 1953). ICB-2

PALMER, Juliette. Her illustrations of animals and children have made Juliette Palmer a well-known artist.
A noted reviewer of books for children has described
her pictures in one book as "beautifully expressive
... really something to see." For boys and girls she
illustrated E. Coatsworth's Cricket and the Emperor's
Son (Norton, 1965) and A Duck for Keeps, by "H. Kay"
[pseud.] (Abelard-Schuman, 1962).

PAPIN, Joseph. He was born in St. Louis, Missouri, and
attended Ohio State University in Columbus. His work
has appeared in many magazines. He and his family
have lived in Matawan, New Jersey. Using artwork of
17th-century London as a basis, he illustrated D. Weiss'

Great Fire of London (Crown, 1968). He also illustrated A. Catherall's Camel Caravan (Seabury, 1968),
and H. Folsom's Famous Pioneers (Harvey House,
1963).

PARKER, Nancy Winslow. Her childhood was spent in
Maplewood, New Jersey, and she later studied at Mills
College in California. In addition to painting, she has
been interested in wood construction. The artist has
also participated in shows associated with the Ameri-
can Kennel Club. She illustrated J. Langstaff's Oh, A-
Hunting We Will Go (a Junior Literary Guild selection;
Atheneum, 1974).

PARKER, Robert Andrew. Artist and professor, graduate
of Chicago Art Institute. He was born in Virginia,
grew up in New Mexico near the Mescelero Apache
Reservation, and later made his home in Carmel, New
York. Robert Parker has been an instructor in Maine
at the Skowhegan School and in New York City at the
School of Visual Arts. A noted painter, his work can
be found in private collections and museums including
the Whitney Museum of American Art. His drawings
appeared in the 1970 Caldecott Honor Book, Pop Corn
& Ma Goodness, by E. Preston (Viking, 1969).

PARNALL, Peter, 1936- . He was born in Syracuse, New
York, and grew up in Connecticut and California. He
received his education at Cornell University and Pratt
Institute School of Art. Peter Parnall has been an art
director for both a magazine and advertising firm. He
and his family have lived in New Milford, New Jersey.
For young people he illustrated M. Shura's A Tale of
Middle Length (Atheneum, 1966), and M. Goodwin's
Underground Hideaway (Harper, 1968). ICB-3

PARRISH, Anne, 1888-1957. Born in Colorado Springs,
Colorado, she later studied at the Philadelphia School
of Design for Women. Both of her parents were distinguished artists. Also an author, Anne Parrish won
the Harper prize in 1925. She lived in Georgetown,
Connecticut, prior to her death on September 5, 1957.
For boys and girls she wrote and illustrated The Story
of Appleby Capple (Harper, 1950). ICB-1, ICB-2

PARRISH, Maxfield, 1870-1966. Born in Philadelphia, he
later studied at the Pennsylvania Academy of Fine Arts

and Haverford College. He also attended Drexel Institute (now called Drexel Institute of Technology). Maxfield Parrish married Lydia Austin, and they resided
in New Hampshire. His first magazine cover for
Harper's Weekly gave him recognition as an artist.
He has received many awards and honors for his work.
The honorary degree of LL.D. was bestowed upon him
by Haverford College. His book illustrations for children include The Arabian Nights, Their Best-Known
Tales, ed. by K. Wiggin (Scribner's, 1909), and E.
Field's Poems of Childhood (Scribner's 1904). ICB-1

PARSONS, Virginia. An American, she has lived in England.
She collaborated with English calligrapher Sheila Waters
to create Animal Parade (Doubleday, 1970). Miss
Waters' maps and manuscripts have received praise
both here and abroad. Miss Parsons also wrote and
illustrated Homes (Garden City Books, 1958) and Night
(Garden City Books, 1958).

PATON, Jane Elizabeth, 1934- . She was born in London
where she later studied at St. Martin's School of Art
and the Royal College of Art. She has lived in Surrey
and often visited with her parents who moved to southern France. The artist once said she used her sister's
children as models for her drawings. She illustrated
the following books for young people: B. Willard's
Dog and a Half (Nelson, 1971), E. Farjeon's Mr. Garden (Walck, 1966), and J. Reeves' Ragged Robin (Dutton, 1961). ICB-3

PAUL, James see KOCSIS, James C.

PAYNE, Joan Balfour, 1923- . She was born in Natchez,
Mississippi and grew up in Minneapolis, Minnesota
where she received her education and studied art. Her
first published work was in collaboration with her mother, writer Josephine Balfour Payne. She married John
Barber Dicks, Jr., who has been a professor of phys-
ics at the University of Tennessee Space Institute in
Sewanee. For children she wrote and illustrated Pan-
gur Ban (Hastings, 1966). She also illustrated M. Jus-
tus' New Home for Billy (Hastings, 1966), and J.
Payne's Stable That Stayed (Pellegrini & Cudahy, 1952).
ICB-2, ICB-3

PAYSON, Dale, 1943- . Born in White Plains, New York,

she later lived in Westport, Connecticut, where she
has worked with the Young People's Division of the
Famous Artists School. She received her education at
Endicott Junior College in Beverly, Massachusetts, and
at the School of Visual Arts in New York. The artist
has also traveled abroad. For boys and girls she illustrated two books by F. Rowland, both for Putnam:
Amish Boy (1970), and Amish Wedding (1971); one by
N. Carlson, Ann Aurelia and Dorothy (Harper, 1968).

PAYZANT, Charles. He has lived in Hollywood. He
     achieved recognition as the creator of a series of
     Christmas cards which depicted America during the
     1900's. Mr. Payzant has also been known for his
     watercolors. For young people he illustrated T. Shan-
     non's Little Wolf (Whitman, 1954) and Trail of the
     Wheel (Golden Gate, 1962).

PERCEVAL, Don, 1908- . Born in Woodford, Essex, Eng-
     land, he grew up in California where he later studied
     at Chouinard Art Institute. He also attended London's
     Royal College of Art and the Heatherley Art School.
     His home has been in Tucson, Arizona. He has been
     both a commercial artist and art teacher as he has
     served on the faculty of Chouinard Art Institute and Po-
     mona College's Art Department. He has become a
     noted painter of the Hopi and Navajo Indians. He illus-
     trated L. Rowntree's Ronnie (1952) and Ronnie and Don,
     (1953), both for Viking. ICB-2

PERL, Susan, 1922- . She was born and raised in Vienna,
     Austria and later lived in Switzerland, Italy, and Egypt.
     After arriving in the United States, she settled in New
     York City where she became a staff member of Vogue
     magazine. Her work has also appeared in Good House-
     keeping and Saturday Review. She has worked in both
     watercolor and pen and ink. In 1965 she received the
     Palma d'Oro Award in the International Cartoonist Ex-
     hibition in Italy. She has illustrated the following juve-
     nile books: S. Russell's Motherly Smith & Brother
     Bimbo (1971), N. Smaridge's Watch Out! (a Junior Lit-
     erary Guild selection; 1965) and M. Conger's Who Has
     Seen the Wind? (1959), all for Abingdon. ICB-3

PERROTT, Jennifer. Her childhood was spent in Newburgh,
     New York, where she later graduated from the New-
     burgh Free Academy. She studied graphic arts at

Pratt Institute in Brooklyn. Miss Perrott has been associated with the Department of Vertebrate Paleontol-
ogy at the American Museum of Natural History in New
York City. Her home has been in Brooklyn. For
young people she illustrated E. DeWaard's The Color
of Life (a Junior Literary Guild selection; Doubleday,
1971).

PETERSHAM, Maud (Fuller), 1890- ; and Miska Petersham,
1889-1960. Authors and illustrators, this husband-and-
wife team have contributed many books for children.
They lived in Woodstock, New York. Maud Petersham
was born in Kingston, New York, the daughter of a
minister. A graduate of Vassar, she did further study
at the New York School of Fine and Applied Arts.
Born Petrezselyem Mihaly in Hungary, he changed his
name to Miska Petersham after his arrival in England.
He attended night classes in London in order to study
art and later came to New York where he continued his
painting. In 1946 the Petershams received the Caldecott Medal for The Rooster Crows (Macmillan, 1945).
They also wrote and illustrated American ABC (Macmillan, 1941), Box with Red Wheels (Macmillan, 1949),
The Christ Child (Doubleday, 1931), and Circus Baby
(Macmillan, 1950). ICB-1, ICB-2, ICB-3, ABYP-2

PETERSHAM, Miska see PETERSHAM, Maud

PETIE, Haris. She was born in Boulder Creek, California,
and attended the Rochester Institute of Technology in
New York. She also studied art under Norman Rockwell in Paris. Her illustrations have appeared in both
magazines and books. Mrs. Petie has made her home
in Tenafly, New Jersey. Her work includes The Earth
Around Us, adapted by H. Collins (Dial Press, 1960),
D. Halacy's Energy and Engines (World, 1967), G. Hal-
sell's Getting to Know Colombia (Coward-McCann (1964),
and T. Phillips' Getting to Know Saudi Arabia (Coward-
McCann, 1963).

PHELAN, Joseph. He graduated from New York's Cooper
Union Art School. During World War II, he served as
a combat artist with the United States Navy. The
books which he has illustrated have reflected his love
of sky and sea. The artist has also worked in advertising agencies and studios as an art director both in
New York City and Chicago. His book for young
people was Whale Hunters (Little, 1969).

PICKARD, Charles. He was born in Yorkshire, England, and studied at the Harrogate School of Art and at London's Royal College of Art. He received the Gold Medal of the Art Directors Club of Philadelphia in 1957. He has lived in London. His work includes J. London's Call of the Wild (Dutton, 1968), R. Weir's Mike's Gang (Abelard-Schuman, 1965) and A. Eisenberg's Worlds Lost and Found (Abelard-Schuman, 1964).

PINCUS, Harriet. The first book which she illustrated, C. Sandburg's The Wedding Procession of the Rag Doll and the Broom Handle and Who Was in It (Harcourt, 1967), was awarded the distinction of being named an Honor Book in the 1967 Book World's Children's Spring Book Festival. According to one of the festival judges, Maurice Sendak, Miss Pincus possesses "a dreamlike quality, and her images have a heartbreaking truthfulness." She also illustrated L. Segal's Tell Me a Mitzi (Farrar, 1970), and Tit for Tat and Other Latvian Folk Tales, retold by Mae Durham (Harcourt, 1967).

PINTO, Ralph. He was born in Brooklyn and attended New York City's School of Visual Arts. The illustrator and his family have resided in Hillsdale, New Jersey. His book illustrations include J. Lester's Knee-High Man (Dial, 1972), M. Rudolph's The Magic Sack: A Lithuanian Folktale (McGraw, 1967), and R. Graves Two Wise Children (Harlin Quist, 1966).

PITZ, Henry Clarence, 1895- . He was born in Philadelphia where he later studied at the Philadelphia Museum School of Art and Spring Garden Institute. Mr. Pitz has been an instructor and the recipient of many awards. His pictures can be found in many permanent collections, and his murals have been created for several public buildings. Mr. Pitz has been professor emeritus of the Philadelphia College of Art. He has lived at Plymouth Meeting, Pennsylvania. His work includes E. Meadowcroft's By Secret Railway (Crowell, 1948), Fools and Funny Fellows, comp. by P. Fenner (Knopf, 1947); and O. Wheeler's Hans Andersen, Son of Denmark (Dutton, 1951). ICB-1, ICB-2, ICB-3

PIUSSI-CAMPBELL, Judy. She was born in South Bend, Indiana, the daughter of writer M. Rudolph Campbell.

After graduating from De Pauw University in Green-
castle, Indiana, she worked in New York City as an illustrator and textile designer. She married Pietro Pi-
ussi and lived in Florence, Italy, where her husband
has been on the staff at the university. Her book illustrations include M. O'Neill's Poor Merlo (Atheneum,
1967), The Talking Crocodile, adapted by M. Campbell (Atheneum, 1968), and O'Neill's Words, Words,
Words (Doubleday, 1966).

PLASENCIA, Peter P. The illustrator attended the Art Students League in New York and studied industrial design
at Pratt Institute in Brooklyn. He also studied in Rome
at the Meschini Institute. His many book illustrations
include A. Stone's The Chemistry of a Lemon (Prentice-Hall, 1966), S. Brandt's How to Write A Report
(Watts, 1968), and J. Throneburg's Man on the Moon
(Knopf, 1961).

PLUMMER, W. Kirtman. He attended Syracuse University,
England's Brighton School of Art, and graduated from
the Philadelphia College of Art. His illustrations have
appeared in Good Housekeeping and Holiday magazines.
His work has been exhibited in the New York City and
Philadelphia Art Directors' shows. For young people
he illustrated R. Wohlrabe's Picture Map Geography of
Western Europe (Lippincott, 1967) and M. Phelan's
Story of the Great Chicago Fire: 1871 (Crowell, 1971).

POGANY, William Andrew, 1882-1955. Willy Pogany was
born in Szeged, Hungary and later studied at Budapest's
Technical School and Academy of Art. His distinctive
drawings can be immediately recognized in a book designed for young people. In addition to his work as a
book illustrator, Pogany was a mural painter and designer of theatrical productions. He lived in New York
City. He illustrated P. Colum's Children of Odin (Macmillan, 1920), and Willy Pogany's Mother Goose (Nelson, 1928). ICB-1

POLGREEN, John. Artist and author. He has lived in
Dobbs Ferry, New York, with his wife Cathleen. Mr.
Polgreen has illustrated numerous books about science.
He collaborated with his wife, an amateur astronomer,
to write and illustrate The Earth in Space (Random,
1963). Mr. Polgreen has belonged to the Association
of Lunar and Planetary Observation of Variable Star

Observers. His juvenile book illustrations include I.
Asimov's Satellites in Outer Space (Random, 1960) and
P. Lauber's This Restless Earth (Random, 1970).

POLITI, Leo, 1908- . Author-illustrator, born in Fresno,
California. When he was seven, his family moved to
Italy. At the age of 15, he was awarded a scholarship
for the Institute of Monza near Milan. Mr. Politi re-
turned to the United States and has lived on Olvera
Street in Los Angeles. In 1950 he received the Caldecott Medal for his picture book, Song of the Swallows
(a Junior Literary Guild selection; Scribner's, 1949).
Other titles include Boat for Peppe (1950), The Butter-
flies Come (1957), Emmet (1971), Juanita (1948), Little
Leo (a Junior Literary Guild selection, 1951), Mieko
(Golden Gate, 1969), The Mission Bell (1953), Moy
Moy (1960), and Saint Francis and the Animals (1959),
all except Mieko, for Scribner's. ICB-1, ICB-2, ICB-
3, ABYP-2

POLSENO, Jo. He received a degree in Fine Arts from
New Haven's Whitney Art School, and he also studied
at the École des Beaux Arts in Marseilles. In addition
to books, his work has appeared in many magazines.
Mr. Polseno has enjoyed sports and has been a pro
football fan. His work includes S. Corbett's Cop's Kid
(Little, 1968), M. Marks' Fine Eggs and Fancy Chickens
(Holt, 1956), B. Freschet's Flight of the Snow Goose
(Crown, 1970), and J. Lonergan's When My Father Was
a Little Boy (Watts, 1961).

PORTER, George. Illustrator and painter, born in Perry,
Florida. He attended the Brooklyn Museum School and
Phoenix Art School in New York, and the Ringling
School of Art in Sarasota, Florida. His home has been
in Katonah, New York. George Porter has painted por-
traits in addition to illustrating magazines and books
for children. His book illustrations include W. St.
John's The Christmas Tree Mystery (a Junior Literary
Guild selection; Viking, 1969) and A. Stapp's Fabulous
Earthworm Deal (Viking, 1969).

PORTER, Jean Macdonald, 1906- . She was born in Ard-
more, Pennsylvania, grew up there and in New Jersey,
and studied at the Philadelphia Museum School of Industrial Art. Her ancestry has included a painter, sculptor, and singer. Her husband Pliny Porter was among

many who encouraged her to draw and paint. Mrs.
Porter made numerous charcoal sketches of service
men and women in hospitals during World War II. She
has also made many sketches of the Soap Box Derby in
White Plains, New York. For boys and girls she illustrated W. Carmichael's Island Voyage (McKay,
1968), R. Froman's Quacko and the Elps (a Junior
Literary Guild selection; McKay, 1964), and M. Wallace's A Race for Bill (Nelson, 1951). ICB-2

POWERS, Richard M., 1921- . His pseudonym is Terry
Gorman. He grew up in Chicago where he was born.
He later made his home in Ridgefield, Connecticut, but
has also lived in Maine, New York, and Vermont. The
artist attended Loyola University and the Chicago Art
Institute. He also studied at the University of Illinois
Art School in Urbana and the New School for Social Research in New York. In addition to his work in book
illustration, Richard Powers has written both children's
and adult books. He has also been a painter. He
served in the Army during World War II. For young
readers he illustrated B. DeRegniers' David and Goliath
(Viking, 1965), B. Dietz's Musical Instrumens of Africa (Day, 1965) and G. Swarthout's Whichaway (Random, 1966). ICB-2, ICB-3

PRICE, Garrett, 1896- . Cartoonist and artist. He was
born in Bucyrus, Kansas, grew up in Saratoga, Wyoming, and attended the University of Wyoming in Lara-
mie. He also studied at the Art Institute in Chicago,
and in New York and Paris. His home has been in
Westport, Connecticut. Garrett Price Served as editorial and sports cartoonist on the Great Lakes Navy
Bulletin during World War I. He has illustrated many
magazine covers and has been on the New Yorker staff
since 1925. For children he illustrated P. Burroughs'
The Honey Boat (a Junior Literary Guild selection;
Little, 1968) and M. Nash's Mrs. Coverlet's Detectives
(Little, 1965). ICB-3

PRICE, Harold, 1912- . Artist and merchant seaman, Harold Price was born in Portland, Oregon and later made
his home in San Francisco, California. He received
his education in New York at the Art Students League
and at the University of Oregon in Eugene. His art
career has included the illustration of pamphlets and
posters for the U.S. Government and the National

Maritime Union. He also created animations of Navy
Training Films. The artist has enjoyed outdoor sports
as hobbies. He illustrated H. Kinney's Lonesome Bear
(Whittlesey House--McGraw, 1949). ICB-2

PRICE, Norman Mills, 1877-1951. Artist and lecturer, he
was born in Brampton, Ontario. He attended the Ontario School of Art and both the Westminster School of
Art and Goldsmiths' Institute in London. He also studied in France at the Académie Julian in Paris. Price
came to this country in 1911 and later became a United
States citizen. His work has included book jackets and
covers for the St. Nicholas Magazine. His illustrations have also appeared in such magazines as Argosy,
Century, and Cosmopolitan. Prior to his death in 1951,
the artist belonged to the Guild of Free Lance Artists.
He served as Honorary President of the Society of Illustrators Library for many years. For children he
illustrated D. Fisher's Paul Revere and the Minute
Men (Random, 1950). ICB-1, ICB-2

PRINCE, Leonore E. Artist, teacher. She graduated from
the University of Southern California in Los Angeles.
Prior to teaching art in the Pasadena public schools,
she was an elementary school teacher. Later she devoted her time to being a free-lance illustrator. Leonore Prince illustrated M. Murray's Nellie Cameron
(a Junior Literary Guild selection; Seabury, 1971).

PROVENSEN, Alice, 1918- ; and Martin Provensen, 1916-
    . Artists, authors, husband-wife team. Both grew
up in Chicago and both attended the University of Cali-
fornia in Los Angeles. She also studied at the Chicago
Art Institute and the Art Students League in New York.
The Provensens and their family have resided in Dutch-
ess County, New York, on a farm near Staatsburg.
Many of their books have been included in the New
York Times yearly listings of the "Ten Best Illustrated
Children's Books." Their work has also been exhibited in the American Institute of Graphic Arts Shows.
Most of their illustrations have been done in watercolor. Together they illustrated Golden Book of Fun
and Nonsense, ed. by L. Untermeyer (Golden Press,
1970). ICB-2, ICB-3

PROVENSEN, Martin see PROVENSEN, Alice

PURSELL, Weimer. Free-lance illustrator and designer.
He attended the Chicago Art Institute and also studied
at the New Bauhaus School of Design. Prior to devoting all of his time to art, Mr. Pursell had been a college instructor. For young people he illustrated J.
Bronowski's Biography of an Atom (Harper, 1965).

PYK, Jan. Artist, born in Stockholm. He has continued his
interests of reading, sailing, and boat building which
began during his childhood in the Swedish Archipelago.
Jan Pyk studied art in Stockholm and after several years
spent in the advertising field, he became a free-lance
illustrator. He and his wife have lived in both New
York and Stockholm. His juvenile drawings can be
found in J. Brindel's Luap (a Junior Literary Guild selection; Bobbs-Merrill, 1972).

PYLE, Howard, 1853-1911. Artist, painter, and teacher (of
N. C. Wyeth, for example). Born in Wilmington, Dela-
ware, he attended the Art Students League in New York.
He died at the age of 58 in Florence, Italy. His drawings have appeared in books by other writers in addition to his illustrations for children. His work has also appeared in Harper's Monthly. For boys and girls
he wrote and illustrated Men of Iron (Harper, 1904),
Otto of the Silver Hand (Scribner's, 1920), and Wonder
Clock (Harper, 1887).

-Q-R-

QUACKENBUSH, Robert Mead, 1929- . Born in California,
he grew up in Phoenix, Arizona, and graduated from the
Art Center School in Los Angeles. Following military
service he studied at the New School for Social Research
in New York City. In addition to book illustration, Mr.
Quackenbush has illustrated for magazines. His work
first appeared in Sports Illustrated in 1962. He has
traveled abroad on magazine assignments and has made
his home in New York City. His favorite medium has
been woodcuts. For young people he illustrated L.
Klein's "D" Is for Rover (Harvey, 1970), E. Clymer's
Horatio (Atheneum, 1968), L. Moore's I Feel the Same
Way (Atheneum, 1967), and M. Bloch's Two Worlds of
Damyan (Atheneum, 1966). ICB-3

QUINTANILLA, Luis, 1895- . Born in Santander, Spain, he

later painted in Paris. In 1938 he arrived in the
United States and has made his home in New York City.
His paintings were included in many permanent collec-
tions; i.e., Chicago Art Institute, Museum of Modern
Art in Madrid, and New York's Metropolitan Museum.
For boys and girls he illustrated M. Schlein's Four
Little Foxes (a Junior Literary Guild selection; Scott,
1953). ICB-2

RAIBLE, Alton Robert, 1918- . He was born in Modesto,
California, and studied at the California College of Arts
and Crafts in Oakland. He has worked in a bank and a
shipyard. Mr. Raible later taught art at the College
of Marin in Kentfield, California. His home has been in
San Anselmo, California. His work includes three books
by Z. Snyder, Season of Ponies (1964), The Velvet Room
(a Junior Literary Guild selection; 1965), and Witches of
Worm (1972), all with Atheneum. ICB-3

RANDALL, Christine. Artist and designer, graduate of Utah
State University. Her work has appeared in magazines,
and her book illustrations include J. Seidelman's Creating with Papier-Maché (Crowell-Collier, 1971).

RASKIN, Ellen, 1928- . She was born in Milwaukee and
studied at the University of Wisconsin. Her work has
appeared in magazines and on book jackets and has re-
ceived much recognition. Her book, Nothing Ever Hap-
pens on My Block (Atheneum, 1966), was designated a
Prize Book by the Herald Tribune in the 1966 Spring
Children's Book Festival. Her home has been in New
York City. Her work includes S. Bartlett's A Book to
Begin on Books (Holt, 1968), V. Cleaver's Ellen Grae
(Lippincott, 1967), and O. Coolidge's The King of Men
(Houghton, 1966). ICB-3

RAVERAT, Gwendolen Mary (Darwin), 1885-1957. She was
born in Cambridge, England, and later studied in London at University College and the Slade School of Art.
After her marriage to French designer Jacques Raverat,
the artist lived in France until his death in 1925. A
wood engraver in addition to book illustrator, Gwendolen
Raverat has belonged to the Royal Society of Painter-
Etchers and Engravers and the Society of Wood-Engrav-
ers. Her illustrations for children include C. Yonge's
Countess Kate (Random, 1960). ICB-2

RAY, Deborah. She married a sculptor and has lived in Philadelphia, Pennsylvania. She attended the Philadelphia College of Art, the Pennsylvania Academy of the Fine Arts, the Albert Barnes Foundation, and the University of Pennsylvania. Deborah Ray also studied in France and Italy. She has had her work exhibited in many shows, and in 1967 was awarded the Mabel Rush Homer Award of Woodmere Art Gallery and a Louis Comfort Tiffany Foundation grant. She illustrated Abdul Abul-Bul Amir & Ivan Skavinsky Skavar (Macrae, 1969).

RAY, Ralph, 1920-1952. He was born in Gastonia, North Carolina, and later attended Grand Central Art School in New York and Ringling Art School in Sarasota, Florida. A nature lover since childhood, Ralph Ray was a painter in addition to being an illustrator of books. The advertising field also utilized this illustrator's talents. He illustrated M. Burgwyn's River Treasure (Oxford, 1947). ICB-2

RAYNES, John. Artist and writer, born in Australia. He grew up in England where he attended the Royal College of Art in London. Mr. Raynes has worked in advertising and has written books in addition to his career as a free-lance illustrator. His work has also appeared in magazines. For young people he illustrated H. Lent's What Car Is That? (Dutton, 1969).

REED, Philip G., 1908- . He was born in Park Ridge, Illinois, and studied at nearby Chicago Art Institute. He later made his home in St. Joseph, Michigan. Philip Reed began learning about the book trade when his father operated a private press in the basement of their house. Later he worked with the Monastery Hill Press. His work has been included in many outstanding permanent collections both in the United States and abroad. A distinguished book for young people which included his magnificent woodcuts was J. Thurber's Many Moons (A.M. & R.W. Roe, 1958). He also illustrated Mother Goose and Nursery Rhymes (Atheneum, 1963). ICB-1, ICB-3

REED, Veronica see SHERMAN, Theresa

REID, Bill. The descendant of a Haida Indian chief (Charlie Gladstone), he has done a great deal of research on

Haida art. He has also created jewelry which has reflected this art form. For boys and girls he illustrated C. Harris' Raven's Cry (Atheneum, 1966).

RETHI, Lili, 1894- . Artist-illustrator, born in Austria.
She became an American citizen after coming to the
United States in 1939. In addition to book illustra-
tion, the artist has had her work exhibited in many
museums. New York University has a permanent ex-
hibit of Miss Réthi's work at the Wallace Clark Center.
For young people she has illustrated C. Robinson's
The First Book of Ancient Egypt (Watts, 1961), D.
Sobol's The First Book of Medieval Man (Watts, 1959),
and J. Ayars Illinois River (Holt, 1968).

REYNA, Marilyn (Hafner) de see HAFNER, Marilyn

RIBBONS, Ian, 1924- . He was born in London and studied at the Beckenham School of Art in Kent and at London's Royal College of Art. He served in the Army in
India and Burma. Mr. Ribbons has been an art instructor in the Colleges of Guildford and Brighton and
at the Hornsey College of Art in London. His interests have included music and travel. He wrote Monday,
21 October 1805 (David White, 1968). He illustrated
I. Southall's Let the Balloon Go (St. Martin's, 1968),
and E. Goudge's Linnets and Valerians (Coward-Mc-
Cann, 1964). ICB-2, ICB-3

RICE, Elizabeth. Her illustrations have appeared in the
books written by Adda Mai Sharp. She has been known
to be interested in all new aspects in the field of art,
and this interest has been reflected in her work. She
illustrated A. Sharp's Secret Places (1955) and wrote
and illustrated Who-oo-oo (1972) and Yippy (1971), all
for Steck.

RICHARDS, John Paul. A gifted young artist from Houston,
Texas, John Richards' work has appeared in several
books. For children he illustrated E. Lapp's Hey,
Elephant! (Steck, 1970).

RINGI, Kjell. A Swedish-born artist and author, Kjell Ringi
came to the United States as a student. In 1967 he received recognition as an artist on a visit to New York.
His work has included books, magazine illustrations,
and paintings. For young people he wrote and

illustrated Magic Stick (Harper, 1968), The Stranger
(a Junior Literary Guild selection; Random, 1968), and
Sun and the Cloud (Harper, 1971).

RIPPER, Charles L., 1929- . He was born in Pittsburgh,
Pennsylvania, where he later attended the Art Institute. Both of his parents were artists, and from early
childhood he received help and encouragement from
them. By the time Charles Ripper was 20 he had illustrated a book. In addition to illustrating books, he
has created paintings for conservation stamps of the
National Wildlife Federation in Washington, D.C. His
home has been in Huntington, West Virginia. He wrote
and illustrated for Morrow Foxes and Wolves (1961),
Ground Birds (1960), and Mosquitoes (1969). ICB-2,
ICB-3

RISWOLD, Gilbert. He was born in Chicago and grew up in
Oak Park, Illinois, and Salt Lake City, Utah. He has
worked in the motion picture industry and on Air Corps
Training Films. His work has received several awards,
which include an award from the Art Directors Club of
Chicago and in 1964 an Award for Excellence from the
Society of Illustrators in New York. The Riswolds
have lived in Newtown, Connecticut. His work in-
cludes A. Johnson's Grizzly (Harper, 1964), O. Wilde's
Happy Prince (Duckworth, 1952), L. Davis' Round Rob-
in (rev. ed., Scribner's, 1962), and N. Carlson's
School Bell in the Valley (Harcourt, 1963). ICB-3

RITCHIE, Trekkie, 1902- . Of Scottish and British descent, Trekkie Ritchie was born in Natal, South Africa.
She grew up there and in England, and later attended
London's Slade School of Fine Art. Her home has
been in Kingston, Sussex, England. Miss Ritchie has
illustrated both educational and "Midget" books. Her
drawings can be found in A. Ritchie's Treasure of Li-
Po (Harcourt, 1949). ICB-2

RIVOLI, Mario, 1943- . Artist and designer, born in New
York City. He studied in New York at the Art Students League, School of Industrial Arts, and the School
of Visual Arts. At one time Mario Rivoli worked in
fashion illustration and fabric design. He was the recipient of the 1965 Society of Illustrators Award. The
artist has lived and operated a shop called "The Tun-
nel of Love" in New York City. His work includes

L. Young's Best Foot Forward (Van Nostrand, 1968),
and two by B. Wersba, Do Tigers Ever Bite Kings?
(a Junior Literary Guild selection; Atheneum, 1966)
and A Song for Clowns (a Junior Literary Guild selection; Atheneum, 1965).   ICB-3

ROBBINS, Frank, 1917- . He was born in Boston, Massachusetts.   His talent was obvious at an early age because by the time he was 14 he had received two scholarships in art.   In addition to illustrating books, Mr.
Robbins has created illustrations for magazines.   He
has also drawn comic strips and exhibited his work in
art shows.   For young people he illustrated H. Liss'
Bowling Talk for Beginners (Messner, 1973).

ROBINSON, Charles.   Attorney and artist, he was born in
Morristown, New Jersey.   After graduation from Harvard College, he attended the University of Virginia
where he received a law degree.   Prior to devoting
fulltime to illustration, Mr. Robinson practiced corpor-
ate law.   He and his family have lived in New Vernon,
New Jersey.   He illustrated S. Levitin's Journey to
America (a Junior Literary Guild selection; Atheneum,
1970).

ROBINSON, Irene Bowen, 1891- . She was born in South
Bend, Washington.   Later she studied in Springfield,
Missouri, at Drury College and in Los Angeles at
Chouinard Art Institute and the Otis Art Institute of
Los Angeles County.   Her childhood experiences on a
farm gave her a lasting love of animals which the art-
ist has depicted in her drawings.   Married to W. W.
Robinson, she has lived in Los Angeles.   In addition
to book illustrations, she has painted both still life
and landscape.   She illustrated her husband's book
The Book of Elephants (rev. ed., Ward Ritchie Press,
1962).   ICB-1, ICB-2

ROBINSON, Jerry.   Artist, author, cartoonist.   Mr. Robinson and his family have lived in New York City.   In
addition to book illustration, the artist has written a
number of books, and his cartoons have been published
nationwide.   At one time Jerry Robinson served as
president of the National Cartoonist Society.   He has
been the recipient of numerous awards including the
Ruben Award.   For children he illustrated A. Stevenson's Israel Putnam (Bobbs-Merrill, 1959), G.

Herman's Let's Go Logging (Putnam, 1962), and two by
R. Wyler, Professor Egghead's Best Riddles (Simon
and Schuster, 1973) and Science Teasers (Harper,
1966).

ROCKWELL, Anne. She spent her childhood in the states of
New Mexico, Arizona, Tennessee, Ohio, and New York.
Later she married artist Harlow Rockwell [which see]
and lived in Old Greenwich, Connecticut. The first
book that she illustrated was included in the American
Institute of Graphic Arts selection of the "Fifty Best
Books of the Year." She has also designed UNICEF
Christmas cards. She wrote and illustrated Monkey's
Whiskers (Parents' magazine, 1971) and Tuhurahura
and the Whale (Parents' magazine. 1971).

ROCKWELL, Gail. Born in New York City, the artist later
graduated from Bard College. Following her marriage
to Norman Rockwell's son Thomas in 1955, she studied at the Art Students League. Her parents have also been artists. The Rockwells have lived on a farm
outside of Poughkeepsie. She has illustrated books
written by her husband in addition to E. Conford's
Dreams of Victory (Little, 1973).

ROCKWELL, Harlow. His home [with Anne Rockwell--which
see] has been in Old Greenwich, Connecticut. Prior
to book illustration, Harlow Rockwell was an art director for an advertising firm. His lithographs and
woodcuts have been on public view and exhibited at the
Library of Congress. Many magazines including Good
Housekeeping, McCall's, and Parents' have published
his work. For young readers he illustrated his wife
Anne's Head to Toe (Doubleday, 1973).

ROCKWELL, Norman, 1894- . Born in New York City, he
studied at the National Academy of Design, Chase Art
School, and the Art Students League. When he was 17
he had received assignments to illustrate several publications. He once served as Art Editor for Boys' Life.
His cover drawings often appeared on the Saturday Evening Post, and he also painted for the Boy Scout calendar for many years. He has lived in Arlington, Vermont. For boys and girls he illustrated Twain's The
Adventures of Huckleberry Finn (Hermitage Press,
1940), R. Coles' Dead End School (Little, 1968), and
J. Wahl's Norman Rockwell Storybook (Simon, 1969).
ICB-1

ROEVER, J. M. She and her husband Wilfried Roever have
    lived in Cocoa Beach, Florida. Engaged in the U.S.
    space program, Mr. Roever has been a systems test
    engineer, and Mrs. Roever has been a technical illus-
    trator. The Roevers have been interested in wildlife
    conservation and visited the Catskill Game Farm in or-
    der to study the Przewalski wild horses for their book
    The Mustangs (Steck, 1971). She also wrote and illus-
    trated for Steck: Rascally Ringtails (1970), and Whoop-
    ing Crane (1971).

ROGERS, Carol. Artist and designer, born in Waco, Texas.
    Her home has been near Austin. She received her
    B.A. degree in design from Texas Woman's University
    at Denton. Carol Rogers has worked in advertising
    and illustrated textbooks in addition to picture books for
    children. She has enjoyed animals and raising flowers
    as hobbies. For young readers she illustrated S. Rus-
    sell's About Bananas (Melmont, 1968) and two of N.
    Zimelman's books, A Good Morning's Work (a Junior
    Literary Guild selection; Steck, 1968), and Once When
    I Was Five (Steck, 1967).

ROJANKOVSKY, Feodor, 1891- . Illustrator, author, born
    in Mitava, Russia. He attended the Academy of Art in
    Moscow. In World War I he was an officer in the Rus-
    sian Army. Feodor Rojankovsky has been a stage
    director and has also worked in a Polish publish-
    ing house. He came to the United States in 1941
    and has lived in Bronxville, New York. In 1956 he
    won the Caldecott Medal for Frog Went A-Courtin', re-
    told by John Langstaff (Harcourt, 1955). Juvenile books
    include two books for Knopf, Animals in the Zoo (1962),
    and Animals on the Farm (1967); J. Graham's A Crowd
    of Cows (Harcourt, 1968), and E. Averill's Daniel
    Boone (Harper, 1945). ICB-1, ICB-2, ICB-3, ABYP-2

ROSE, Gerald, 1935- . He was born in Hong Kong and
    studied at the Royal Academy in London. His wife, a
    schoolteacher and author, encouraged him to illustrate
    children's books. In 1960 he was awarded England's
    Kate Greenaway Medal. Mr. Rose has taught in the
    Graphic Design School of the Maidstone College of Art.
    He and his wife have lived in Kent, England. His work
    includes E. Rose's The Big River (Norton, 1962), L.
    Pender's Dan McDougall and the Bulldozer (Abelard-
    Schuman, 1963), B. Ireson's The Story of the Pied

<u>Piper</u> (Barnes, 1961); L. Bourliaguet's <u>A Sword to Slice Through Mountains and Other Stories</u> (Abelard, 1968). ICB-3

ROSENBLUM, Richard. He graduated from New York's Cooper Union and has made his home in Brooklyn with his family. He has worked in both commercial art and animation design. His first book illustrations appeared in L. Baum's <u>A Kidnapped Santa Claus</u> (Bobbs-Merrill, 1969).

ROSS, John, 1921- . Artist, lecturer, teacher, born in New York City. He and his artist-wife Clare Romano Ross have lived in Englewood, New Jersey. Mr. Ross attended New York's Cooper Union School of Art and also studied in France and Italy. Both Mr. and Mrs. Ross have lectured and lived abroad and have received many art awards. Both have also been on the staffs of Pratt Institute in Brooklyn and the New School for Social Research in New York. Mr. Ross has been a past President of the Society of American Graphic Artists. For young people he illustrated <u>Sprints and Distances</u>, comp. by L. Morrison (Crowell, 1965). ICB-3

ROTH, Arnold. Free-lance illustrator, he and his wife have lived in Princeton, New Jersey. Mr. Roth's work has appeared in the following magazines: <u>Punch</u>, <u>Holiday</u>, and <u>Sports Illustrated</u>. For boys and girls he illustrated J. Schwartz's <u>Go On Wheels</u> (McGraw, 1966), C. Fadiman's <u>Wally the Wordworm</u> (Macmillan, 1964), and J. Yolen's <u>The Witch Who Wasn't</u> (Macmillan, 1964).

ROWAND, Phyllis. The daughter of a newspaper editor, she was born in Vermont. She achieved her reputation as a children's book illustrator without formal art school training. She became interested in books for children following the birth of her daughter. Her home has been in Rowayton, Connecticut. She illustrated R. Krauss' <u>Bears</u> (Harper, 1948). ICB-2

RUTH, Rod. Mr. Ruth has worked in an art studio in Chicago. As a young man he traveled from Yucatan to the Yukon where he became a dog team driver for a fur trading post. He has always loved the out-of-doors and once said: "My life-long interest in wildlife in its natural environment is stronger than ever. So

is my concern for the desperate need of preserving our
rapidly dwindling wilderness areas." He and his family have made their home in Park Ridge, Illinois. For
young people he illustrated J. May's Alligator Hole
(Follett, 1969).

RUZICKA, Rudolph, 1883- . Born in Bohemia, he came to
the United States at an early age. He received his education in Chicago at the Art Institute and in New York
at the School of Art. He has lived in New York City
and later in Boston, Massachusetts. Rudolph Ruzicka
has been a writer, a wood engraver, and designer of
type. His work has been exhibited in museums and the
Library of Congress. Mr. Ruzicka has been the recipient of numerous awards including the 1935 American Institute of Graphic Arts Gold Medal. He has been
a Fellow of the American Academy of Arts and Sci-
ences and an Associate of the National Academy of Design. He has also belonged to the Society of Printers
and other notable organizations. His decorations can
be found in R. Greenough's Home Bible (Harper, 1950).
ICB-1, ICB-2

-S-

SADER, Lillian. Artist-designer. After graduating from the
Chicago Art Institute, she continued her studies at the
University of California at Berkeley. Exhibitions of
her work have been held at Art Director's shows in
San Francisco and Chicago and in museums and galleries. Lillian Sader has been associated with one of
the leading design studios in this country. Her home
has been in Berkeley, California. For children she illustrated H. Jacob's Garland for Gandhi (Parnassus,
1968), and P. Hitchcock's The King Who Rides a Tiger
and Other Folk Tales from Nepal (Parnassus, 1967).

SAGSOORIAN, Paul. A native New Yorker, he attended
schools in New York City and the U.S. Army Map Making School. After completing his art studies, Paul
Sagsoorian became a free-lance artist and has worked
in publishing firms, art studios, and advertising agencies. The American Institute of Graphic Arts honored
him in 1957 by selecting one of his illustrated books as
one of the "Fifty Best Books of the Year." His drawings can be found in J. Williams' Danny Dunn and the
Smallifying Machine (McGraw, 1969).

SANDBERG, Lasse E. M. , 1924- . He was born in Stockholm, Sweden, and studied at Anders Beckman's Art
School. He has been a cartoonist and photographer in
addition to illustrating books for boys and girls. He
has won several awards including the 1965 Elsa Beskow
Plaque (Swedish Librarians' prize for best children's
book illustrations). The Sandbergs have lived in Karl-
stad, Sweden. He and his wife collaborated on: Boy
With Many Houses (Delacorte (1970), Come On Out,
Daddy (Delacorte, 1971), and What Anna Saw (Lothrop,
1964). ICB-3

SANDIN, Joan. Born in Watertown, Wisconsin, she spent
her childhood in the southwestern part of the United
States. She graduated from the University of Arizona
at Tucson. Prior to making her home in New York
City, she traveled in Europe. As a member of the
New York Council of American Youth Hostels, she has
enjoyed taking young people on camping and cycling
trips. She illustrated M. Wojciechowska's "Hey What's
Wrong With This One?" (1969), and T. Lewis' Hill of
Fire (1971), both for Harper.

SANDOZ, Edouard, 1918- . He spent part of his childhood
in Europe and later graduated from Harvard. He has
been particularly interested in the medieval period of
history and has served on a Heraldry Committee at
Harvard. Prior to his service in the Navy where he
made a distinguished record, he was an assistant
graphic arts curator at Harvard. The artist's home
has been in Cambridge, Massachusetts. For young
people he illustrated O. Coolidge's Trojan War (Houghton, 1952). ICB-2

SANDSTROM, George F. A noted artist of natural history,
George Sandstrom was born in Argentina and graduated
from Argentina's University of Litoral in Rosario. After coming to the United States in 1955, he became
well-known for his nature drawings of shells and minerals. His work has appeared in encyclopedias and
magazines. His farm studio in Chester County, Pennsylvania enabled him to do research at nearby natural
history museums in New York, Philadelphia, and
Washington, D.C. The artist has belonged to several
natural history organizations. With Marita Sandstrom
he illustrated R. Abbott's ..Sea Shells of the World
(Golden Press, 1962. He also illustrated R. Abbott's
Seashells of North America (Golden Press, 1968).

SANDSTROM, Marita see under SANDSTROM, George F.

SAPIEHA, Christine. Born in Poland, she came to the
United States in 1939. She studied at Georgetown University and the Parsons School of Design. Miss Sapieha
has been Assistant Art Director of the Reporter and
once did illustrations for the British School of Archaeol-
ogy in Greece. She has also worked for the Metropolitan Museum of Art in New York City. She illustrated
L. Poole's Fireflies in Nature and Laboratory (Crowell,
1965), and W. Stephens' Hermit Crab Lives in a Shell
(Holiday, 1969).

SARI see FLEUR, Anne

SAVAGE, Steele, 1900- . He was born in Detroit, Michigan, and later made his home in New York City. He
studied at the Detroit School of Fine Arts, Chicago Art
Institute, and the Slade School of Fine Art in London.
In addition to book illustration, Mr. Savage has been a
magazine illustrator, set and costume designer, and advertising artist. He once lived and painted in the West
Indies. For children he illustrated C. Sellew's Adventures with the Giants (Little, 1950), C. Judson's Andrew
Carnegie (Follett, 1964), M. Komroff's Bible Dictionary
for Boys and Girls (Winston, 1957) and V. Voight's
Patch, a Baby Mink (Putnam, 1965). ICB-2

SCHACHNER, Erwin. He was born in Austria and came to
the United States in 1940. A graduate of the Philadelphia Museum School, he also studied at Pratt Institute
in Brooklyn, New York. He has worked in advertising,
printing, and illustrated for magazines. His wood and
linoleum cuts have been exhibited in New York and
Philadelphia. Mr. Schachner has lived in New York
City. He created the wood engravings for M. Chase's
The Story of Lighthouses (Norton, 1965). He also illustrated O. Gibbons' Cryes of London Town (Putnam,
1968).

SCHILLING, Betty. She studied at Mary Hardin-Baylor College in Belton, Texas and at the Cranbrook Academy of
Art in Bloomfield Hills, Michigan. Her home has been
in Scottsdale, Arizona. Besides the enjoyment of writing and drawing stories for children, the artist has
been interested in the practice of yoga. She illustrated
E. Haney and R. Richards' Yoga for Children (Bobbs-
Merrill, 1973).

SCHINDELMAN, Joseph, 1923- . He was born in New York,
    studied at the Art Students League, WPA art classes,
    and New York City College. He has worked in radio
    and has been an art director in an advertising agency.
    He has lived in Bayside, New York. A book which he
    illustrated was selected as one of "ten best-illustrated
    books of 1963" by the New York Times. His work in-
    cludes R. Dahl's Charlie and the Chocolate Factory
    (Knopf, 1964), J. Raymond's The Marvelous March of
    Jean François (Doubleday, 1965), L. Harris' Maurice
    Goes to Sea (Norton, 1968), and J. Bosworth's Voices
    in the Meadow (a Junior Literary Guild selection;
    Doubleday, 1964). ICB-3

SCHOENHERR, John Carl, 1935- . He was born in New
    York City, studied at Pratt Institute and the Art Stu-
    dents League, and later lived on a farm in Stockton,
    New Jersey. In addition to book illustration for both
    children and adults, he has illustrated science fiction
    magazines and paperback book covers. Mr. Schoenherr
    has belonged to the National Speleological Society, the
    New York Zoological Society, and the Society of Illus-
    trators. He was winner of first prize at the National
    Speleological Society Salon in 1963 and was the recipi-
    ent of the World Science Fiction Award in 1965. The
    artist has also been honored by the Society of Illustra-
    tors. For children he illustrated two books by M.
    Miles, Eddie's Bear (1970), Mississippi Possum (1965),
    both for Little. He also wrote and illustrated Barn
    (Little, 1968). ICB-3

SCHONGUT, Emanuel. Artist-teacher. After graduating
    from Pratt Institute, he did further study at the Pratt
    Graphic Art Center and Art Students League. Mr.
    Schongut has been an art instructor at Pratt and has al-
    so designed and illustrated book jackets. His work has
    appeared in such magazines as Ingenue and Harpers.
    For children he illustrated L. Chaffin's John Henry Mc-
    Coy (Macmillan, 1971) and I. Asimov's Tomorrow's
    Children: 18 Tales of Fantasy and Science Fiction
    (Doubleday, 1967).

SCHREIBER, Georges, 1904- . Born in Brussels, Belgium,
    he studied in Germany at Kunstgewerbeschule, Elber-
    field, and at the Academy of Fine Arts in Berlin and
    Düsseldorf. He came to the United States at the age of
    24 and ten years later became a naturalized citizen.

His illustrations have appeared in many magazines, and
he has designed posters for the U.S. Treasury Depart-
ment. Mr. Schreiber's work has been included in the
permanent collections of many museums and colleges.
He married Lillian Yamin, and they have lived in New
York City. His work includes J. Sauer's Light at Tern
Rock (Viking, 1951), C. Bishop's Pancakes---Paris
(Viking, 1947), and A. Dalgliesh's Ride on the Wind
(Scribner's, 1956). ICB-2

SCHREITER, Rick, 1936- . Born in Boston, Massachusetts,
he studied at Harvard and the Rhode Island School of
Design. He later made his home in New York City.
He has done a great deal of work in black-and-white.
Several of his books were included in the 1967 Graphis,
a publication concerned with "the artistically valuable
children's book." He wrote and illustrated The De-
licious Plums of King Oscar the Bad (Harlin Quist,
1967). He illustrated E. Merriam's Miss Tibbett's
Typewriter (Knopf, 1966). ICB-3

SCHUCKER, James. Mr. Schucker developed an early inter-
est in art. He always liked animals, especially horses.
The artist and his family have lived in Quakertown,
Pennsylvania. For boys and girls he illustrated three
books by W. Farley for Random House: Big Black
Horse (1953), Little Black, a Pony (1961), and Little
Black Pony Races (1968).

SCHULE, Clifford H. Artist and portrait painter, Clifford
Schule has become well-known especially in New York
and Pennsylvania. His home has been in Philadelphia.
He served in the Eighth Air Force as official artist
during World War II. His book illustrations can be
found in F. Lane's Nat Harkins, Privateersman (Holt,
1956), and M. Thomas' Sing in the Dark (Winston,
1954). ICB-2

SCHUYLER, Remington, 1884-1955. Born in Buffalo, New
York, he attended Washington University in St. Louis,
the Art Students League in New York, and also studied
abroad. His father was a critic on the St. Louis Post-
Dispatch and his mother was an artist and musician.
He was active in Boy Scouts and wrote several of their
Merit Badge pamphlets. He taught art and was Artist
in Residence at Missouri Valley College in Marshall,
Missouri. He illustrated H. McCraken's Great White
Buffalo (Lippincott, 1946). ICB-1, ICB-2

SEARLE, Ronald, 1920- . He was born in Cambridge, England, where he later studied at the Cambridge School
of Art. In 1939 he joined the Army and remained in
it until 1946. He spent three of these seven years as
a prisoner of war in Japan. As a free-lance artist,
he has created both book and magazine illustrations.
The artist has lived in London. For young people he
illustrated Dickens' Oliver Twist, ed. by Doris Dickens
(Norton, 1962). ICB-2

SEGAWA, Yasuo, 1932- . He was born in Okazaki City,
Japan. He received first prize in the Japan Tourist
Poster Contest in 1959 and 1960. In Tokyo he has
painted and worked in sculpture using both European
and Japanese techniques. For young people he illus-
trated M. Maeda's How Rabbit Tricked His Friends
(Parents' magazine, 1969) and B. Lifton's The Many
Lives of Chio and Goro (Norton, 1968).

SEIGNOBOSC, Françoise, 1900-1961. Her pseudonym is Françoise. Born in Lodève, Hérault, France, she later
studied at the Collège Sévigné in Paris. She used to
spend her winters there and her summers on a farm
in the south of France. Her books were first published in Paris; however, her childlike drawings were
later enjoyed by many children in America. For
Scribner's, she wrote and illustrated The Big Rain
(1961), Minou (1962), and Small-Trot (a Junior Literary
Guild selection, 1952). ICB-1, ICB-2, ICB-3

SEITZ, Patricia. Artist-teacher. She graduated from the
Maryland Institute of Art in Baltimore where she also
taught an art class for children. She and her husband,
also an artist, have lived in Minneapolis, Minnesota.
She illustrated S. Martin's Ride On! Ride On! An
Easter Season Story for Children (Augsburg Publishing
House, 1968).

SELIG, Sylvie. Born in France, she studied at the École
des Beaux Arts in Paris. Her work has received recognition in France and also won the 1968 Graphic Prize
for Children at the International Children's Book Fair
in Bologna, Italy. She and her husband have made
their home in Paris. She illustrated A. Surany's
Etienne-Henri and Gri-Gri (Holiday, 1969), and V.
Thompson's Hawaiian Legends of Tricksters and Rid-
dlers (Holiday, 1969).

SENDAK, Maurice, 1928-   .   Author-illustrator, born in
    Brooklyn, New York. He attended the Art Students
    League. During high school he illustrated his first
    book. He has made his home in New York City.
    Meindert DeJong's The Wheel on the School (Harper,
    1954) with pictures by Maurice Sendak won the New-
    bery Medal in 1955. Other juvenile books include
    five books for Harper: In the Night Kitchen (1970),
    Nutshell Library (1962), The Sign on Rosie's Door
    (1960), Very Far Away (1957), and Where the Wild
    Things Are (winner of the 1964 Caldecott Medal,
    1963).   ICB-2, ICB-3, ABYP-2

SEVERIN, Mark, 1906-   .   He grew up in England and later
    made his home in Brussels. He received his educa-
    tion in Belgium at Ghent University and Ghent Academy.
    He served in the Belgian Army during World War II.
    Mark Severin has designed stained glass, wall decora-
    tions, and stamps. He has been an official graphic de-
    signer for the government of Belgium. Mr. Severin
    has also worked in both metal and wood engraving. He
    has occupied Belgium's only chair of engraving at the
    Institute Supérior des Beaux Arts in Antwerp. The
    artist has enjoyed Japanese art, nature, gardening, and
    a collection of bookplates and engravings as hobbies.
    His drawings can be found in Beowulf the Warrior, re-
    told by I. Serraillier (Walck, 1961).   ICB-2

SEWARD, Prudence.   She studied at Northwood College, Har-
    row Art School, and the Royal College of Art. She has
    been a member of the Royal Watercolor Society and the
    Society of Painter-Etchers and Engravers. In fine line
    drawings she illustrated J. Robinson's Charley, (Mc-
    Cann, 1969).

SHARP, William, 1900-   .   Artist, cartoonist, designer,
    muralist, he was born in Lemberg, Austria. He came
    to the United States in 1934 and has lived in New York
    at Forest Hills, Long Island. William Sharp studied in
    Austria at the Academy for Arts and Industry, and he
    also did further study in England, France, Germany,
    and Poland. At one time the artist designed stained-
    glass windows and painted murals. He has also been
    a newspaper and magazine cartoonist. His illustrations
    for children include H. Lothrop's Five Little Peppers
    and How They Grew, "by M. Sidney" [pseud.] (Grosset
    1948) and E. Vance's The Tall Book of Fairy Tales
    Retold, (Harper, 1947).   ICB-1, ICB-2

SHARPE, Caroline. She attended Eastbourne School of Art
in Sussex, England. She has not only been interested
in drawing for children but has also helped boys and
girls with physical handicaps. She wrote and illustrated Ben and Clementine (Abelard, 1971). She also
illustrated E. Luginbuhl's Red Wood Man (Abelard,
1971).

SHAW, Charles. A native of Texas, he has made his home
in Austin. His work has been exhibited in art directors' shows in Texas and Colorado. In addition to
book illustration, Mr. Shaw has worked in advertising
firms. For children he illustrated two works by E.
Pedersen, House Upon a Rock (a Junior Literary Guild
selection; Atheneum, 1968) and Petticoat Fisherman
(Atheneum, 1969).

SHEKERJIAN, Haig and Regina. A husband-and-wife team.
Mrs. Shekerjian graduated from the New School for Social Research and from Skidmore College, and her husband was a graduate of the Rochester Institute of Technology. Together they created the sensitive illustrations which appeared in B. DeRegniers' The Boy, the
Rat, and the Butterfly (Atheneum, 1971).

SHEKERJIAN, Regina see SHEKERJIAN, Haig

SHENTON, Edward, 1895- . Artist and teacher, born in
Pottstown, Pennsylvania. He attended the Philadelphia
Museum School of Industrial Art and the Pennsylvania
Academy of the Fine Arts. He also studied in Paris.
He married writer Barbara Webster and has illustrated
her books. Their home has been in West Chester,
Pennsylvania. Mr. Shenton has been associated with
Philadelphia's Moore College of Art as head of its Department of Illustration. In addition to teaching and illustrating, he has also written books and stories for
magazines. For children he illustrated C. Burland's
Finding Out about the Incas (Lothrop, 1962), H. Morrow's On to Oregon (Morrow, 1946). He also wrote
and illustrated On Wings for Freedom (Macrae Smith,
1942). ICB-1, ICB-2

SHEPARD, Ernest Howard, 1879- . Born in St. John's
Wood, England, he received his education at St. Paul's
School and studied at the Heatherley and Royal Academy
Schools. His first picture was exhibited in 1901 at
the Royal Academy, and he began his career as a

Punch artist in 1907.   He has held a Commission in the
Royal Artillery and served in France in 1916.   He
later made his home in Lodsworth, Sussex, England.
His illustrations serve as a vital part of A. A. Milne's
memorable story, Winnie-the-Pooh (Dutton, 1926), as
well as Milne's When We Were Very Young (Dutton,
1924), The House at Pooh Corner (Dutton, 1928), and
Christopher Robin Book of Verse (Dutton, 1967).   He
also illustrated K. Grahame's The Wind in the Willows
(Scribner's, 1933; 1st pub. in 1908).   ICB-1, ICB-2,
ICB-3

SHEPARD, Mary Eleanor, 1909- .   She was born on Christmas Day in England, the daughter of distinguished illustrator Ernest Shepard.   She studied in Paris and at the
Slade School of Fine Art and the Central School of Art
in London.   She married a former editor of Punch
named E. V. Knox, and they have lived in London.
Her work has received several awards, and she has
had exhibitions in London galleries.   She illustrated
two books by P. Travers, both for Harcourt: Mary
Poppins (1934), and Mary Poppins from A to Z (1962).
ICB-2, ICB-3

SHERMAN, Theresa, 1916- .   Her pseudonym is Veronica
Reed.   She married David Rosenberg and has lived in
Manhattan where she was born.   Her childhood was
spent in Brooklyn, and she has lived in France.   In
addition to private study, Theresa Sherman attended
both the American Artists School and Art Students
League in New York.   She has exhibited her work in
galleries, conducted painting and ceramic classes for
adults, and taught painting, puppetry, and sculpture to
children.   She illustrated I. Black's Big Puppy and
Little Puppy (Holiday, 1960), M. Holland's Muggsy
(Knopf, 1959) and M. Crowley's Pringle and the Lavender Goat (Walck, 1960).   ICB-2

SHILSTONE, Arthur.   Artist and traveler, he has made his
home in West Redding, Connecticut.   Mr. Shilstone has
visited the Far East and South America in addition to
his travels in this country.   Many magazines have published his work including Reader's Digest, Life, and
Sports Illustrated.   The artist has been the recipient of
two awards of excellence presented by the Society of Illustrators.   His drawings can be found in M. Reynolds'
Puerto Rican Patriot (Crowell-Collier, 1969).

SHIMIN, Symeon, 1902- . He was born in Astrakhan, Russia and came to the United States at the age of ten. He studied at Cooper Union and painted in George Luk's studio; however, most of his art training came from studying paintings in the museums of Spain and France. He has painted murals in the Department of Justice building in Washington, D.C. and the United States Post Office building in Tonawanda, New York. He held his first one-man exhibition in 1961. The artist married a sculptor and has lived in New York City. His work includes G. Cretan's All Except Sammy (a Junior Literary Guild selection; Little 1966), B. Schweitzer's One Small Blue Bead (Macmillan, 1965), R. Wilson's Outdoor Wonderland (Lothrop, 1961) and A. Glasgow's Pair of Shoes (Dial, 1971). ICB-2, ICB-3

SHINN, Everett, 1876-1953. He was born in Woodstown, New Jersey, and was educated at Spring Garden Institute in Philadelphia, the Pennsylvania Academy of the Fine Arts, and he also studied art abroad. He began his career as a draftsman in a locomotive works and later became a staff artist on the Philadelphia Press. Mr. Shinn created a mural for the Trenton, New Jersey, City Hall and was a motion picture art director. He was elected an Associate of the National Academy. Prior to his death in 1953, the artist lived in New York City. For young people he illustrated The Everett Shinn Illustrated Edition of the Night Before Christmas, by C. Moore (Winston, 1942) and O. Wilde's The Happy Prince, and Other Tales (Winston, 1940). ICB-1, ICB-2

SHORE, Robert, 1924- . Painter, sculptor, born in New York City. He studied at the Cranbrook Academy of Art in Michigan and at the Art Students League in New York. In 1952 he was awarded a Fulbright Fellowship and in 1966 received the Gold Medal from the Society of Illustrators. He has taught at the School of Visual Arts and has lived in New York City. For children he illustrated E. Clymer's The Big Pile of Dirt (Holt, 1968) and W. Morey's Home Is the North (Dutton, 1967). ICB-3

SHORTALL, Leonard. He was born in Seattle, Washington, attended the University of Washington, and later made his home in Westport, Connecticut. His illustrations have appeared in such national magazines as Farm

Journal and Woman's Day. He has also written and il-
lustrated his own books and worked in advertising. His
drawings can be found in D. Sobol's Encyclopedia Brown
Keeps the Peace (Nelson, 1969) and H. Felton's Pecos
Bill and the Mustang (Prentice-Hall, 1965). ICB-2,
ICB-3

SHULEVITZ, Uri, 1935- . Artist and author, born in War-
saw, Poland. He grew up in Poland, France, and Is-
rael where he studied at the Tel Aviv Academy of Art.
After coming to the United States in 1959, he continued
his studies at the Museum of Art in Brooklyn, New
York. His work has received recognition from the
American Institute of Graphic Arts and the Society of
Illustrators. He married an artist and has lived in
New York City. He was awarded the 1969 Caldecott
Medal for A. Ransome's The Fool of the World and the
Flying Ship (Farrar, 1968). He wrote and illustrated
The Moon in My Room (Harper, 1963) and Soldier and
Tsar in the Forest (Farrar, 1972). Other juvenile
books he illustrated include S. Ish-Kishor's The Carpet
of Solomon (Pantheon, 1966) and M. Stolz's Maximilian's
World (Harper, 1966). ICB-3, ABYP-2

SIBAL, Joseph. Born in Vienna, he came to the United
States when he was quite young. Mr. Sibal studied at
the Art Students League, the National Academy of Design, and the Polytechnic Institute in Brooklyn. Prior
to painting birds, he was an industrial artist. He has
visited zoos throughout the United States and Europe,
and in 1952 his paintings of birds were exhibited in New
York City libraries. They were later published in Life
magazine. For young people he illustrated W. Wise's
Amazing Animals of Latin America (Putnam, 1969) and
Giant Birds and Monsters of the Air (a Junior Literary
Guild selection; Putnam, 1969).

SIBERELL, Anne. She was born in California and attended
UCLA and the Chouinard Art Institute in Los Angeles.
Mrs. Peter Siberell and her family have lived in New
Canaan, Connecticut. In addition to her work as an il-
lustrator, she has been both a print maker and painter.
She has also worked for an architectural firm. For
children she illustrated J. Beatty's A Donkey for a King
(Macmillan, 1966), I. Eastwick's Rainbow over All (Mc-
Kay, 1967) and J. Montgomery's Wrath of Coyote (Mor-
row, 1968).

SIBLEY, Don, 1922- . He was born in Hornell, New York, and later made his home in Roxbury, Connecticut. He completed his education at Pratt Institute in Brooklyn after serving as a pilot in World War II. His career has included advertising and promotion work in addition to children's book illustration. These include R. Burch's Skinny (Viking, 1964), S. Meader's Snow on Blueberry Mountain (Harcourt, 1961), and R. Burch's Tyler, Wilkin, and Skee (Viking, 1963). ICB-3

SIDJAKOV, Nicolas, 1924- . He was born in Riga, Latvia. He attended the École des Beaux Arts in Paris in order to study painting. He has been a free-lance designer and illustrator. He married an American girl in Paris, but they have lived in the United States since 1954. He has had a studio in San Francisco and has lived in Sausalito, California. His first illustrations in children's books appeared in L. N. Baker's adaptation of an old English Christmas carol, The Friendly Beasts (Parnassus, 1957). He also illustrated two books written by R. Robbins: Baboushka and the Three Kings (winner of the 1961 Caldecott Medal; Parnassus, 1960) and The Emperor and the Drummer Boy (Parnassus, 1962). He also illustrated I. Elmer's Lodestone and a Toadstone (Knopf, 1969). ICB-1, ICB-2, ICB-3, ABYP-2

SIEBEL, Fritz (Frederick), 1913- . Artist and designer, born in Vienna, Austria. He studied in Vienna at the Academy of Art. He served in the Czechoslovakian Army for two years before coming to this country. The artist and his family have lived in Rye, New York. Fritz Siebel has been both an industrial designer and commercial artist. He has done television animation and magazines have used his drawings. Most of his book illustrations were done in color, and he has used color separation with his pen and ink designs. For children he illustrated, all for Harper, P. Parish's Amelia Bedelia (1963), M. McClintock's David and the Giant (1960), and C. Bonsall's Tell Me Some More (1961). ICB-3

SILVERMAN, Burton Philip, 1928- . Illustrator, painter, born in Brooklyn, New York. Burt Silverman studied at the Art Students League and at Columbia University in New York. He has worked in a studio apartment overlooking the Hudson River in New York City. For young people he illustrated P. Bentley's <u>The Adventures of Tom Leigh</u> (a Junior Literary Guild selection; Doubleday, 1966), and S. Hirsch's <u>Globe for the Space Age</u> (Viking, 1963). ICB-3

SILVERMAN, Melvin Frank, 1931-1966. Illustrator, painter, teacher. Born in Denver, Colorado, Mel Silverman studied and graduated from the Chicago Art Institute. Prior to his death at the age of 35, he worked as a display designer in New York City. He also taught graphics in Israel at Ein Harod. His paintings can be found in permanent collections in museums and universities. For children he illustrated A. Sondergaard's <u>My First Geography of the Panama Canal</u> (Little, 1960). He also wrote and illustrated <u>Hymie's Fiddle</u> (World, 1960). ICB-3

SIMON, Howard, 1903- . Born in New York City, this artist and painter has lived in the West, Ozark Mountains, and in France. He married writer Mina Lewiton and has resided in Stanfordville, New York. Mr. Simon received his education at the University of the State of New York and the National Academy of Design. He also studied in Paris at the Académie Julien. He has taught art at New York University. His work has been exhibited in numerous museums and in private collections. The artist has illustrated classics and designed books. For young people he illustrated D. Boehm's <u>Blazer the Bear</u> (Sterling, 1953) and M. Lewiton's <u>Faces Looking Up</u> (Harper, 1960). ICB-1, ICB-2, ICB-3

SIMONT, Marc, 1915- . Illustrator-author, born in Paris. He studied in Paris at the André Lhote School, Académie Julien, and the Académie Ranson. He also studied in New York at the National Academy of Design. Marc Simont's work has included magazine illustrations, portraits, and visual aids for the Army. Mr. Simont and his family have lived in West Cornwall, Connecticut, and in New York City. In 1957 he received the Caldecott Medal for his illustrations in <u>A Tree Is Nice</u>, written by J. M. Udry (Harper, 1956). He also illustrated J. Schwartz's <u>The Earth Is Your Spaceship</u> (McGraw, 1963) and J. Chenery's <u>Wolfie</u> (Harper, 1969). ICB-2, ICB-3, ABYP-2

SLOBODKIN, Louis, 1903- . Sculptor, illustrator, author.

He grew up in Albany, New York and studied at the
Beaux Arts Institute of Design in New York. He has
illustrated children's books for various authors, including James Thurber's Many Moons (Harcourt, 1943),
the winner of the 1944 Caldecott Medal. Mr. Slobodkin married Florence Gersh. Juvenile contributions
include Adventures of Arab (Macmillan, 1946), Amiable
Giant (Macmillan, 1955), Circus, April 1st, (Macmillan,
1953), Dinny and Danny (Macmillan, 1951), Excuse Me!
Certainly! (Vanguard, 1959), Hustle and Bustle (Macmillan, 1948), Space Ship under the Apple Tree (Macmillan, 1952), and Wilbur the Warrior (Vanguard,
1972). ICB-1, ICB-2, ICB-3, ABYP-2

SMITH, Alvin, 1933- . He was born in Gary, Indiana, and
graduated from the State University of Iowa. He received his master's degree from the University of Illinois and did additional work at Teachers College, Columbia University. Atlanta University Permanent Collection of Contemporary American Art and the Dayton
Art Institute had his paintings in their collections. He
has taught art in Kansas City, Kansas, Dayton, Ohio
and at Queens College of the City of New York University. He and his wife Pauline, a teacher, have lived
in New York City. In addition to illustrating the 1965
Newbery Award winner, M. Wojciechowska's Shadow of
a Bull (Atheneum, 1964), he also illustrated F. Bon-
ham's The Nitty Gritty (Dutton, 1968) and M. Wojciechowska's Odyssey of Courage: Cabeza de Vaca (Atheneum, 1965). ICB-3

SMITH, Lawrence Beall, 1909- . Born in Washington,
D.C., he grew up in Indiana and Illinois. He received
his education in Chicago at the Art Institute and the
University of Chicago. He married an artist and has
lived in Cross River, New York. The artist served
as an artist war correspondent during World War II.
For boys and girls he illustrated O. Nash's Girls Are
Silly (Watts, 1962), W. Hays' Mary's Star (Holt, 1968),
and P. Horgan's Toby and the Nighttime (Ariel Books,
1963). ICB-3

SMITH, Ned. Artist, photographer. His illustrations have
appeared in many magazines in addition to books. Ned
Smith has also been a natural history writer. He has
made his home in Pennsylvania. For young people he
illustrated G. Sand's Iron-tail (Scribner's, 1971).

SMITH, William Arthur, 1918- . Born in Toledo, Ohio, he
later studied at the University of Toledo and Toledo
Museum School of Design. He also attended Keane's
Art School, Académie de la Grande Chaumière and
École des Beaux Arts in Paris. During World War II,
he served in the Army in China. He has worked in
oil, watercolor, and lithography, and his paintings have
been exhibited both in this country and abroad. Mr.
Smith has served as President of the American Watercolor Society and has been associated with the National
Academy of Design. He has divided his time between
a home in New York City and Bucks County, Pennsylvania. For young people he illustrated S. Lim's More
Folk Tales from China (Day, 1948). ICB-1, ICB-2

SNYDER, Jerome, 1916- . Art director and illustrator,
born in New York City. He married an artist, and
they have lived in Brooklyn. He has done magazine illustrations and worked in advertising. Jerome Snyder
has been Art Director for Scientific American magazine
and prior to this was Art Director for Sports Illustrated. The artist has been the recipient of many
awards from New York's Art Directors Club and the
Society of Illustrators. For young people he illustrated P. Ressner's Jerome (Parents' magazine, 1967),
G. Kirtland's One Day in Elizabethan England (Harcourt,
1962), R. Silverberg's Scientists and Scoundrels (Crowell, 1965), and A. Rand's Umbrellas, Hats, and Wheels
(Harcourt, 1961). ICB-3

SOFIA see ZEIGER, Sophia

SOLBERT, Ronni G., 1925- . She was born in Washington,
D. C., grew up in Chicago and Rochester, New York,
and later graduated from Vassar. She studied at the
Cranbrook Academy of Art and received a Fulbright
Fellowship to India. She has taught art to children and
worked for the International Red Cross Conference in
Stockholm. In 1959 she had a one-woman show at the
Museum of Modern Art. Her home has been in New
York City. Books which she illustrated for young
people include three by J. Merrill, Black Sheep (Pan-
theon, 1969), The Pushcart War (Scott, 1964), and The
Superlative Horse (a Junior Literary Guild selection;
Scott, 1961), and M. Neville's Woody and Me (Pantheon,
1966). ICB-2, ICB-3

SOMMERSCHIELD, Rose. In 1969 Mrs. Bengt Sommers-
    chield won a Grand Prix for Animation at the Nyon,
    Switzerland, Film Festival for her film "You Can."
    She has also been the recipient of numerous awards
    from the New Jersey and New York Art Directors
    Clubs, the Hollywood Radio and TV Society, and the So-
    ciety of Illustrators. For young people she illustrated
    E. Bloome's Dogs Don't Belong on Beds (Doubleday,
    1971).

SOPER, Eileen Alice, 1905- . She was born in Enfield,
    Middlesex, England, the daughter of the noted illustra-
    tor, etcher, and engraver, the late George Soper. Her
    home has been in Welwyn, Hertfordshire, the place of
    her childhood. Miss Soper was tutored by her father
    and received no formal art training. Her work has
    been exhibited at the Royal Academy in London. In ad-
    dition to book and magazine illustration, Eileen Soper
    has written books for both children and adults. For
    boys and girls she wrote and illustrated Dormouse
    Awake (Macmillan, 1948). ICB-1, ICB-2

SOREL, Edward, 1929- . He was born in New York City
    where he later studied at Cooper Union. He has done
    caricature and political satire, and his work has ap-
    peared in the Realist and Ramparts. One of the found-
    ers of Push Pin Studios, he has also been a staff ar-
    tist for Esquire and CBS. He has received awards
    from the American Institute of Graphic Arts and the
    Art Directors Club of New York. He married Nancy
    Caldwell, and they have lived in Carmel, New York.
    His work includes J. Cowley's The Duck in the Gun (a
    Junior Literary Guild selection; Doubleday, 1969), N.
    Sherman's Gwendolyn the Miracle Hen (Golden, 1961),
    W. Miller's King Carlo of Capri (Harcourt, 1958), and
    W. Cole's What's Good for a Five-Year-Old (Holt, 1969).
    ICB-3

SOTOMAYOR, Antonio, 1904- . He was born and raised in
    Bolivia. He studied at Escuela de Bellas Artes in La
    Paz and at the Hopkins Institute of Art (California
    School of Fine Arts) in San Francisco where he later
    made his home. He has worked in terra cotta includ-
    ing an exhibit for the 1939 San Francisco World's Fair.
    The artist also created a drawing for the tenth anniver-
    sary of the United Nations held in San Francisco's Cow
    Palace. For young people he illustrated Q. Hawkins'
    The Best Birthday (Doubleday, 1954). ICB-2

SPIER, Peter, 1927- . He was born in Amsterdam, Holland, where he attended Rijksakademie voor Beeldende Kunsten. He served in the Royal Netherlands Navy and later was junior editor of Elsevier's Weekly in Holland. In 1951 he came to Houston, Texas, where Elsevier's had a branch office. His book The Fox Went out on a Chilly Night (Doubleday, 1961) was runner-up for the Caldecott Medal in 1962. Mr. Spier became an American citizen and has lived in Port Washington, Long Island, New York. For Doubleday he illustrated Crash! Bang! Boom! (1972), L. Davis' Island City (a Junior Literary Guild selection; 1961), London Bridge Is Falling Down! (1967), and To Market! To Market! (1967). ICB-2, ICB-3

STAHL, Benjamin Albert, 1910- . Ben Stahl was born in Chicago and later made his home in Weston, Connecticut, and Sarasota, Florida. He received a scholarship to the Chicago Art Institute when he was 12. He has created illustrations for magazines, adult book jackets, and children's books. His work "Way of the Cross" is in the permanent exhibit of Florida's Sarasota Museum of the Cross. He has painted in oil or casein. Mr. Stahl lived in Amsterdam for three years when he served as Director of Art Education for the Famous Artists Schools International. For young people he illustrated M. Sachs' A Pocket Full of Seeds (Doubleday, 1973). ICB-3

STANDON, Edward Cyril, 1929- . Artist and cartoonist, born in London. He later attended St. Martin's School of Art. He has been a musician and worked in animation in addition to his work as a book illustrator. He has illustrated many of his wife, Anna's stories, which include Flower for Ambrose (Delacorte, 1967), and The Tin Can Tortoise (Coward, 1965). ICB-3

STANLEY, Diana, 1909- . Born in London, she grew up in Gloucester where she later attended Cheltenham Ladies College. She also studied in London at the Regent Street Polytechnic and at the Byam Shaw School of Drawing and Painting. The artist married Professor C. A. Pannett and resided in Basingstoke, Hampshire. A hand injury she received during World War II restricted her art work in later years, but she learned to paint with her left hand. She has been a draftsman, etcher, teacher, and wood engraver in addition to an illustrator.

Her drawings can be found in M. Norton's The Borrowers (Dent, 1952). ICB-2

STEIG, William, 1907- . New Yorker cartoonist, author, born in New York City. Mr. Steig's family have been artists. His daughter Lucy has been a painter, and Jeremy has been a jazz flautist. The Steigs have lived in Greenwich Village. Roland the Minstrel Pig (Windmill, 1968), was his first book for children. He also created Amos and Boris (Farrar, 1971), CDB! (Simon, and Schuster, 1968), and Sylvester and the Magic Pebble (1970 Caldecott Medal winner; Windmill, 1969).

STEIN, Harve, 1904- . Born in Chicago, Illinois, where he later studied at the Art Institute. He also attended the Académie Julien in Paris and the Art Students League in New York. Mr. Stein has been head of the Illustrations Department of the Rhode Island School of Design. His home has been in Noank, Connecticut. He illustrated J. Tottle's Benjamin Franklin: First Great American (Houghton, 1958), and S. Garst's Custer: Fighter of the Plains (Messner, 1944). ICB-2

STEINBERG, David Michael. Artist, teacher, musician. He attended Harvard and Columbia Universities, and the Université de Paris. Some of his illustrations have been done in collaboration with his father, Isador Steinberg. Chemistry and astronomy have been his hobbies, and he has worked in research laboratories in biochemistry. In addition to his art work, David Steinberg has taught French literature and has written songs. He has belonged to Phi Beta Kappa and Mensa. For children he illustrated D. Halacy's Bionics (Holiday, 1965).

STEPTOE, John, 1950- . Painter, author. When he wrote and illustrated Stevie (Harper, 1969), he said: "I am a painter and not yet an artist. I don't just happen to be black I also happen to have the ambition of being a fine painter. This is the beginning of my life and this book is one of the things that happened to me so far." John Steptoe was born in Brooklyn. His picture books are filled with vivid, colorful, realistic illustrations and written in "ghetto English." These books include: Train Ride (Harper, 1971), Uptown (Harper, 1970). He also wrote and illustrated Birthday (Holt, 1972).

STEVENS, Mary E., 1920-1966. She was born and grew up

in Bar Harbor, Maine. She received her education at
Boston's Vesper George School of Art and the Art Students League in New York. In addition to illustrating
books for children, Miss Stevens also illustrated stories for Story Parade and Child Life magazines. Puppetry, sports, and the theatre were her special interests. Prior to her death in 1966 at the age of 46,
Miss Stevens lived in Manhattan. Juvenile books she
illustrated include E. Guilfoile's Have You Seen My
Brother? (Follett, 1962), B. Cleary's The Real Hole
(Morrow, 1960), E. Parkinson's Terrible Troubles of
Rupert Piper (Abingdon, 1963), and B. Cleary's Two
Dog Biscuits (Morrow, 1961). ICB-2, ICB-3

STEWART, Arvis L. Born in Texas, he later made his
home in New York City. He attended the Texas Tech-
nological College in Lubbock where he studied art and
design. The artist has enjoyed carpentry, fishing, and
nature as special interests in addition to printmaking
and the fine arts. He illustrated R. Hutchins' Cicada
(Addisonian, 1971), and C. Zolotow's The New Friend
(Abelard, 1968).

STEWART, Charles William, 1915- . Born in the Philippine Islands, his early years were spent in Scotland and
England. He later made his home in London. Charles
Stewart received his art training at Radley College and
the Byam Shaw School of Drawing and Painting where
he later became Senior Master in 1955 after being an
art instructor. Mr. Stewart has been interested in
Oriental art. His work has been exhibited at the Royal
Academy. The artist has belonged to the Art Workers'
Guild and the Society of Industrial Artists. For young
people he illustrated B. Picard's The Faun and the
Woodcutter's Daughter (a Junior Literary Guild selec-
tion; Criterion, 1964), and The Lady of the Linden
Tree (Criterion, 1962). ICB-2

STIRNWEIS, Shannon. He was born in Portland, Oregon and
studied at the Los Angeles Art Center School. He once
served abroad with the United States Army as an illustrator of instructional materials. Mr. Stirnweis has
made his home in New York City. His work includes:
L. Waller's Book to Begin on Numbers (Holt, 1960);
M. Besser's Cat Book (Holiday, 1967), C. Joy's Getting to Know Tanganyika (Coward-McCann, 1962), S.
Gudmundson's Getting to Know the British West Indies
(Coward-McCann, 1962).

STOBART, Ralph. A resident of London, England, he has
    been greatly interested in the education of preschool
    children. In addition to being a free-lance artist, Mr.
    Stobart has done volunteer work in an English nursery
    school. The first book which he illustrated for boys
    and girls was L. Ogle and T. Thoburn's <u>A B See</u> (Mc-
    Graw, 1973).

STOBBS, William, 1914- . He was born in South Shields,
    England, and has lived in Richmond, Surrey, England.
    He studied at King Edward VI School of Art and re-
    ceived both a B.A. and M.A. degree in the History of
    Art from Durham University. Prior to being Principal
    of Maidstone College of Art, Mr. Stobbs was associ-
    ated with the London School of Printing and Graphic
    Arts as Head of the Design Department. He has be-
    longed to the Society of Industrial Artists. He illus-
    trated R. Syme's <u>Amerigo Vespucci</u> (Morrow, 1969) and
    A. Chekhov's <u>Kashtanka</u> (Walck, 1961), and R. Syme's
    <u>Walter Raleigh</u> (Morrow, 1962). ICB-2, ICB-3

STONE, David K. This artist has created both illustrations
    and book jackets for textbooks and stories. He grew
    up in Oregon and graduated from the University of Ore-
    gon at Eugene. He also attended the Art Center in Los
    Angeles and studied in Mexico. For young people he il-
    lustrated M. Jones' <u>The Bible Story of the Creation</u>
    (Rand-McNally, 1967) and J. Shore's <u>What's the Matter
    with Wakefield?</u> (a Junior Literary Guild selection;
    Abingdon, 1974).

STONE, Helen, 1904- . Born in Englewood, New Jersey,
    she attended the Art Students League and the New York
    School of Fine and Applied Art. She also studied in
    Paris. She has been a teacher and worked in the field
    of commercial art in addition to illustrating books for
    young people. Mrs. Stone has traveled in Europe and
    the West Indies and has made her home in East Hamp-
    ton, Long Island, New York. Her work includes A.
    Bennett's <u>Little Witch</u> (Lippincott, 1953), P. McGinley's
    <u>Plain Princess</u> (Lippincott, 1945) and F. Branley's <u>Snow
    Is Falling</u> (Crowell, 1963). ICB-1, ICB-2, ICB-3

STOVER, Jo Ann. She grew up on a farm near Peterborough,
    New Hampshire, and attended the New England and Mas-
    sachusetts Schools of Art. She married painter Paul
    Pollaro and has lived on Cape Cod and in New York

City.   Jo Ann Stover has been an art teacher, painter,
illustrator, and author.   Her work has been exhibited
in many galleries.   For boys and girls she illustrated
B. Horvath's The Cheerful Quiet (a Junior Literary
Guild selection; Watts, 1969) and E. Evans' That Lucky
Mrs. Plucky (McKay, 1961).

STUBIS, Tālivaldis.   He was born in Riga, Latvia, and
studied art at the University of Wisconsin.   His work
has appeared in the advertisements of the Broadway
shows, "Camelot" and "Funny Girl."   He also drew an
advertisement for the movie "Night of the Iguana."   He
and his wife Patricia have lived in New York City.
His work includes D. Foster's A Pocketful of Seasons
(a Junior Literature Guild selection; Lothrop, 1961),
R. Wyler's Prove It! (Harper, 1963), and R. Wyler's
Real Science Riddles (Hastings, 1972).

SUBA, Susanne, 1913- .   She was born in Budapest, Hungary, grew up in Europe and the United States, and has
lived in New York City.   She has also traveled and
lived in Europe.   She received her education in Brooklyn, New York at the Friends School and Pratt Institute.   She was a recipient of a grant for painting from
the Michael Karolyi Memorial Foundation.   Miss Suba
has received many awards for her work in advertising
including the Medal Award presented by the Art Directors Club of Chicago.   Many of her books have been
listed in the American Institute of Graphic Arts Fifty
Books of the Year Exhibits, and her art work has been
exhibited in many museums.   For children she illustrated V. Haviland's Favorite Fairy Tales Told in Germany (Little, 1959), M. Vance's A Flower from Dinah
(Dutton, 1962), and D. Johnson's Su An, (Follett, 1968).
ICB-1, ICB-2, ICB-3

SWAYNE, Zoa Lourana (Shaw), 1905- .   Born in Torrington, Wyoming, part of her childhood was spent in Washington including a memorable Christmas on Puget Sound's
Whidby Island.   Later she lived in Idaho on a wheat
ranch.   Mrs. Swayne, a teacher, received her education at Albion State Normal in Idaho and the University
of Idaho.   Married to attorney Sam Swayne, her home
has been in Orofino, Idaho.   She illustrated her husband Sam Swayne's book based on a tale told by his
father and grandfather, entitled Great-Grandfather in
the Honey Tree (Viking, 1949).   ICB-2

SWEAT, Lynn. Mr. Sweat spent his boyhood in Nederland,
Texas and later made his home in Weston, Connecticut. In the 1966 Society of Illustrators' Annual Show in
New York he was the recipient of an Award of Excellence. He has also received medals in graphic arts in
both the West and Southwest. His work has appeared in
J. Seidelman's The Rub Book (Crowell-Collier, 1968),
and P. Parish's Sheet Magic (Macmillan, 1971).

SWENEY, Frederic, 1912- . He was born in Hollidaysburg,
Pennsylvania, and studied at the Cleveland Institute of
Art. He has worked in advertising and also as an artist for the Cleveland Press. He has taught art for a
number of years at the Ringling School of Art in Sarasota, Florida. For young people he illustrated F. Russell's Frightened Hare (1966), and Hawk in the Sky
1965), both for Holt. ICB-3

SZEKERES, Cyndy. She was born in Bridgeport, Connecticut, and graduated from Pratt Institute in Brooklyn,
New York. She married artist Gennaro Prozzo and
has lived in Brooklyn Heights. She illustrated P. Parish's Jumper Goes to School (Simon, 1969), and A.
Holl's Moon Mouse (Random, 1969).

SZYK, Arthur, 1894-1951. Born in Lodz, Poland, he studied art in Cracow and at the Académie Julien and
École des Beaux Arts in Paris. In 1940 he came to
the United States and became an American citizen. His
paintings on George Washington hang in the Roosevelt
Museum at Hyde Park, New York. He has also illustrated for magazines including war cartoons which
were published during World War II. He was married
to Julia Likerman. Prior to his death, Mr. Szyk lived
in Connecticut. He illustrated an edition of Andersen's
Fairy Tales transl. by E. Lucas (Grosset, 1945).
ICB-2

-T-

TAIT, Agnes, 1897- . Born in New York City, she later
studied at the National Academy of Design. Her work
has included murals and the painting of portraits in
addition to the illustrating of books. The artist's lithographs have been included in the collections of the Library of Congress, Yale University, and the New York

Public Library. Her home has been in Santa Fe, New
Mexico. She illustrated J. Spyri's Heidi (Lippincott,
1948). ICB-2

TAIT, Douglas. Artist, teacher. He has been on the faculty of Simon Fraser University in British Columbia.
Mr. Tait has contributed illustrations for many of the
university's publications. For young people he illustrated C. Harris' Secret in the Stalakum Wild (a Junior Literary Guild selection; Atheneum, 1972).

TEE-VAN, Helen (Damrosch). Artist, muralist, native New
Yorker. She married Dr. John Tee-Van, General Director of New York's Zoological Park and Aquarium.
Her illustrations have appeared in scientific publications
and in both Collier's and Britannica Encyclopedias.
Well-known for her illustrations of animals, flowers,
and undersea life, Mrs. Tee-Van has served as artist
on several expeditions with the Tropical Research Department of the Zoological Society of New York. In
addition to painting murals for zoos and museums, she
has exhibited her work in New York at the Museum of
Natural History and the Metropolitan Museum. For
children she illustrated C. Pope's Reptiles Round the
World (Knopf, 1957) and A. Milotte's Story of an Alas-
kan Grizzly Bear (Knopf, 1969). She also wrote and
illustrated Insects Are Where You Find Them (Knopf,
1963).

TENGGREN, Gustaf, 1896- . Artist and painter, born in
Sweden. He came to the United States in 1920
and has lived in West Southport, Maine. He received
his education in Sweden at the Valand School of Fine
Arts in Gothenburg and the Slojdforeningens School.
He has illustrated books for children both in this country and in Scandinavia. His work has been exhibited
abroad, and he has traveled and painted in Mexico,
Nova Scotia, and Yucatan. His hobbies have included
boating, chess, and fishing. Mr. Tenggren has received many awards and honors for his book illustrations. For children he illustrated K. Jackson's Pi-
rates, Ships and Sailors (Simon and Schuster, 1950),
O. Wheeler's Sing for Christmas (Dutton, 1943), and
K. Jackson's Tenggren's Cowboys and Indians (Simon
and Schuster, 1948). ICB-1, ICB-2

TENNIEL, John, 1820-1914. English cartoonist and

illustrator, born in London. For nearly fifty years
John Tenniel contributed political cartoons to <u>Punch</u>.
He became well-known for his book illustrations for
children, especially Lewis Carroll's <u>Alice's Adven-</u>
<u>tures in Wonderland</u> (Macmillan, 1865) and <u>Through</u>
<u>the Looking Glass and What Alice Saw There</u> (Macmil-
lan, 1872). (Mr. Tenniel was listed in "A Bibliogra-
phy of Illustrators," p. 441, ICB-1.)

THOLLANDER, Earl Gustave, 1922- . Artist, painter,
born in Kingsburg, California, he grew up in San Francisco. He received his education at San Francisco
City College and the University of California at Berkeley. The artist also studied at the Art League of California and at San Francisco's Art Institute and Academy of Art. He began his career in the advertising
field and also worked as a newspaper artist. Mr.
Thollander has enjoyed travel and has made "drawing
trips" to Mexico, Europe, and the Orient. His home
has been in San Francisco. His book illustrations include R. Franchere's <u>Cesar Chavez</u> (Crowell, 1970),
P. Martin's <u>Jump Frog Jump</u> (a Junior Literary Guild
selection; Putnam, 1965), and B. Ritchie's <u>To Catch a</u>
<u>Mongoose</u> (Parnassus Press, 1963). ICB-3

THOMAS, Glen. He was born in Sterling, Illinois. He has
always been interested in railroads and has traveled on
many types of trains in various countries. Mr. Thomas has specialized in all types of transportation in his
work as an illustrator. For your people he illustrated
S. Farrington's <u>Giants of the Rails</u> (Garden City, 1944).

THOMPSON, Mozelle. Artist and teacher, born in Pittsburgh,
Pennsylvania. He attended the Carnegie Institute of
Technology (now Carnegie-Mellon University) and the
Art Students League in New York. He also studied in
Paris and New York on a scholarship at the Parsons
School of Design. In addition to book illustration, Mr.
Thompson has worked in display and fashion design.
He has also been an instructor at the Fashion Institute
of Technology. His book illustrations first appeared in
S. Yezback's <u>Pumpkinseeds</u> (a Junior Literary Guild se-
lection; Bobbs-Merrill, 1969). He also illustrated J.
Johnson's <u>Lift Every Voice and Sing</u> (Hawthorn, 1970).

THOMPSON, Ralph. The son of a farmer, this British artist was born in Thorner, Yorkshire. He later made

his home in Cookham, Berkshire. He attended both
the Leeds and Royal Colleges of Art in England. Life
in the country provided material for his drawings, illustrations, and lithographs. The artist has endeavored
to create authentic pictures of animals and became a
Fellow of the Zoological Society of London. For children he illustrated G. Durrell's The New Noah (Viking,
1964). ICB-2

THOMSON, Arline K., 1912- . She was born in Lawrence,
Massachusetts, and later studied at the Massachusetts
School of Art in Boston and Columbia University. The
first book she illustrated was R. Woody's Student
Dancer (Houghton, 1951). She married a University of
Maine professor and has lived in Old Town, Maine.
Besides art, she has been interested in the ballet. Her
work includes: R. Woody's Janey and the Summer
Dance Camp (Knopf, 1956), and A. Molloy's Secret of
the Old Salem Desk (a Junior Literary Guild selection;
Ariel Books, 1955). ICB-2

THORNE, Diana, 1894- . Canadian artist and etcher, she
was born in Winnipeg, Manitoba. She later married
Arthur North and made her home in Philadelphia. She
attended art schools abroad (London, Germany, France
and Scotland). In addition to book illustration, Diana
Thorne has done portraits, sculpture, and etchings.
She also illustrated and designed magazine covers. Her
work has been exhibited in galleries and museums
throughout this country. She has belonged to the Royal
Society of Painters and Sculptors, the Philadelphia Art
Alliance, the Boston Arts Club, and the National Soci-
ety of Women Painters and Sculptors. She illustrated
B. Shurtleff's Awol the Courier (Bobbs-Merrill, 1951),
M. Henry's Little Fellow (Winston, 1945); she also
wrote and illustrated Dogs (Saalfield, 1932). ICB-1,
ICB-2

TOLFORD, Joshua, 1909- . He was born in Thorp, Wisconsin, and studied at the Layton School of Art in Milwaukee and the School of the Museum of Fine Arts in
Boston. He also studied under Anthony Thieme in
Rockport, Massachusetts. He and his artist wife have
belonged to the Folly Cove Designers and have made
their home in Rockport. His work includes H. Beatty's
Blitz (Houghton, 1961), C. Jackson's Bud Plays Junior
High Football (Hastings, 1957), H. Beatty's Trumper

(Houghton, 1963), and R. Chase's Wicked John and the Devil (Houghton, 1951). ICB-2

TOMES, Margot Ladd, 1917- . Artist, designer, born in Yonkers, New York. She studied art at Pratt Institute in Brooklyn. Her cousins are author-illustrator William Pène du Bois, designer Raoul Pène du Bois, and painter Guy Pène du Bois. Her sister Jacqueline has also illustrated children's books. In addition to book illustration, Margot Tomes has designed fabrics, wallpaper, and book jackets. Her home has been in New York City. For young people she illustrated A. Fisher's In the Woods, in the Meadow, in the Sky (Scribner's, 1965) V. Day's Landslide! transl. from French by Margaret Morgan (Coward-McCann, 1964), and L. Skorpen's Plenty for Three (Coward, 1971). ICB-3

TOPOLSKI, Feliks, 1907- . Artist and muralist, he was born in Warsaw, Poland. He studied in Warsaw at the Mikolaj Rey School and the Academy of Art. He also attended the Officers' School of Artillery Reserve in Poland. In 1935 he traveled to England to create pictures for the Jubilee and later became the Official Polish War Artist of Poland (in exile) during World War II. Mr. Topolski became a British subject in 1947 and has lived in London. One of his many murals "Cavalcade of Commonwealth" can be found in Singapore's Victoria Memorial Hall. His work has been exhibited in numerous countries and are in permanent collections of museums and galleries. For children he illustrated A. Bontemps' Lonesome Boy (a reissue; Houghton, 1967). ICB-2

TORREY, Helen, 1901- . She was born in Cambridge, Massachusetts, and grew up in England. She studied at the Liverpool School of Art and the San Francisco School of Fine Arts. After a publisher granted her permission to illustrate several books, she moved from California to New York in order to make her home. Later she lived on Long Island in Setauket where she has made and sold ceramic jewelry in addition to illustrating books. Her drawings can be found in G. Ceder's Ethan, the Shepherd Boy (Abingdon, 1948). ICB-2

TORREY, Marjorie, 1899- . She was born in New York City and later studied art there at the National Academy of Design and at the Art Students League. She

began her career drawing cartoons for tapestries which
was followed by work as a magazine illustrator. Later
the artist lived in California with her husband, writer
Roy Chanslor and devoted her time to drawing children. Her work includes Favorite Nursery Songs,
comp. by P. Ohanian (Random, 1956) and O. Wheeler's
Sing in Praise (Dutton, 1946). ICB-2

TOSCHIK, Larry, 1922- . Born in Milwaukee, Wisconsin,
the artist later made his home in Phoenix, Arizona.
He received his art training at both the Layton and
Risko Art Schools and also attended the Famous Artists
Schools. His early interest in nature and history combined with frequent visits to the Milwaukee Public Museum led to his career as an artist. His drawings can
be found in M. Magoon's Ojibway Drums (Longmans,
1955). ICB-2

TOTO, Joe. Illustrator and art director, born in Brooklyn,
New York. He attended the Parsons School of Design
and graduated from New York University. Joe Toto
has been associated with an advertising agency as an
art director. He has traveled throughout the United
States and has lived in New York in Croton-on-Hudson
with his family. His first book illustrations can be
found in K. Mandry's How to Make Elephant Bread
(a Junior Literary Guild selection; Pantheon, 1972).

TOWNSEND, Lee, 1895- . He grew up in the midwest and
later studied at the Chicago Art Institute and Beaux
Arts, New York. Prior to illustrating books for children, Mr. Townsend illustrated for the magazine
Youth's Companion. The artist has been especially interested in drawing horses and once owned a thorough-
bred. His home was near Milford, New Jersey. His
work includes J. Baumann's Idaho Sprout (Morrow,
1950), and F. Frost's Maple Sugar for Windy Foot
(McGraw, 1950). ICB-2

TOWNSEND, Richard F. He grew up in Mexico, served
three years in Germany with the U.S. Army, and later
obtained a master's degree in Latin American art history. The artist also studied in Peru on a Fulbright
Scholarship where he did research and drawings of both
colonial Spanish and American art. For children he illustrated E. Credle's Little Pest Pico (Nelson, 1969).

TRESILIAN, Cecil Stuart, 1891- . Art instructor and illustrator, he was born in Bristol, England. He studied at the Regent Street Polytechnic School and attended the Royal College of Art on a Royal Exhibition Scholarship. In the past he has served as Master of the Art Workers' Guild and as President of the Society of Graphic Artists. He has also belonged to the Savage Club. His home has been in Winslow near Bletchley Bucks, England. The War Museum in London has his drawings in its collection which he made as a prisoner of war during the first World War. For children Stuart Tresilian illustrated E. Blyton's Castle of Adventure (Macmillan, 1946) and Circus of Adventure (St. Martin's Press, 1953). ICB-1, ICB-2, ICB-3

TRIER, Walter, 1890-1951. The artist was born in Prague, Czechoslovakia, where he later studied at its art school. He also attended the Munich Academy of Art. Although he was not encouraged to become an artist at art school, Mr. Trier pursued his dream and created illustrations, murals, and paintings. He began illustrating books in Berlin, and he had exhibitions of his work in Edinburgh and London. He illustrated Baron Munchhausen, retold by E. Kästner; transl. by R. and C. Winston (Messner, 1957). ICB-1, ICB-2

TRIPP, Wallace. Born in Boston, Massachusetts, he studied graphic arts at the Boston Museum School. He later worked toward obtaining a master's degree in English from the University of New Hampshire. In addition to art, his interests have included classical music and aviation. He has lived in Hill Center and Hancock, New Hampshire. For boys and girls he illustrated F. Holman's The Holiday Rat, and the Utmost Mouse (Norton, 1969).

TROY, Hugh, 1906-1964. Artist and muralist, he was born in Ithaca, New York, where he later attended Cornell University. He served as a Captain in the 21st Bomber Command during World War II. Prior to his death on July 7, 1964, the artist lived in Garrison, New York, and Washington, D.C. In addition to his art career, Hugh Troy also was a writer. For young people he illustrated R. Sawyer's Enchanted Schoolhouse (a Junior Literary Guild selection; Viking, 1956). ICB-1, ICB-2, ICB-3

TROYER, Johannes, 1902- . Born in Austria (following
     World War I this particular region became part of
     Italy), he studied there and in Germany. He has been
     a calligrapher and illustrator for American, Swiss, and
     German publishers. He designed several postage
     stamps for the principality of Liechtenstein and has al-
     so designed type faces. Mr. Troyer came to the
     United States in 1949 and lived in New Rochelle, New
     York. He returned to Europe to make his home in
     1961. His work includes M. Mason's Baby Jesus (Mac-
     millan, 1959), A. Baker's The Golden Lynx and Other
     Tales (Lippincott, 1960), and W. Cole's Poems for Sea-
     sons and Celebrations (World, 1961). ICB-2, ICB-3

TUNNICLIFFE, Charles Frederick, 1901- . British artist
     and farmer. Born in Langley, East Cheshire, he later
     made his home in Bodorgan, Anglesey, Wales. He at-
     tended both the Macclesfield and Manchester Schools of
     Art and London's Royal College of Art. His early days
     spent on the farm provided authentic background in later
     years for his art work. Charles Tunnicliffe has worked
     in oil and watercolor and has done wood engraving and
     etching. For children he illustrated H. Williamson's
     Tarka the Otter (Watts, 1964). ICB-2

TURKLE, Brinton Cassaday, 1915- . Artist, designer,
     writer, born in Alliance, Ohio. He studied at Carnegie
     Institute of Technology in Pittsburgh, Pennsylvania, be-
     fore attending art school in Boston. After further
     study at Chicago's Institute of Design, Mr. Turkle be-
     gan his career in book illustration in Santa Fe, New
     Mexico. He later made his home in New York City.
     His main interest has been the theater, and he has
     been both an actor and director. He has worked in ad-
     vertising, and his theatrical caricatures have appeared
     in newspapers. He has also been the author of sever-
     al children's books. Juvenile books which he wrote
     and illustrated include: Adventures of Obadiah (Viking,
     1972), The Magic of Millicent Musgrave (a Junior Lit-
     erary Guild selection; Viking, 1967), and Obadiah the
     Bold (Viking, 1965). He also illustrated M. Farquhar's
     Indian Children of America (Holt, 1964). ICB-3

-U-V-

ULREICH, Nura Woodson, 1899-1950. Her pseudonym is

Nura. An artist, sculptor, and teacher, she was born in Kansas City, Missouri, where she later attended the Art Institute. She also studied in Chicago at the Academy of Fine Arts and in New York at the Art Students League. After her marriage to painter Buk Ulreich, she studied painting and sculpture in Europe. In addition to her art career, Nura Ulreich has been a writer and lithographer. Her work has been exhibited in various museums in this country. For children she used her pseudonym to write and illustrate The Kitten Who Listened (Harper, 1950). ICB-1, ICB-2

UNGERMANN, Arne, 1902- . He was born in Odense, Denmark. His early art training was in lithography, but he studied other art forms in Germany, Austria, and France. His career began in the advertising department of a Copenhagen newspaper, and he later became associated with this same newspaper's Sunday supplement as an illustrator. The artist's home has been in Copenhagen. For young people he illustrated J. Sigsgaard's Nils All Alone (Oxford, 1947). ICB-2

VALLI see VAN DE BOVENCAMP, Valli

VALPY, Judith. She was born in Malaya in Southeast Asia. Judith Valpy later returned to England with her family. Upon her return, she studied art in London. She has illustrated D. Ross' Letters from Foxy (Pantheon, 1968) and Yeats' Running to Paradise, ed. by K. Crossley-Holland (Macmillan, 1968).

VAN ABBE, Salaman, 1883-1955. He was born in Holland and received his education in London, Amsterdam, and Paris. Later he made his home in Putney, London. A versatile artist, Van Abbé was a painter, etcher, and illustrator. President of the Art Workers' Guild, he also was a member of the Royal Society of British Artists, Savage Club, London Sketch Club, and the Ridley Art Club. He was also an Associate of the Royal Society of Painter-Etchers. His work received several awards. For young people he illustrated T. Hughes' Tom Brown's School Days (Dutton, 1951). ICB-2

VAN DE BOVENCAMP, Valli. Illustrator and designer, born in Bucharest, Romania. She has used Valli as her professional name. She came to the United States as a

child and later made her home in New York City where
she has been associated with NBC as a free-lance designer of animation and promotional films.   Miss Van
de Bovencamp received her education at Finch College
and Columbia and Michigan Universities.   She also
studied in Geneva and Paris.   She illustrated S. Simon's Soap Bubbles (Hawthorn, 1969), and B. Kohn's
Talking Leaves (a Junior Literary Guild selection;
Hawthorn, 1969).

VASILIU, Mircea, 1920- . He was born in Bucharest, Rumania, and received a law degree from the University
of Bucharest.   He later studied art at the Corcoran
School of Art in Washington, D.C. and the Art Students
League in New York.   He had his first book published
at 13.   Mircea Vasiliu has written and illustrated books
for both children and adults.   He and his wife have
lived in Riverdale, New York.   His work includes N.
Sherman's Miss Agatha's Lark (Bobbs-Merrill, 1968),
L. Gould's Royal Giraffe (Dutton, 1971), and P. Lauber's The Story of Numbers (Random, 1961).   ICB-2,
ICB-3

VAUGHAN, Anne, 1913- . Born in Worcester, Massachusetts, she later made her home in Natick with her husband, Windsor A. Mallett.   She studied in Boston at the
School of the Museum of Fine Arts and in Fountaine-
bleau, France at the École des Beaux Arts.   In addition to book illustration, Anne Vaughan has designed
toys and textiles.   She has also been on the staff at the
Worcester Art Museum School.   Her book illustrations
include L. Carveth's Moro Boy (Longmans, 1949), and
A. DeLeeuw's Nobody's Doll (Little, 1946).   ICB-1,
ICB-2

VAUGHAN-JACKSON, Genevieve, 1913- . Born in England,
she spent part of her childhood in Ireland and studied
in France at the Sorbonne, Atelier Armand-Delille,
Ville d'Avray, Seine et Oise, and at the Central School
of Arts and Crafts in London.   She came to the United
States in 1937.   Married to geologist John A. Shimer,
she has lived in New York City.   She illustrated two
books for M. Venn, Day and a Night in the Arctic
(1970) and The North American Wolf (1965), both for
Hastings.   She was author of Carramore (Hastings,
1968).   ICB-2

VENTURA, Piero. Historian, architect, and graphic designer. He has worked in the field of advertising and
has been the recipient of several awards for various
advertising campaigns. He has been a resident of Milan, Italy, where he has served as creative director
of an advertising agency. For young people he illustrated G. Sperandio's Vanuk Vanuk (Doubleday, 1973).

VESTAL, Herman B. Prior to making his permanent home
in New Jersey, Herman Vestal had lived in other
states. He has been in both the Coast Guard and Merchant Marine. The artist attended Pratt Institute in
Brooklyn and the National Academy of Design in New
York. In addition to illustrating books, his work has
appeared in such magazines as Reader's Digest and
Outdoor Life. He has also worked in advertising. For
children he illustrated N. Stirling's Exploring for Lost
Treasure (Garden City Books, 1960), F. Sutton's Illustrated Book about Africa (Grosset, 1959), and A. Em-
ery's A Spy in Old Detroit (McNally, 1963).

VICTOR, Joan Berg, 1937- . Born in Chicago, she graduated from Tulane University in New Orleans and received her master's degree from Yale University. Her
drawings and paintings have appeared in many galleries
throughout America. She also had a one-woman show
in New York City where she has made her home. Her
work includes M. Bloch's Aunt America (Atheneum,
1963), H. Pauli's The First Christmas Gifts (Washburn, 1965). She wrote and illustrated Sh-h! Listen
Again (World, 1969), and Where Is My Monster?
(Crown, 1971). ICB-3

VOSBURGH, Leonard. He was born in Yonkers, New York,
went to school in North Plainfield, New Jersey, and
spent summer vacations in the Mohawk Valley of New
York. He studied art at Pratt Institute and the Art
Students League in New York. Prior to illustrating
books, he worked in advertising. His watercolors have
been exhibited at the National Academy and the Ameri-
can Watercolor Society. His work includes C. Wilson's
Crown Point, the Destiny Road (McKay, 1965), C. De-
Leeuw's Fear in the Forest (Nelson, 1960), H. Pauli's
Gateway to America (McKay, 1965), and E. Parkinson's
Never Go Anywhere with Digby (Abingdon, 1971).

VOUTE, Kathleen, 1892- . A commercial artist and

illustrator, she was born in Montclair, New Jersey.
She studied in New York at the Art Students League
and the Grand Central School of Art.   She also attended art classes at the Y.W.C.A. and the George Pearse
Ennis Art School.   In addition to book and magazine
illustration, the artist has created jacket designs and
maps.   Her watercolors of the New England states have
been exhibited in several cities.   Kathleen Voute has
belonged to both the New Jersey and American Water
Color Societies.   For children she illustrated N. Fra-
zier's The Magic Ring (a Junior Literary Guild selection; Longmans, 1959), and A. Seckar's Zuska of the
Burning Hill (Oxford, 1952).   ICB-2

-W-

WABBES, Maria.   Her pseudonym is Florence.   She has
been instrumental in the preparation of a special page
for children published in the newspaper Le Soir.   Florence has also been a textile designer for children's
wear.   She illustrated G. Van Hout's Caroline at the
King's Ball "by J. Le Paillot" [pseud.] (Parents' magazine, 1972).

WADOWSKI-BAK, Alice.   Artist-teacher, born in New York
near Buffalo.   She received degrees from Syracuse and
Buffalo Universities.   She has been an art instructor
at New York City's Academy of the Sacred Heart.   In
addition to illustrating books, her work has also appeared in such magazines as Jubilee and Woman's Day.
For children she illustrated L. Wibberley's Encounter
Near Venus (Farrar, 1967), and D. Spicer's Owl's Nest
(Coward, 1968).

WAKEMAN, Marion Freeman, 1891-1953.   She was born in
Montclair, New Jersey and graduated from Smith Col-
lege.   She also studied in Switzerland.   In 1942 she was
awarded a prize from the National Association of Water
Color Artists.   Her work has been included in the
Smith College Museum and exhibited at the Architectur-
al League of New York, the National Academy of Design,
Montclair Art Museum, the Pennsylvania Academy of
Fine Arts, and at the shows of the National Association
of Water Color Artists.   For young people she illus-
trated R. Hatch's The Lobster Books (Houghton, 1951).
ICB-2

WALFORD, Astrid, 1907- . She was born in Lisbon, Portugal. Her childhood was spent in both Portugal and
England. Later she attended St. Martin's School of
Art in London. Prior to Astrid Walford, her name
was Astrid Kate Oatelayé Cumpston. At the age of 37
she began her work in illustration. The artist's home
has been in London. For young people she illustrated
J. Scott's Hudson of Hudson's Bay (Schuman, 1951).
ICB-2

WALKER, Charles W. He was born in Hempstead, Long Is-
land, and later made his home in Yorktown Heights,
New York. He studied art at Syracuse University's
College of Fine Arts. In addition to illustrating books,
the artist has also worked in advertising. For boys
and girls he illustrated W. Harter's The Dog That
Smiled (Macmillan, 1965), and J. Bosworth's White
Water, Still Water (Doubleday, 1966).

WALKER, Nedda. Born in Canada, her childhood was spent
in Boston. She studied art at the Pennsylvania Academy in Philadelphia and also studied privately in Eur-
rope. In addition to illustrating books for boys and
girls, she has been a portrait painter. Her work includes M. Vance's Elizabeth Tudor, Sovereign Lady
(Dutton, 1954), and R. Trent's In the Beginning (Westminster Press, 1949). ICB-2

WALLERSTEDT, Don. Designer and illustrator. He studied
at the University of Nebraska in Lincoln and obtained
his M.F.A. in illustration from the Art Institute in
Kansas City. In addition to illustrating books, Mr.
Wallerstedt has been associated with a publishing firm
as an art coordinator. For children he illustrated M.
Gremmels' The Cat Who Knew the Meaning of Christmas (Augsburg, 1972).

WALTER, Frances. Born in San Diego, she attended school
in Los Angeles, and later lived in Santa Monica. Pri-
or to studying art at the Art Center School in Los Angeles, she was on the staff of Walt Disney Productions.
She has been interested in rock collecting and has enjoyed animals. For boys and girls she illustrated V.
Thompson's Ah See and the Spooky House (Golden Gate
Junior Books, 1963).

WALTERS, Audrey. Artist and cartoonist, born in

Philadelphia, Pennsylvania. Her summer home (a Victorian cottage) on Cape May provided the background for many of her drawings. In addition to books, Mrs. Walters has done magazine illustrations. She has also created animated cartoons. For children she illustrated L. Klein's <u>Just Like You....</u> (Harvey House, 1968).

WALTRIP, Mildred, 1911- . She was born in Kentucky and studied art at the Chicago Art Institute. Following graduation, she traveled and studied in Europe for a year on a fellowship. She has done free-lance work in New York and Chicago. Mildred Waltrip has created displays for stores and painted murals in addition to her book illustrations which include G. Barr's <u>Entertaining with Number Tricks</u> (McGraw, 1971), and F. Smith's <u>First Book of Water</u> (Watts, 1959).

WALWORTH, Jane. Artist and designer. She was born in Evanston, Illinois, and later made her home in New York City. In addition to book illustration, Jane Walworth has been an art director of an encyclopedia for three years. For children she illustrated V. Trader's <u>Menehunes</u> (Doubleday, 1972).

WARD, John, 1917- . The son of an antique dealer, he was born in England and later made his home in Folkstone. He attended the Hereford School of Art and did further study at the Royal College of Art in London. He completed his education after serving with the British Army during World War II. At one time John Ward did stilllife interiors, fashion designs, and portraits for <u>Vogue</u> magazine. The artist has belonged to the Royal Portrait Society, the New English Art Club, the Royal Academy, and the Royal Water Colour Society. In addition to illustration and portrait painting, Mr. Ward has been interested in architecture and antiques. His drawings can be found in C. Beaton-Jones' <u>So-Hi and the White Horse</u> (Vanguard, 1957). ICB-2

WARD, Lynd Kendall, 1905- . Artist, author. He married writer May McNeer whom he met while attending Columbia University. When they were first married, they lived in Leipzig, where Mr. Ward studied graphic arts. He has written many books with his wife, and he has been an outstanding illustrator. Mr. Ward has been equally proficient in watercolor, lithography, and oil. They have lived in Leonia and Cresskill, New Jersey.

He illustrated McNeer's The American Indian Story
(Ariel Books, 1963) and E. Forbes' America's Paul
Revere (Houghton, 1946). He was awarded the Calde-
cott Medal in 1953 for his book The Biggest Bear
(Houghton, 1952). He also wrote and illustrated Nic
of the Woods (Houghton, 1965). ICB-1, ICB-2, ICB-3,
ABYP-2

WATERS, Sheila see under PARSONS, Virginia

WATSON, Aldren Auld, 1917- . Born in Brooklyn, New
     York, he received his early education in Quaker
     schools and later attended Yale University in New Hav-
     en, Connecticut, and the Art Students League in New
     York. His interests have included cartography and
     bookbinding. He has also been a map draftsman for
     textbooks and Time magazine. Following World War
     II in which he and his wife served as field workers for
     the American Friends Service Committee, the artist
     made his home in Putney, Vermont. Aldren Watson
     has illustrated many of his wife's books. His draw-
     ings can also be found in A. White's Prehistoric Amer-
     ica (Random, 1951), and M. Bartlett's Where the
     Brook Begins (Crowell, 1961). ICB-1, ICB-2, ICB-3

WATSON, Howard N. Artist and teacher. His home has
     been in Germantown, Pennsylvania. Mr. Watson has
     been on the staff at the Philadelphia College of Art.
     His work has often been exhibited at art galleries in
     the East. For boys and girls he illustrated V. Shar-
     off's Garbage Can Cat (Westminster, 1969).

WATSON, Wendy. She was born in Putney, Vermont, the
     daughter of artist Aldren Watson. She graduated from
     Bryn Mawr College in Pennsylvania. In addition to the
     books which she has illustrated for children, Wendy
     Watson has also been the author of several juvenile
     stories. Her work includes M. Calhoun's Magic in the
     Alley (Atheneum, 1970), Y. Speevack's The Spider
     Plant (Atheneum, 1965), and K. Hitte's When Noodle-
     head Went to the Fair (Parents' magazine, 1968).

WATTS, Bernadette. English illustrator. London has been
     her home, but the artist has traveled extensively and
     lived in Europe. It was on the Continent that she ac-
     quired a special interest in European folktales. She
     used both gouache and pastel in her illustrations for

the book she retold and illustrated for children, the
Grimms' <u>Mother Holly</u> (Crowell, 1972).

WEAVER, Jack, 1925- . He was born in Philadelphia,
Pennsylvania, and studied at the Philadelphia Museum
School of Art. During World War II, he served as a
tank gunner in Europe. He has worked in advertising
as an artist in addition to his work as an illustrator of
books for young people. Mr. Weaver and his family
have lived in Levittown, Pennsylvania. He wrote and
illustrated <u>Mr. O'Hara</u> (Viking, 1953). He also illustrated K. Robertson's <u>Ice to India</u> (Viking, 1955).
ICB-2

WEAVER, Robert. Artist, professor. Mr. Weaver has
been a member of the staff of Pratt Institute and the
School of Visual Arts. His work has appeared on the
covers of various magazines including: <u>Fortune</u>,
<u>Sports Illustrated</u>, and <u>Life.</u> The Society of Illustra-
tors has awarded him a Gold Medal. He and his fam-
ily have made their home in New York City. For boys
and girls he illustrated J. Lexau's <u>Me Day</u> (Dial,
1971).

WEBB, Françoise. Of French descent (François Boucher,
the French painter), Françoise Webb was born in Brussels and came to America when she was 12 years old.
She and her family have lived in Englewood, New Jersey. She received her education in Virginia at the
Richmond Professional Institute. In addition to book illustration, she has worked in commercial art for an
airline. Her drawings can be found in E. Clifford's
<u>The King Who Was Different</u> (Bobbs-Merrill, 1969).

WEBBER, Irma Eleanor (Schmidt), 1904- . Artist and author, she was born in San Diego, California. She later
made her home in Riverside and Berkeley. She studied
both art and botany at the University of California, receiving her M.A. and Ph.D. degrees there. In addition to writing and illustrating, she has also been associated with the U.S. Department of Agriculture. The
artist married John Milton Webber, and her children
inspired her to write and illustrate stories. These include: <u>Bits That Grow Big</u> (1949), <u>Thanks to Trees</u>
(1952), and <u>Up Above and Down Below</u> (1943), all for
Scott publishers. ICB-1, ICB-2

WEGNER, Fritz, 1924- . Born in Vienna, Austria, he
    studied at St. Martin's School of Art in London. He
    later taught graphic design at St. Martin's. Mr. Weg-
    ner's drawings have often appeared in British publica-
    tions. His home has been in Highgate, North London.
    For boys and girls he illustrated A. Maurois' Fatty-
    puffs & Thinifers (Knopf, 1968), and W. Mayne's House
    on Fairmont (Dutton, 1968). ICB-2

WEIL, Lisl. She was born in Vienna, Austria, and studied
    at Wiener Kunstgewerbeschule. Prior to coming to the
    United States in 1939, she worked on a Viennese news-
    paper and magazine. She has conducted a weekly tele-
    vision show ("Children's Sketch Book") and drawn pic-
    tures to music on the concert stage (Little Orchestra
    Society's children's concerts at Lincoln Center). She
    and her husband have lived in New York City. For
    Houghton she wrote and illustrated Bitzli and the Big
    Bad Wolf (1960), Eyes So-o Big (1964), and Mimi (1961).
    She also illustrated M. Sharmat's 51 Sycamore Lane
    (Macmillan, 1971). ICB-2, ICB-3

WEINHEIMER, George. His home has been in Schenectady,
    New York. In addition to his work as an illustrator of
    children's books, Mr. Weinheimer has been a principal
    of an elementary school. He has also conducted a chil-
    dren's art program over educational television. The
    Weinheimer household has included four children plus a
    large assortment of pets. For boys and girls he illus-
    trated J. Unterecker's The Dreaming Zoo (Walck, 1965).

WEISGARD, Leonard, 1916- . Born in New Haven, Con-
    necticut, this illustrator-author attended Pratt Institute.
    He has worked on magazines and designed sets for the
    ballet. Mr. Weisgard has lived in Danbury and Rox-
    bury, Connecticut. Numerous authors have had their
    books illustrated by him. His illustrations in The Lit-
    tle Island, written by M. W. Brown (Doubleday, 1946),
    won the 1947 Caldecott Medal. His books include: Be-
    ginning of Cities (Coward, 1968), Mr. Peaceable Paints
    (Scribner's, 1956), Pelican Here, Pelican There (Scrib-
    ner's 1948), and Silly Willy Nilly (Scribner's, 1953).
    ICB-1, ICB-2, ICB-3, ABYP-2

WEISS, Emil, 1896-1965. Illustrator, newspaper artist, de-
    signer. Born in Olmutz, Moravia, Austria, he later
    lived in England and New York City where he died in

1965. He received a degree in architecture from Austria's University of Vienna. Emil Weiss was a war artist during World War I. He later became well-known for his sketches which appeared in newspapers in Prague, Czechoslovakia and London, England. He also designed costumes and film sets. After service with the British Army during World War II, Mr. Weiss was commissioned by the Royal Engineers Hall of Fame to sketch various Generals of the British Army. He has also served as a press artist to the United Nations. For children he illustrated R. Burch's D. J.'s Worst Enemy (Viking, 1965), L. Paul's Papa Luigi's Marionettes (Washburn, 1962), and E. De Gering's Seeing Fingers (a Junior Literary Guild selection; McKay, 1962). ICB-3

WELLS, Rosemary. Artist, author, designer. She attended the Museum School in Boston, Massachusetts, and later made her home in New York City. Rosemary Wells has become well-known for her picture book illustrations which include R. Service's The Shooting of Dan McGrew & The Cremation of Sam McGee (Young Scott, 1969). Juvenile books which she wrote and illustrated First Child (Hawthorn, 1970), and Martha's Birthday (Bradbury, 1970).

WENDE, Philip. This artist has illustrated a number of books for boys and girls; many of which have been about animals. He has no doubt been inspired by family pets which include a turtle named Sidney, Hector the dog, and two Siamese cats. He has made his home in New York City. For young people he illustrated R. Littell's Gaston's Ghastly Green Thumb (Cowles, 1969), and Left & Right with Lion & Ryan (Cowles, 1969).

WENNERSTROM, Genia Katherine, 1930- . Her pseudonym is Genia. Born in New York City, she attended the New School for Social Research and New York University. She also studied at Pratt Institute in Brooklyn. She married an artist whom she met at Pratt and has lived in Forest Hills. In addition to books, she has illustrated greeting cards, magazines, and fashions. She also designed a 90-foot sign for a mountain top in New Jersey. For children she illustrated L. Budd's Tekla's Easter, (Rand, 1962). ICB-3

WERTH, Kurt, 1896- . Born in Leipzig, Germany, Mr.

Werth received his education at Leipzig's Academy for
Graphic Arts. He began his career in book illustra-
tion in Munich. German magazines also published his
drawings. When the Hitler regime came into power,
the Werth family came to the United States. He be-
came an American citizen and has lived in New York
City. For young people he illustrated W. Mantle's
Chateau Holiday (Holt, 1965), H. Wilson's Herbert's
Space Trip (Knopf, 1965), L. Bason's Isabelle and the
Library Cat (Lothrop, 1966), and C. Zolotow's A Tiger
Called Thomas (a Junior Literary Guild selection; Lothrop, 1963). ICB-2, ICB-3

WEST, Walter Richard, 1912- . He was born in Darling-
ton, Oklahoma, and later graduated from the University
of Oklahoma. He also attended Bacone College, University of Redlands, and the University of Tulsa. During World War II, Dick West served in the Navy. He
has had one-man shows, and his work has been included in the National Gallery of Art, Chappell Art Gallery
in Pasadena, and the William Rockhill Nelson Gallery
of Art. In 1949 and 1955 he was prize winner of the
National Indian Show in Tulsa's Philbrook Art Center.
Associated with Bacone College, his home has been in
Muskogee. He illustrated G. Penney's Tales of the
Cheyennes (Houghton, 1953). ICB-2

WHITE, David Omar. He studied in California at the Clare-
mont Graduate School under Henry Lee McFee. He has
done satiric drawings in addition to his book illustrations. His own children have provided inspiration for
several of his picture books. For young people he illustrated T. Berger's Black Fairy Tales (Atheneum,
1969), and M. Bacon's Sophia Scrooby Preserved (Little, 1968).

WHITEBEAD, Baida. Cherokee Indian, born in Oklahoma,
she studied with Los Angeles painter Lorser Feitelson.
In 1956 and 1958 she was awarded scholarships from
the Huntington Hartford Foundation. Her paintings have
been exhibited in many places including three in Cali-
fornia, the Cabot Hopi Indian Village in Desert Hot
Springs, the Janis Gallery in Van Nuys, and the Santa
Paula Art Festival; in the Newport Gallery in Newport,
Rhode Island, and at the Honolulu Academy of Fine
Arts. For boys and girls she illustrated S. Russell's
Navaho Land (Melmont, 1961).

WHITTAM, Geoffrey William, 1916- . English illustrator.
He was born near Southampton where he later attended
the School of Art. He also studied in London at the
Central School of Arts and Crafts. During World War
II, he was awarded a Distinguished Service Cross. In
later years as a free-lance artist, Mr. Whittam illustrated books, book jackets, and created magazine illustrations. His home has been in Surrey. His work includes A. Catherall's Death of an Oil Rig (Phillips,
1969), and M. Edwards' Dolphin Summer (Hawthorn,
1971). ICB-2

WIESNER, William, 1899- . He graduated from the University of Vienna with degrees in engineering and architecture. He has been an interior decorator, architect,
and designer. He also once operated a shadow-puppet
theater. He and his wife have worked in textile design,
and their work was in the Metropolitan Museum's 1945
exhibit entitled "American Fabrics and Fashions." The
Wiesners have lived in New York City. He illustrated
C. Wilson's Hobnob (a Junior Literary Guild selection;
Viking, 1968), and C. Potter's Tongue Tanglers (World,
1962). ICB-2, ICB-3

WILDSMITH, Brian Lawrence, 1930- . He was born in
Penistone, Yorkshire, England, grew up in Sheffield,
and studied at the Barnsley School of Art, London's
Slade School of Fine Art, and University College in
London. Prior to doing free-lance work, he was an
art teacher. He was awarded the 1962 Kate Greenaway Medal for his book ABC (Watts, 1962). His other
books, all for Watts, include Brian Wildsmith's Birds
(1967), Brian Wildsmith's Fishes (1968), Brian Wildsmith's 1, 2, 3's (1965), Brian Wildsmith's Puzzles
(1971), and Wild Animals (1967). ICB-3

WILKIN, Eloise Burns, 1904- . Born in Rochester, New
York, she grew up there and in New York City. She
studied at Rochester Institute of Technology. Following school, she went to New York City where she began her career in book illustration. She has lived in
Canandaigua, New York. For boys and girls she illustrated M. Reely's Seatmates (Watts, 1949), and M.
Lovelace's Tune Is in the Tree (Crowell, 1950). ICB-
1, ICB-2

WILKON, Jozef, 1930- . The son of an artist, he was

born near Cracow, Poland. He grew up in Wieliczka
and studied in Cracow at Jagiellonski University and the
Academy of Art. His home has been in Warsaw. His
book illustrations have been published by Polish, German, and French publishers. Jozef Wilkon has been
the recipient of many awards including both the 1960
and 1962 Polish Editors' Award for the "Most Beautiful
Book of the Year." He also won the "Most Beautiful"
German book award in 1965. For young readers he illustrated R. Schnell's Bonko (Scroll Press, 1970), and
P. Schaaf's The Crane with One Leg (Warne, 1964).

WILLCOX, Sandra. She spent her childhood in St. Paul and
     later studied at the University of Minnesota. Prior to
     teaching art in schools of the Caledonia-Orange Super-
     visory School District in Newbury, Vermont, Mrs. Will-
     cox taught art at Peacham Academy in Peacham, Ver-
     mont. Her husband has been a writer and sculptor,
     and they have lived in Peacham. For young people she
     illustrated B. Clayton's Ditto (a Junior Literary Guild
     selection; Funk, 1968).

WILSON, Charles Banks, 1918- . Art instructor and illus-
     trator, he was born in Oklahoma. A childhood spent
     around Indian tribes in northeastern Oklahoma provided
     authentic background for his art work in later years.
     His home has been in Miami, Oklahoma. His many
     historical works include a mural in Wyoming's Teton
     National Park in the Jackson Lake Lodge. The artist's
     main interest has been in lithographs and paintings of
     today's Indian. The Smithsonian Institution, the Metro-
     politan Museum, and the Library of Congress have ex-
     hibited his work. He illustrated L. Neyhart's Henry's
     Lincoln (Holiday, 1945) and R. Stevenson's Treasure
     Island (Lippincott, 1948). ICB-2

WILSON, Edward Arthur, 1886- . Born in Glasgow, Scot-
     land, he later studied at the Chicago Art Institute and
     Howard Pyle's School in Wilmington, Delaware. Al-
     though he has lived the majority of his life in America,
     he spent some years of his childhood in Rotterdam,
     Holland. Mr. Wilson's talents have included: stage de-
     signs, advertising art, and the designing of book-plates
     and furniture. The recipient of many awards, his
     prints are in the Library of Congress, Metropolitan

Museum, and the New York Public Library. The artist's home has been in Truro, Massachusetts. His work includes J. Jennings' Clipper Ship Days (Random, 1952), and R. Stevenson's Treasure Island (Heritage Press, 1941). ICB-1, ICB-2

WILSON, Gahan. Artist, cartoonist, born in Evanston, Illinois. He studied art in Chicago and Paris and later made his home in New York. Mr. Wilson has enjoyed traveling which has included Tibetan mountain climbing and several expeditions down the Amazon. For young people he illustrated J. Beatty's Matthew Looney's Invasion of the Earth (Scott, 1965).

WILSON, John. Born in Houston, he graduated from Boston's School of the Museum of Fine Arts and received a B.S. in Education from Tufts University in Medford, Massachusetts. Mr. Wilson has been honored with many awards. His work has been exhibited in the United States and Jerusalem and can be found in private collections. For boys and girls he illustrated A. Adoff's Malcolm X (Crowell, 1970), J. George's Spring Comes to the Ocean (Crowell, 1966), and J. Lexau's Striped Ice Cream (Lippincott, 1968).

WILSON, Peggy. She was born and grew up in Galveston, Texas. She received her education at Texas Woman's University in Denton and San Francisco State College. Miss Wilson has lived in New York City since 1965. Her work has been exhibited throughout the Southwest in both galleries and museums. The New York Times selected her first children's book P. Appiah's Ananse the Spider (Pantheon, 1966) as one of the "Ten Best Illustrated Children's Books" for 1966. The artist has worked with a felt pen in black-and-white. Her book illustrations for children include A. Jablow's The Man in the Moon (Holt, 1969). ICB-3

WINTER, Milo Kendall, 1888-1956. He always lived in the Midwest. Born in Princeton, Illinois, he grew up in Grand Rapids and Detroit, Michigan, and later made his home in Lake Forest, Illinois. The artist attended Chicago's Art Institute and also studied abroad. Milo Winter has stated that he always enjoyed juvenile illustration best. His drawings for children include J. Verne's Twenty Thousand Leagues Under the Sea, transl. by P. S. Allen (Rand McNally, 1922). ICB-1, ICB-2

WISKUR, Darrell. Free-lance artist and illustrator, he has
    resided in Aurora, Illinois, with his family. He stud-
    ied art in Chicago at the Academy of Fine Art and the
    School of Professional Art. The artist has enjoyed
    fishing, hunting, and nature as hobbies. Most of his
    time has been devoted to illustrating children's books,
    among which was A. Carpenter's Kentucky (Children's
    Press, 1967).

WONG, Jeanyee, 1920- . Artist, illustrator, painter.
    Born in San Francisco, California, she later made her
    home in New York City. Jeanyee Wong received her
    art training at New York's Cooper Union School of Art.
    She also had private study in illustration and woodcut-
    ting. She has worked in calligraphy, design, and
    sculpture in addition to book illustration. For young
    readers she illustrated M. Farraday's Chemical His-
    tory of a Candle (Crowell, 1957), and J. Bothwell's
    The Story of India (Harcourt, 1952). ICB-2

WONSETLER, John Charles, 1900- . Artist and muralist,
    he was born in Camden, New Jersey. He later made
    his home in Chatham, New Jersey. John Wonsetler
    was awarded the first prize in illustration when he
    graduated from the Philadelphia Museum School of In-
    dustrial Art in 1925. In addition to books and maga-
    zines, the artist has illustrated numerous textbooks.
    His drawings can be found in C. Meigs' Fair Wind to
    Virginia (Macmillan, 1955). ICB-1, ICB-2

WOOD, Leslie, 1920- . Born in England, she grew up in
    Stockport, Cheshire, and later made her home in Poyn-
    ton, Cheshire, England. The artist attended British
    schools including the Regional College of Art in Man-
    chester. She was awarded a traveling scholarship and
    visited only galleries and art exhibitions in London due
    to World War II. For young people she illustrated M.
    Baker's Hi-Jinks Joins the Bears (Farrar, 1969).
    ICB-2

WOODWARD, Alice Bolingbroke, 1862- . She was born in
    London and later studied at London's Royal College of
    Art and Westminster Art School. She also attended
    Académie Julien in Paris. As a young person, she
    used to make drawings for her father, a noted geolo-
    gist at the British Museum. During World War I, she
    drew maps for the Naval Intelligence Bureau. Later

she made her home in Hertfordshire. In addition to illustrating books, her work has appeared in the Illustrated London News. She illustrated O. Goldsmith's History of Little Goody Two Shoes (Macmillan, 1924). ICB-1

WORM, Piet, 1909- . Born in Holland, he later studied at the Technical School for Architects and Holland's Royal Academy of Art. He worked as an architect in South Africa where he met people who were instrumental in introducing him to a New York literary agent. In this way Piet Worm began his career as an illustrator of children's books. He has lived in Amsterdam. For boys and girls he wrote and illustrated Three Little Horses (Random, 1954). ICB-2

WRONKER, Lili (Cassel), 1924- . Born in Berlin, she grew up in Germany and England. Her family came to the United States in 1940. Lili Cassel married Israeli Brich Wronker in 1952, and they have resided in Jamaica, New York. Mrs. Wronker studied in New York at both the Art Students League and the Brooklyn Museum Art School. One of her chief hobbies has been a collection of international children's books. In addition to book illustrating, her career has included advertising and teaching. She has also created book jackets and has become a noted calligrapher. Her drawings can be found in Happy New Year 'Round the World, ed. by L. Johnson (Rand, 1966). ICB-2, ICB-3

WULFF, Edgun Valdemar, 1913- . His pseudonym is Edgun. Born in New York City, he later made his home in Hartsdale, New York. His early years were spent in New York and Denmark. He received his education at the Cooper Union School of Art. His illustrations can be found in two books "retold by" M. Hatch, More Danish Tales (Harcourt, 1949), and 13 Danish Tales (Harcourt, 1947). ICB-2

WYETH, Newell Convers, 1882-1945. Artist-muralist, known as N. C. Wyeth. He was born in Needham, Massachusetts, and studied with artist Howard Pyle. At one time he lived in Colorado and New Mexico. He encouraged his son Andrew to learn to paint and draw. For boys and girls he illustrated Anthology of Children's Literature, ed. by E. Johnson (Houghton, 1970), J. Cooper's The Deerslayer (Scribner's, 1925), The

Little Shepherd of Kingdom Come (Scribner's, 1931),
and P. Creswick's Robin Hood (McKay, 1917).

-Y-Z-

YAMAGUCHI, Marianne Illenberger, 1936- . Born in Cuya-
hoga Falls, Ohio, she studied at Bowling Green State
University and the Rhode Island School of Design. She
married Tohr Yamaguchi, and they have lived and studied in Australia. She illustrated her husband's books
...The Golden Crane (Holt, 1963) and Two Crabs in
the Moonlight (Holt, 1965). She wrote Finger Plays
(Holt, 1970). ICB-3

YANG, Jay. Born in Taiwan, he later came to the United
States where he studied at the University of Pennsylvania. After receiving his Master of Fine Arts degree
from the University, he became a designer in New
York City. For young people he illustrated S. Fleischman's The Wooden Cat Man (Little, 1972).

YAP, Weda, 1894- . Born Louise Drew Cook in Philadelphia, she grew up there and in Bar Harbor, Maine.
She studied at the Museum School of Industrial Art in
Philadelphia, New York's Art Students League, and the
Winold Riess Art School. Mrs. Yap received private
instruction in the graphic arts and portrait painting.
She also studied abroad in Italy, France, and Germany.
At one time the artist traveled and lived in China and
other countries of the Far East. She worked as a ma-
rine draftsman during World War II. Her home has
been in Morristown, New Jersey. For children she il-
lustrated N. Larrick's Junior Science Book of Rain,
Hail, Sleet & Snow (Garrard, 1961), R. Feravolo's
Junior Science Book of Weather Experiments (Garrard,
1963), and P. Buck's Stories for Little Children (John
Day, 1940). ICB-2

YASHIMA, Taro, 1908- . Born in Kagoshima, Japan, he
later studied art at the Imperial Art Academy of Tokyo
and at the Art Students League in New York. His
paintings have been included in several permanent collections, and he has illustrated for magazines in addition to books. His wife has also been an artist, and
they have made their home in Los Angeles, California.
In an article entitled "On Making a Book for a Child,"

in the February 1955 issue of the <u>Horn Book</u> magazine,
he wrote: "But I think the theme of these [books for
children] should be, 'This earth is beautiful! Living is
wonderful! Believe in humankind!'" His work includes <u>Crow Boy</u> (a Junior Literary Guild selection;
Viking, 1955), and <u>Seashore Story</u> (Viking, 1967).
ICB-2, ICB-3

YOUNG, Ed.   Artist, illustrator, teacher, born in Shanghai,
China. He has been on the staff of Pratt Institute
where he has taught visual communication. In 1968 a
book which he illustrated, J. Yolen's <u>The Emperor and
the Kite</u> (World, 1967), was designated a runner-up for
the Caldecott Medal. He and his wife, a ceramicist,
have lived in New York City. His work includes R.
Weiss' <u>Bird from the Sea</u> (Crowell, 1970), <u>Chinese
Mother Goose Rhymes,</u> ed. by R. Wyndham (World,
1968), and J. Udry's <u>The Mean Mouse, and Other
Mean Stories</u> (Harper, 1962).

ZALLINGER, Jean Day, 1918- . She was born in Boston,
grew up in Braintree, Massachusetts, and graduated
from the Massachusetts College of Art and the Yale
School of Fine Arts. She married artist Rudolph Zallinger, and they have lived in New Haven, Connecticut.
In addition to illustrating books for young people and
the Wildlife Federation, her work has appeared in <u>Col-
lier's</u> Encyclopedia. For young people she illustrated
R. Andrews' <u>In the Days of the Dinosaurs</u> (Random,
1959), A. Crosby's <u>Junior Science Book of Pond Life</u>
(Garrard, 1964), and L. Zappler's <u>Natural History of
the Tail</u> (Doubleday, 1972). ICB-3

ZIMNIK, Reiner, 1930- . He was born and grew up in
Beuthen, Upper Silesia (now East Germany). His home
has been in Munich, Germany. He worked as a carpenter in Bavaria after his father was killed in World
War II. He later attended the Academy of Fine Arts
in Munich. Reiner Zimnik has been both an illustrator
and writer. He has worked in black-and-white with
pen and ink. His drawings can be found in B. DeRegniers' <u>Snow Party</u> (Pantheon, 1959). He also wrote and
illustrated <u>The Bear and the People</u>, transl. from German by N. Ignatowicz (Harper, 1971), and <u>The Little
Roaring Tiger</u> (Pantheon, 1961). ICB-2, ICB-3

ZEIGER, Sophia, 1926- . Her pseudonym is Sofia. Although she was born in New York City, part of her
childhood was spent in Greece.   Later she studied at
the Franklin School of Professional Arts.   She received inspiration in her work from studying and painting the countryside of both Mexico and Greece.   Besides painting, the artist has done woodcuts and was
awarded a first prize in 1956 at the New School for Social Research.   She married Arthur Zeiger, a professor at New York's City College.   Her work for young
people includes D. Clewes' Roller Skates, Scooter and
Bike (Coward, 1966). ICB-2, ICB-3

ZEMACH, Margot, 1931- . She was born in Los Angeles,
California, grew up in New York City, and attended the
County Art Institute in Los Angeles.   She also studied
at the Jepson and Kann Art Institutes and was awarded
a Fulbright Scholarship to study in Vienna, Austria, in
1955-56.   She married history professor and writer
Harve Zemach, and they have lived in Newton Centre,
Massachusetts.   She illustrated the picture book Salt,
adapted by H. Zemach (Follett, 1965), which won recognition in the 1965 Book Week's Spring Book Festival.
She was awarded the Caldecott Medal in 1974 for her
illustrations in Duffy and the Devil, "A Cornish tale retold by Harve Zemach" (Farrar, 1973).   Other juvenile
books she illustrated include R. Mincieli's Harlequin
(Knopf, 1968), and J. Williams' The Question Box (Norton, 1965).   ICB-3

TITLE INDEX*

---

*Illustrator's name is given in parentheses, number refers to page where title is cited.